THE MAKING OF PSYCHOTHERAPISTS
AN ANTHROPOLOGICAL ANALYSIS

JAMES DAVIES

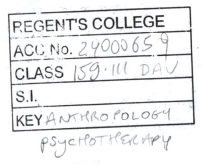
First published 2009
by Karnac Books Ltd.
118 Finchley Road
London NW3 5HT

British Library Cataloguing in Publication Data
A C.I.P. is available for this book from the British Library.

ISBN-13: 978-1-85575-656-4

Printed and bound in Great Britain.

www.karnacbooks.com

CONTENTS

Acknowledgements

The process of writing a book is rarely free of all difficulty. To the following people I owe a great debt of gratitude for helping me through the more demanding times. I first wish to thank Professor David Parkin for his kindness, goodwill, and invaluable guidance, as well as for providing me with the priceless example not only of how a scholar should work (but also, unbeknown to him) of how a scholar should *be*. What a precious model he provided. I am also greatly indebted to my discussions with Dr Matias Spektor—a most dear friend and always a positive force behind the scenes. Important others who challenged and/or helped me were especially Dr Ben Hebbert (a true companion), Dr Audrey Cantile, Dr Elisabeth Hsu, Professor Wendy James, Professor Roger Goodman, Dr Maria Luca, Professor Tanya Luhrmann, Professor Andrew Samuels, Professor Peter Fonagy, Joe Yarbourgh, Rob Waygood, Professor Roland Littlewood, Dr Adrianne Baker, Dr Simcha Brooks, Professor Richard Sholzt, Mark Knight, Nancy Browner, and, more recently, Rev James Wilkinson. To all of you I offer my deepest gratitude. Finally, I owe especial thanks to Dr Karem Roitman who gave me the great benefit of her close reading of the text, her sensible advice, astute commentary, as well as her tireless encouragement and support.

I must also thank the training institutes that allowed me access to their staff and students, and all the interviewees and informants who kindly gave up their time for the benefit of this research. I wish to thank for their assistance the librarians at Regent's College

School of Psychotherapy and Counselling, the Institute of Psycho-analysis, Oxford University, Senate House (University of London), Cambridge University. My gratitude also to my colleagues and students at Roehampton University, and especially to Professor Del Lowenthal for his constant backing and encouragement.

Financial help for this book came through the generous assistance of the Equity Trust Fund (John Fernald Award), and from various sources from St Cross College and the University of Oxford —to all these benefactors I am greatly indebted. I also owe deep gratitude to the staff and members of St Cross College, Oxford, whose kind and stimulating company (often during a lunch) offered solace during the dips in research.

Finally, I wish to thank my parents and family for their support, encouragement and love. If this book is to be dedicated to anyone at all, then let me dedicate it to them.

INTRODUCTION

In this book I shall analyse from an anthropological perspective the training of psychoanalytic psychotherapists. I undertake this anthropological task since psychotherapy not only constitutes a clinical practice, a professional association, and a way of making a living, but also a moral and cultural community with wide social influence and standing. If we wish to study how the values, practices, and knowledge of this distinct community are maintained and reproduced over time, we must investigate the sites, the training schools, where these cultural forms are transmitted. In this book I offer a detailed survey of the hidden institutional devices used in psychoanalytic training to help reproduce this world of shared practice and meaning. I ask why and how such devices are used, I discern their meaning and consequences, I explore how they profoundly alter the outlook of trainees and practitioners, and finally I show how they shape the fortunes and functioning of the therapeutic community itself. By taking the reader by the hand through the core stages of therapeutic training, while at the same paying close attention to what trainees do, say and feel as they pass through these stages, we will see how professional training not only grooms trainees as practitioners, but as specific types of persons who also become the main agents of community maintenance. We will see how trainees are coaxed into supporting an avowedly secular enterprise that can offer rewards (i.e. a new orientation to life, increased status and a deep sense of belonging) reminiscent of certain political or religious movements; an enterprise

1

which also advances behind its professional façade a robust 'political' and 'ideological' regime of wider social ambition and significance. We will see, then, how these training institutes, or what I
refer to as *institutions of affirmation*, work to create practitioners
who will sustain the values and hegemony of the psychoanalytic
tradition itself, usually vis-à-vis other therapeutic institutes and
schools. Whether institutes are successful in their aims, and whether these aims are actually proving to undermine the status and
standing of the profession itself, are other important questions I
shall explore.

This book, then, is not only written for social/cultural anthropologists interested in the new field of 'professional socialisation'
(the study of how professional institutions transform persons and
social practices, as well as *create* social structures), and for psychotherapists who wish to understand why their community is divided internally as well as set against more powerful social institutions (medicine and academe), but also for current and prospective
students of psychotherapy who wish to understand the formidable
institutional forces to which they are invariably subject; forces
which leave their inevitable imprint not only upon their
clinical/professional practices and beliefs but also upon their deeper subjective selves. Finally, it is hoped that for those with a general
interest in psychotherapy this book will offer a stimulating introduction to the behind-the-scenes features of this alluring professional world.

ANTHROPOLOGY OF PROFESSIONAL SOCIALISATION

Studying how powerful institutions (training or otherwise) transform the subjectivities of those individuals passing through them
has always had an important place in anthropological enquiry. As
this book therefore falls within this established field of study, let it
first be seen as providing an example of how this particular species
of social enquiry proceeds. By reviewing some of the work already
written in this area to familiarise the reader with this existing research, not only will we see the relevance such work has for understanding psychotherapeutic training, but we will also uncover the
central methods and deeper aims underpinning this book.

To start, from the early days of the American 'culture and personality school' (Bateson and Mead 1954; Benedict 1934; Kardiner 1939) to the more recent British work in the anthropology of learning and cognition (Tyler 1969; Dougherty 1985; Bloch 1998) there has always been an anthropological interest in how individuals adopt the cultural beliefs and practices of their specified group; beliefs and interests that ultimately come to guide their lives in particular and predictable ways. While most of this research has admittedly focused on how children are socialised into their social group, a smaller collection of anthropologists have studied 'adult' socialisation: including adult conversions, transformations, and 'cognitive restructuring' (Heelas 1996; Luhrmann 1989, 2001; Goffman 1961; Gusterson 1996). Within this smaller body of work we find investigations of professional training, or what I shall refer to here as 'professional socialisation'. These studies by and large explore how individual subjectivity is shaped and transformed in professional training contexts, largely with the aim of socialising trainees into the particular professional group. They further investigate how the 'transformed persons' these professional trainings produce come to support and perpetuate the existing institutional practices that underpin the professional community at large. These researchers thus study not only what professionals produce and reproduce (i.e. the artefacts—linguistic, symbolic, material—left by individuals), but also the social factors and institutional devices that precede and fashion us as individuals who produce in prescribed directions (Gusterson 1996: 3).[1] In exploring psychoanalytic socialisation, then, I investigate this interplay between individuals and the training institutes to which they are subject; institutes that through strategies of self-survival seek to self-perpetuate over time.

ANTHROPOLOGICAL ETHNOGRAPHIES OF PROFESSIONAL SOCIALISATION

Investigating how individuals are transformed to help construct and maintain social reality is a common thread binding anthropological studies of professional socialisation. Simon Sinclair's (1997) anthropology of medical training is a case in point. He starts by showing how medical training takes place not only in the obvious 'official' and 'front-stage' educational contexts (e.g. in seminars, lecture rooms, and on ward rounds), but also in many 'backstage' and 'unofficial' locations—in the bar, on the games field, and during more 'theatrical' social events. Students' lives are thus inundated by institutional demands and directives (p.16). It is this more penetrating education that leads students to acquire deep professional 'dispositions' (professional habits of thought, feeling and action), which 'fit' with their profession's existing norms and expectations—a 'fit' which ensures that these professional mores are transmitted and maintained (p.32). At the end of Sinclair's work he calls for the reform of medical training, largely because the 'dispositions' being transmitted to trainee doctors support a medical system that undermines the health of both trainees and doctors. But since the trainee's capacity and willingness to undertake reform is largely weakened by the ordeals of training, he concludes that changes to the medical system must come from without. One vehicle for change consists in educating doctors to become more critically and sociologically aware of what they do and how they do it; this, he believes, will increase the young doctor's awareness of the side-effects that medical training not only produces in the medic and the medical profession, but also in society at large. Sinclair advocates that cultivating critical awareness of the taken-for-granted norms and practices of medical culture is the first step in reforming those aspects of biomedical training, practice and belief that generate harmful consequences for self and society (p.326).

Tanya Luhrmann (2001) in her highly acclaimed anthropology of psychiatric training is also interested in the effect professional training has upon self and society. Unlike Sinclair, Luhrmann does not use the language of 'dispositions' to define that which professional socialisation instils in trainees. Rather she prefers the language of 'moral and technical instincts'—these are the qualities trainees need to develop in order to enter with the professional community. While still retaining an approach similar to Sinclair, she seeks to understand how sets of authoritative practices and ideas change how persons subject to them feel, act, and think. By following the training of young psychiatrists in the United States she arrives at an understanding of why psychiatrists come to think, diagnose, and practice in the world as they do. Psychiatry in recent decades has become a divided profession, creating almost two different and competing kinds of practitioner. She shows comparatively how the biomedical and psychodynamic traditions each produce very different moral and technical instincts in psychiatrists. This has led to competing perceptions of illness, disease, prognosis, and treatment within the one psychiatric social space. By studying socialisation at the local level she explores the interplay between practitioner, system, and society: as biomedicine is ever more wooed by corporate pharmacology, old psychodynamic practices die away. Psychiatric socialisation is thus adapting to the wants and aims of powerful insurance and pharmacological companies. And as new trainees are subtly socialised into complicity with corporate and 'pharmacological' aims and interests, not only does a new clinical hegemony prevail, but a new kind of practitioner is produced.

In many ways both these studies presuppose Goffman's (1961) early idea that institutions (themselves pressured by outside forces) transfigure persons via 'direct assaults on the self.' With this phrase he was describing, albeit in the case of asylums, how individuals adapt to institutional expectations and demands simply in order to acquire the security and rewards that conformity brings. One of the unintended consequences of such 'fitting in' is to accept as 'normal' the institutional imperatives that bear upon the individual. People often prefer to remain in warm accord with their social surroundings than to suffer the difficulties non-conformity can create. Conformity when 'naturalised' legitimates actions which are rewarded by institutional paybacks; this sets in place relationships of mutual confirmation and constitution between persons and the systems in which they operate.

As we shall see, and as both Becker *et al* (2002 [1977]: 437) and Sinclair (1997: 327) assert to be the case in medical socialisation, psychoanalytic institutes prefer a student body that conforms with authoritative demands; and the institutes clearly resist any kind of autonomous student culture or sub-culture which might challenge the status quo.[2] Institutes, by and large, prefer a trainee community that is predominantly compliant with the wishes of the leadership. Revolt against established procedures is institutionally resisted by processes of what I come to call 'exclusion', 'secondary elaboration', and by the fashioning of 'imaginations' and 'dispositions' sympathetic to institutional demands. These devices attempt to render trainee innovation into a form of dissent, to brand trainee protests as symptoms of pathology, and to exile any inconsistent student ideas behind walls of private doubt. Thus through a variety of strategies trainees' intellectual and cultural life becomes subject to institutional expectations. This stimulates a mood of conformity in which the inculcation of dispositions that 'conserve' rather than 'challenge' the tradition is easily performed; inculcations which, from the standpoint of the institutes, keep any threats to their 'regime of truth' at bay.

How and why the rewards of conformity can lead individuals to embody contradictions, warranted or unwarranted certainties, or new ways of seeing, practising, and imagining, has its history of interest in anthropology.[3] For instance, Hugh Gusterson (1996) in his anthropology of science offers a detailed account of the moral transformations nuclear physicists undergo as their professional training proceeds: he sets out to discover how once politically liberal young men, hesitant about nuclear arms proliferation, were gradually transformed by their training into keen weapons scientists. As they progressed through their studies the adventure of entering a secret group, of making light of their work, and of developing a sense of technical mastery, were principle instigators of their personal transformations. For Gusterson, the rewards these acquisitions brought gradually dulled the concerns that were once impediments to their becoming professionals—such new acquisitions, because of their allure, prompted individuals to rationalise their old objections away.

Like the process of becoming a physicist, becoming a psychotherapist offers attractive and seductive rewards: those of belonging, of a new identity, and of new mastery—namely, it offers incentives as desirable as the 'economic and status rewards' identified by certain sociologists of the professions (see Rustin 1985). Professions first and foremost need new recruits—thus investigating what inspires newcomers to train is to unearth alternative sources of community maintenance. One of my contentions is that psychotherapeutic training transforms more than just 'cognitive processes' and instils more than just 'clinical expertise', it also initiates persons into a moral and social community. Learning is then not simply a process of 'knowledge acquisition' or a process of 'technical and cognitive instruction' but a process of 'becoming'—

becoming a full participant, an accepted member, and finally, a kind of person.[4]

PIERRE BOURDIEU—A POINT OF THEORETICAL ORIENTATION?

To make explicit one theoretical tradition influencing my analysis of psychoanalytic training, let me offer a brief sketch of Pierre Bourdieu's socio-anthropological theory in order to highlight which of his concepts may usefully illuminate hidden aspects of psychoanalytic socialisation. Although Bourdieu's work is notoriously difficult to understand, principally because of the language he uses (Jenkins, 1992: 162-72), there is no doubt that once we have understood his concepts of 'habitus', 'disposition', and 'cultural field' we will find them useful aids in our analysis of psychoanalytic training.

Let me start with Bourdieu's concept of 'habitus'. This refers to a collection of habits of thought, feeling and action that 'dispose' individuals to behave in certain socially and culturally predictable ways (Bourdieu 1977a: 78-9). For example, an individual whose habitus was developed within an individualistic and capitalistic society may well display actions, thoughts and feelings that are consistent with the values and aims of that society—he may be industrious, competitive, and keen on making profit, he may display a marked capacity to sever ties in order to move with the demands of market etc. The particular habits of thought and action that comprise the individual's 'habitus' Bourdieu refers to as 'dispositions'. 'Dispositions' are ways of being and acting which help individuals to 'fit' with the 'fields' in which they are located—this is to say, dispositions are those embodied actions, thoughts and feelings that his or her community rewards and expects. But what does Bourdieu mean by 'field'? He is not talking here about a geographically bounded concrete space, such as a nation state or a city state. Rather he uses the word 'field' as a kind of metaphor to denote an area in which people and institutions engage in shared practices and behaviours—thus we can speak of the fields of 'academe' of the 'media' of 'politics' and indeed of 'psychotherapy'. Such fields are not circumscribed by geographical bounds but rather by bounds of interest, shared values, knowledge and belief.[5]

In sum, a 'habitus' (an orientation to life) consists of a set of 'dispositions' (acts and feelings) which generate 'practices' (social actions) characteristic and supportive of the shifting and dynamic 'fields' (e.g. academe or politics) with which they are congruent.

The first step in using these concepts to help our analysis of psychotherapeutic training is to note that certain education theorists have employed them to understand other educational contexts.[6] For instance, students can be taught to develop certain thoughts and acts (i.e. dispositions) by means of either 'overt' or 'covert' modes of learning.[7] This is to say, many of the strategies or 'devices' used in institutes to transform trainees into professionals are not necessarily overt educational tools nor clear pedagogical strategies or techniques. Rather they are often hidden, covert or 'unintentional' educational devices that operate outside the awareness of both learners and teachers, and which can therefore only be revealed through close analytical enquiry. As I intend to expose such hidden devices at work in therapeutic training, I shall follow Lave and Wenger's (1991: 40) distinction between 'learning' and 'intentional instruction'. That is to say, as people learn things beyond what they are openly and 'intentionally' taught, intentional instruction can never account for all that is learnt, for far more is learnt than what is intentionally taught—things always seep in through the back-door, so to speak.

As we shall see, psychotherapy students learn by overt and explicit educational 'devices', but more importantly by devices that are covert, insensible or hidden from both they and their teachers: I shall show that through shrouded devices that work to 'transfigure the trainee's imagination', to 'socially induce anxieties and uncertainty', to 'alter the trainees sense of personhood' and to 'instil a sense of clinical mastery', that is, I shall show that through devices not always explicitly recognised by the trainees and institutes as such, trainees learn to accept as true the professional reality with which they are presented. In fact, we might go so far as to say that it is these covert and insensible modes of learning (rather than overt and intentional devices) which constitute the most powerful factors and forces facilitating the making of psychotherapists.

While Bourdieu's ideas are therefore helpful, as I am predominantly interested in how individual dispositions are *established* in trainees, it is necessary to go beyond his work and analytic standpoint. As Sinclair points out (1997: 22), Bourdieu's study is mainly concerned with the adult *practice* of dispositions (how dispositions shape adult behaviour), rather than with how dispositions are transmitted to new generations. Bourdieu is therefore less attentive to the various devices by which persons are inculcated with dispositions that transform them to both 'fit with' and perpetuate existing institutional norms and preferences. For example, by focusing on the practice of established dispositions, Bourdieu's work resembles Ernest Gellner's (1985) study *The Psychoanalytic Movement*. Gellner investigated how the theory of psychoanalysis constitutes a self-protecting 'anatomy of belief'—namely, a system of intellectual props and practices which tries to protect the psychoanalytic system from external critics or internal dissent. Like Bourdieu, he was less concerned with the institutional devices used to transmit these systems over time, preferring instead to analyse how such systems maintained their dominance in the present.

Gellner thus studied the *transformed* practitioner, whereas it is with the *processes of transformation* that I am concerned. For if we are truly to understand why professionals practise in the world as they do (why individual lawyers, doctors, academics, actors, psychotherapists, and so on, all bear the idiosyncratic stamps of their particular professional regime) we must investigate the sites where their professional dispositions are officially transmitted. Through exposing the overt and covert devices that facilitate learning, then, we will uncover the idiosyncratic 'type' of graduate the psychoanalytic institute seeks to produce; a type largely complicit with and supportive of existing institutional structures and interests. A type therefore, and as I shall argue, which may be securing the demise of the community so far as the values and structures with which the trainee is compelled to comply may well be the very values and structures that are serving to undermine the vitality of the profession itself. In other words, are these institutes, despite their avowed intentions, sowing the seeds of the therapeutic community's own demise?

How far trainees are mere pawns in the hands of more powerful institutional and social forces will also be a theme of my research. While it is clear that trainees have a good deal of influence over how their transformation into 'professional status' proceeds, it is also clear that they are never entirely free from influential social and institutional forces which shape their development in a prescribed direction. For example, along with social theorists such a F. Furedi (2004), R. Sennet (1976), E. Gellner (1985), and Heelas (1996) we can argue that the erosion of traditional 'communities of belief' in modern society has led many individuals to seek security in new systems of meaning. For such individuals the psychotherapeutic calling offers a surrogate moral and professional home. What is precisely appealing about the therapeutic system as taught in the institutes, is that it is cast as a bounded configuration of ideas: pure, discrete, and logically consistent. It is taught as a circumscribed, totalising body of knowledge that provides a comprehensive explanatory system in terms of which self, society and other can be understood. The 'modernist' manner in which the psychoanalytic world-view is transmitted discourages the uncertainly and 'the doubt in discourse' characteristic of the post-modernist period. It is this totalising aspect of the psychoanalytic project that could appeal to those dislocated from old social allegiances (to state, community, church etc.), as it replaces lost frames of orientation with a new conceptual system which is itself buttressed by authoritative and powerful symbols and institutions.

If the demise of traditional communities and belief can help make the assimilation of psychoanalytic dispositions more attractive to candidates, and can thus be said to more smoothly aid their transition into a surrogate professional and moral home, then we must, in the first place, partly locate one factor bearing upon the practitioner's transformation in this fall of traditional communities in modern society. The second external factor aiding the trainee's transformation is located in the institutes themselves, which aim to create practitioners who will support and perpetuate the wider psychoanalytic cause.

To say that trainees are influenced and transformed by these powerful, external forces, however, is not to say that trainees have no influence over their own transformations—for indeed many trainees do resist the smooth and total assimilation of the psycho-analytic world-view. To invoke David Parkin's (1995: 145) insight for a moment—individuals find it difficult to completely convert to new modes of meaning and thought, for old meanings and ideas resist total disavowal and often re-emerge for re-integration. However, those individuals in training who resist the unques-tioned assimilation of psychoanalytic knowledge, and who to some extent therefore assert their own vision of things, often encounter institutional opposition. For these trainees there is a clear struggle between the official practice that they are taught to adopt, and the integrated practice that they might privately believe. For them the knowledge that the institutes impart, instead of being assimilated purely and completely, is often latticed or integrated with existing knowledge to create something entirely new. Old knowledge that resists complete disavowal can therefore affect and colour what is being taught. These influences often confound the kind of pure as-similation which institutes everywhere seem to prefer.

While the training institute therefore may wish for the smooth and unruffled transformation of its trainees, for some this does not occur successfully. For these trainees there may be opposition and dissent which on occasion may be formalised in innovation. This is to say (and to take issue with Sinclair's contention [1997: 321-27] that rigid forms of training produce professionals unlikely to change the system), the more formal and firm the training struc-ture, the more likely dissent, fracture, and on occasion some kind of defiant and creative innovation. Ironically, rigid institutions may ultimately beget their own transformation via the opposition they invariably generate. By asserting this position I also depart from Bourdieu who speaks of agency as arising only from the cultiva-tion of 'cultural literacy' (awareness of the world one is in): it may also arise from rigid structures which create the subjective condi-tions for inevitable opposition—rigidity, so to speak, is often the source of its own demise.[8]

In the end, in discussing psychotherapeutic training it goes without saying that questions pertaining to the truth or falsity of psychotherapeutic ideas are of anthropological interest only in so far as what people believe (both inside and outside the community) has a bearing upon the social reality of the community itself.[9] Thus the psychologist's, intellectualist's or philosopher's concern about whether a given theory or belief is objectively true is replaced here with a phenomenological concern about the social significance of beliefs that are held to be 'true' (Kapferer 1983: xix). As Mauss and Hubert tell us, 'beliefs exists because they exist objectively as social facts' (Hubert and Mauss 1981 [1964]: 101), implying that the objective truth of a belief and the social consequences of its being believed to be true are quite separate things. In this work I am concerned with the social implications of a set of beliefs held to be true, not with making epistemological or normative judgements about their truth or falsity.[10] In fact, if this study offers critical comments at all, then these do not pertain to the ideas the profession believes and expounds, but only to the institutions which purport to protect, steward and transmit these ideas.

WHY THIS BOOK MATTERS

In this monograph, and within the broad parameters of the orientation outlined above, I wish to make use of an older and deeply insightful body of anthropological theory by applying it to this novel contemporary context. With this method, rather than breaking with traditional anthropological approaches, I seek to affirm the worth of tested anthropological ideas by reworking them in the context of a critical 'repatriated anthropology' (Gusterson 1996: 3). But before I proceed to outline why I believe this book matters, let me first provide a brief outline of each chapter in turn.

In chapter one I provide a history of the institutional development of psychotherapy in Britain, identifying three broad historical trends that have influenced the state of the community today: the expansion of psychotherapy during the twentieth century; the proliferation and stratification of training schools that has accompanied this growth; and the growing attack psychoanalytic psychotherapy has sustained during the last quarter of the twentieth century.

In chapters two and three we move into the first stage of psychoanalytic socialisation: *pre-training therapy* (i.e. the personal psychotherapy all candidates undergo before entering the institute). In short, we learn that the therapeutic encounter, like any ritual encounter, takes place in a bounded 'psychotherapeutic frame' which delimits the spatial, temporal and relational dimensions of the session. We further learn how within this frame trainees come to imagine themselves and the world differently. This cultivation of a 'psychoanalytic imagination' constitutes a form of 'institutional vetting' ensuring that only those who have taken to the therapeutic experience self-select to proceed into the institute.

In chapter four I show how the 'psychoanalytic imagination' is appealed to within the institutes to legitimate the training they offer. By studying the next phase of training, *the seminar encounter*, we will see how status imbalances within institutes are legitimated by analytic ideas, and how the transmission of 'text-based', 'secret', and 'personal' knowledge shields this knowledge from criticism. In short I argue that the educative atmosphere in seminars is by and large more 'affirmative' than 'critical', more 'sectarian' than 'academic'.

In chapter five we focus on how institutions manage trainee dissent, describing how trainees are taught to direct their doubts away from the system (the ideas) and onto other receptacles (patients, outsiders, competitors). I then illustrate through selected case studies instances where trainee doubt, being unsuccessfully redirected, settles on the paradigm itself causing 'dissent' from the orthodox position. How dissent has been managed historically by the institution provides insight into why the community lies in a fractured state today.

In chapter six we turn to the next phase of training—*clinical supervision*, focusing especially on the psychoanalytic understanding of aetiology. By analysing an extended case study ('the case of Arya'), and the socio-historical biases shaping Freud's early thinking, I illustrate how and why the analytic understanding of aetiology can be seen as limited. I further show how such aetiological assumptions are subtly affirmed in clinical supervision, leading practitioners to treat patients in predictable ways.

In chapter seven we will see how covert institutional pressures make trainees susceptible to the instruction on offer. By linking the ordeals and stresses of socialisation to trainees' dependency on seniors, we find that the social conditions of the institute covertly render trainees susceptible to embodying the commitments, preferences, and the expansive ideology that seniors embrace.

Finally, in chapter eight I reveal that the psychoanalytic habitus not only supports a species of clinical practice, but a way of life. Here we acknowledge three 'projects' that the psychoanalytic myth supports: the ethical, the political, and the communal. By analysing the core values analytic training inculcates, and by exploring the profound personal meaning therapy comes to have for practitioners, I provide the background against which the deeper significance of training can be revealed—initiation into a 'self-redemptive', socio-political movement of wide social aspiration and influence.

In all chapters I make use of a wide variety of anthropological concepts to illuminate the core stages of therapeutic training. In this sense my work is less a 'case-study' showing where existing anthropology is mistaken, than an 'example' of how existing anthropological theory can unravel social phenomena in the psychotherapeutic context. In Jeremy MacClancy's (2002: 11) phrase, I 'study up' with anthropological insights in hand, showing how individuals are socialised into systems of meaning that support and which are refracted in the community's social structure. In other words, I show how institutes can train individuals to recreate and sustain the social structures of the community itself.

Applying the anthropological imagination to the psychotherapeutic context, along with contributing to the growing ethnographic record of professional socialisation, I offer a novel perspective on certain problems afflicting the psychotherapeutic profession itself. Many psychotherapists have traditionally sought to understand the fracturing and inter-rivalry within their own community by means of psychoanalytic ideas. To use Needham's phrase, such psychotherapists have reverted to a theoretical 'psychologism' to analyse community dynamics: applying ideas devised to study individuals to investigate social life and institutions. In this sense they mistakenly by-pass what sociological or anthropological theory could tell us about their social and community dynamics.

For instance, Cremerius (1990: 125) explains the inter-school rivalries that beset the profession in terms of unresolved *Oedipal rivalries.* 'To the extent to which [they] remain unresolved,' says Cremerius, 'intellectual powers are eroded and hate, jealousy and phallic rivalry define the relationships within the association (p.125). Lousada (2000: 470), alternatively, suggests that the inability of psychotherapy schools to create working partnerships is due to their inability to form *libidinal cathexis*—if such cathexis could take place then partnership might ensue. Frattaroli (1992: 132-42) argues that psychotherapy's history of schism and factionalism is due to the institutionalisation of an *internalised split* Freud never resolved between the contradictory views that neurosis is primarily intra-psychic (repressed drives) or inter-psychic (insufficient relationships). If this split could be reconciled then these divisions might fall away. While Bruzzone et al (1985: 411), stress that the regression students experience in their therapy (making them use words such as 'mummy' and 'daddy' to refer to their therapists, and use phrases such as a 'good feed' to refer to a good training experience) is replicated during their training in the institute. Students then may feel persecuted and paranoid in the institute just as they might in therapy when in regression. Finally, Figlio (1993: 326) argues that because trainees internalise key figures—such as the therapist and the institute—when they encounter others holding onto different (often opposing) internalised figures a mutual hostility ensues.

I could continue to pile up many more examples of how community dynamics have been explained by psychotherapists in terms of psychoanalytic concepts.[11] This fact tells us not only something about the community in question, but that therapists themselves, as so many expressed to me, hold deep concerns about the warring and fractured state of their profession; an institutionalised rivalry not only impeding the process of statutory regulation, but also the cross-fertilisation of ideas necessary for theoretical development and reform, and—one might add—improved practice.

Not all therapists, of course, have resorted to explaining community dynamics in terms of psychoanalytic ideas. Some have understood wider tensions in more practical terms of how candidates are selected and trained (Cremerius 1990; Kleinman 1998); and how creativity is discouraged in training institutes (Kernberg 2006, 1996). Indeed, in recent years a new body of literature has proposed reforms to psychoanalytic education more broadly (Gaza-

Guerrero 2002a, 2002b; Kernberg 2006; Levine 2003; Mayer 2003). This literature is unified in suggesting that many of the problems it believes the community now faces (diminishing creativity, ongoing conservatism and interschool rivalry) must be challenged at the institutional level either by divesting self-interested groups of any legal authority to define what is legitimate or illegitimate practice (Whan 1999: 312); by introducing openness, pluralism and authenticity into training institutes (Samuels 1993); by diversifying and broadening the curriculum to facilitate in candidates better empathetic and introspective perceptiveness (Berman 2004; Samuels 1993); or by establishing institutional mechanisms by which the power of executive and educational committees can be devolved (Kernberg 2006). Strategies such as abolishing the traditional training analysis (Mayer 2003), undermining retrogressive dependency upon the theoretical faiths of the past (Garza-Guerrero 2002b), developing more objective criteria for training assessment (Tuckett 2003), and strengthening the intellectual, scholarly and research context within which psychoanalytic education takes place (Auchincloss & Michels 2003), have all been championed as possible remedies to the demise of creativity in the institutes, and to the rise and entrenchment of rivalrous relations between different psychotherapeutic schools.

While this project is not directly about making sense of such problems and the rivalries as well as the entrenched positions they engender, it is my belief that an anthropology of psychotherapeutic socialisation can bring fresh light to old troubles while avoiding being prescriptive or normative. Anthropologists have long known that much human conduct is orientated to, and shaped by, the demands and pressures of the environments in which people find themselves. If institutes harbour definite expectations in relation to which trainees must organise their behaviour and professional aims, then what these expectations demand of trainees (either openness or antipathy toward 'other' schools) will influence how they act as professionals, and finally whether the community will move towards a more creative pluralism or simply remain in its fractured state. Indeed, if change is to occur in the community then what may require alteration are the circumstances and situations people have to contend with. '[I]f this were done', as Becker has stated, 'students would probably adapt to the changed situation and develop quite different kinds of perspectives' (Becker *et al* 2002: 442). What Becker, Samuels, Sinclair, Luhrmann and others have shown is that any kind of community reform must start with a deep reflexive inspection of the sites or places where the community's values, practices and beliefs are transmitted and sustained—and in so far as this study comprises such an investigation it may thus indirectly inform and contribute to the unravelling of these social problems.

PSYCHOANALYTIC / PSYCHODYNAMIC PSYCHOTHERAPY EXPLAINED

Before discussing my fieldwork methods, I would first like to identify the exact kind of practitioner and training upon which my research is focused. The most obvious confusion I must first anticipate concerns the differing roles of psychologist, psychiatrist, and psychotherapist. A psychologist is someone whose professional life involves researching and applying psychology (e.g. in the different fields of education, forensics, criminality, etc.). Psychological theories charter different aspects of mental life such as cognition (memory, perception, learning), and behaviour (social and individual). Thus psychologists are not clinicians. If they see patients at all they only do so if they have submitted to an additional doctoral or postgraduate training in clinical psychology, in such instances they are referred to as 'clinical psychologists'.[12] Psychiatrists, on the other hand, are medical doctors who specialise in diagnosing and treating mental illness. They concentrate mainly on pharmacological intervention. Like psychologists, some psychiatrists have had an additional psychotherapeutic training, usually at one of the independent psychotherapeutic institutes that I have studied here, but most have only a rudimentary training during their own psychiatric residency. As to how much psychotherapy psychiatrists study and employ is largely at their own and their supervisor's discretion, although psychiatric departments now insist that trainees undertake some form of psychotherapeutic instruction during their residency.[13]

To turn now to the psychotherapist, he or she is a clinician who is usually a trained member of a psychotherapeutic training body recognised by one of the two major accrediting bodies: the BPC (British Psychoanalytic Council) or the UKCP (the United Kingdom Council for Psychotherapy). A psychotherapist need not be a psychiatrist or psychologist, and the majority of psychotherapists are neither, although all must have some form of undergraduate or 'equivalent' experience (i.e. in nursing, social work, or teaching etc.). The fact that the British psychotherapeutic field is wide, diversified, and unpredictably protean, comprising myriad schools and contending traditions, makes the term 'psychotherapist' greatly unspecific. It denotes an array of practitioners from 'psychoanalysts' to 'cognitive behavioural therapists' to 'humanistic therapists' and 'existentialist therapists'. In Britain alone there are eight *traditions* of psychotherapy recognised by the UKCP, each one comprising an assemblage of varying *schools*. With this tangle of divergent forms it is crucial to define the precise kind of psychotherapy upon which my research will chiefly focus. Broadly put, I focus on the training and practice of practitioners within the *psychodynamic or psychoanalytic tradition* which is by far the largest and most established psychotherapeutic tradition in Britain.

'Psychodynamic' psychotherapy is the term I shall use in this book to characterise all those psychotherapies stemming from Freud's original teaching. Under the rubric of 'psychodynamic psychotherapy' I shall include '*psychoanalytic psychotherapists*' and '*psychoanalysts*'. Thus in this book I shall uses the terms 'psychodynamic' and 'psychoanalytic' interchangeably. Psychoanalysts can be distinguished from all other psychodynamic psychotherapists in Britain by virtue of being trained at the *Institute of Psychoanalysis*. The term 'psychoanalyst' then, in Britain today, denotes an institutional affiliation rather than a species of psychotherapy distinct from other psychodynamic forms. Where psychoanalysis is most obviously distinct clinically is in requesting that its trainees (and often patients) submit to five-times-weekly analysis (a practice which is supposed to facilitate a 'deeper' analysis), while other psychoanalytic and psychodynamic trainings request only three-times-weekly contracts or less. The social significance of these distinctions, and there are many, I will return to at a later point.

The mainstream tradition of psychodynamic or psychoanalytic psychotherapy includes the great pioneers of psychotherapy such as Sigmund Freud (1856-1939), Carl Gustav Jung (1875-1961), Melanie Klein (1882-1960), Karen Horney (1885-1952), Donald Winnicott (1896-1971), Jacques Lacan (1901-81) and Erik Erikson

(1902-1994). Thus it comprises many schools which have links both institutionally and theoretically. As I shall focus on these institutional linkages at later points, here I shall very briefly focus on the theoretical.

The common thread linking the *psychodynamic or psychoanalytic tradition* (in distinction from, say, the humanistic or cognitive / behavioural tradition) is that its numerous schools all agree that mental functioning is a 'dynamic' phenomenon (deriving from the Greek *dunasthi* 'to have strength or power'). The psyche is seen as structured into permeable segments (e.g. ego and unconscious) which interact dynamically to the degree that thought, emotion, and behaviour, both adaptive and psychopathological, are believed to be influenced by these interactions. For instance, Freud believed that we have strivings, feelings, and wishes of which we are not entirely conscious, but which we resist coming into our awareness —mainly because we fear losing our group's approval if such stifled elements are felt and expressed. As the 'repression' of these fearful and socially unacceptable elements largely occurs in early childhood, childhood is posited as the key phase of human biography—hence the psychoanalytic mantra 'the child is the father of the man'. That these strivings are largely repressed does not mean that they cease to exist. Rather they retain their dynamism and if not adequately sublimated they express themselves in distorted ways. Hence Freud's explanation of neurotic symptoms as repressed strivings that resurface in disguised forms—although we may be aware of the suffering they bring, we may remain oblivious as to their origins and meaning. Part of the therapist's task is to make these forces and their meaning conscious to the patient so he or she can be freed from the destructive compulsions they establish in the personality.

Different psychodynamic schools have emphasised the centrality of different aspects of psychodynamics. For purposes of clarity I shall summarise these approaches under a broad distinction largely adopted by the British community today (a distinction I elaborate in appendix one). This is between the *analytical psychodynamic psychotherapists* (classical Freudian psychoanalysts who stress the instinct theory—e.g. Freud, Ernest Jones, K. Abraham), and the *interpersonal psychotherapists* (including the 'Kleinians' and the 'Independents' otherwise known as the 'object relations' therapists—namely Donald Winnicott, Harry Guntrip, and William Fairbairn). However, such is the common ground of both perspectives that in the BPC they fall under the broad category of the 'psychoanalytic'.

TO WHOM I RESTRICT MY RESEARCH

In this paper I restrict my research to the *institutions of psychodynamic or psychoanalytic psychotherapy*, which are largely integrative (teaching both the analytic and interpersonal approaches). Despite this integrative approach, which is the hallmark of modern British psychodynamic and psychoanalytic training, some institutions lay special emphasis on the teaching of one key school (e.g. the Lincoln Centre is integrative with a special emphasis on Kleinian therapy, while the Institute of Psychoanalysis is integrative with a special emphasis on the analytic approach).

As my fieldwork focused on psychodynamic and psychoanalytic institutions, in what sense might my research apply to the Institute of Psychoanalysis, the only institute that refers to its graduates as psychoanalysts? I believe my research is largely applicable for the following reasons: firstly, the model of psychoanalytic psychotherapy training that I am investigating is based on that offered at the Institute. Most of the teachers at these schools are psychoanalysts, while most members of their senior committees comprise psychoanalysts. Thus most of the people I interviewed and befriended were being taught and schooled by psychoanalysts, while many of my interviews were conducted with analysts or with those trained by them. Furthermore, as many psychoanalytic schools are seeking psychoanalytic status (so they might join the IPA—the 'International Psychoanalytic Association'—and call their graduates 'psychoanalysts'), they are careful to bring into alignment their methods of teaching with those of the Institute of Psychoanalysis. Finally, the major psychodynamic training institutes belong under the same accrediting body, the BPC (British Psychoanalytic Council) which standardises trainings across the board, including the Institute of Psychoanalysis. Thus structurally speaking these trainings are largely comparable. For these reasons, although my research is strictly speaking an ethnography of psychoanalytic socialisation, my research has considerable applicability to the understanding of psychoanalysis.[14]

The practical and—one must say—difficult business of gaining entrance to, and conducting fieldwork within, psychodynamic training institutes, is something I must now address. Previous anthropologists who have sought entrance have commonly met with rejection. Ernest Gellner's proposal to study ethnographically the British Psychoanalytic Society, for instance, was never given approval. According to the then president, D.W. Winnicott, the institute would rather arrange some such investigation at a later date with a social scientist of their specification than hand this role to a self-appointed researcher (their investigation has yet to materialise).[15] Dr Audrey Cantile's proposal some years later was also rejected on similar grounds—it seems that the institute was again reluctant to trust a non-therapist and thus possible antagonist with research responsibilities.[16] However, things were different for Dr D. Kirsner, himself a sociologist and psychologist, who was more successful in gaining access to institutes in the United States and Australia, perhaps because of his 'clinical psychologist' status. But again in the case of the British institute he met with rejection. For this reason his subsequent book *Unfree Associations* (2000), regrettably enough, is empty of data concerning the British context.

While the doors of the Institute of Psychoanalysis remained closed to these scholars, I too, when approaching this and other British psychodynamic institutes, experienced my share of standing out in the cold[17]—a fact raising an important question: With the obvious reticence of psychoanalytic institutes to open their doors to outside investigation, which is itself an interesting social fact, how then did I gain access? The answer is best made by my immediate admission that I was not always an 'outsider', for my story begins with my formal training in psychodynamic psychotherapy at a well-known training institute in London; a training that I put aside after two years to pursue other interests. At the point of leaving, although my interest in psychotherapy and my desire to train remained alive, I had little intention of returning to study the process anthropologically, this idea only materialised some time later.

The fact that I was already affiliated with the therapeutic profession made my returning to train and my gaining access to other trainings a more straightforward affair. This does not mean that there were no ethical concerns regarding my return, which was participatory and observational in the truest sense, but that my previous training put stoppers on open doors that would have otherwise closed shut. Before looking at the ethical issues surrounding my return, let me first outline the particular form my participant observation took.

My fieldwork has included two years of formal training (not counting first years of previous study) at a psychotherapeutic institute in London. This incorporated my attending weekly seminars at the institute and sitting more than 200 hours of clinical supervision (psychoanalytic). Accompanying these commitments I have engaged in a full three years of individual psychotherapy. Along with these institutional activities, in the second year of my fieldwork I took up the activity of seeing patients (three patients weekly for outpatient psychodynamic psychotherapy in the NHS). My NHS placement also included my attending weekly psychodynamic peer supervision, and frequent one-on-one supervision with the centre's senior supervisor (a psychoanalyst).

During the second year of my fieldwork I resided in London for ten months. This enabled me not only to become more immersed in these formal commitments, and also to observe and attend seminars at a neighbouring institute as a 'guest', but also to spend countless hours in informal discussions with psychoanalytic trainees. At this point I was also able to conduct many hours of formal interviews with both training and qualified practitioners, which I have supplemented with 200 surveys sent out to psychoanalytic practitioners around the country. Alongside my participatory activities I undertook a thorough inspection of two psychoanalytic trainings, one within the BPC, and one in the UKCP. This inspection included interviewing trainees and tutors as to the structure and experience of training; inspecting curricula, assessment criteria, institutional histories and theoretical preferences, institutional relations with neighbouring institutes, as well as interviewing trainees as to their experience of the training to which they were subject.

In all these encounters whenever possible I have made known my research intentions.[18] That I was both insider and outsider seemed rarely to place me in an ambiguous position in respect of my colleagues. From those accepting me as an 'insider' to the profession (e.g. those with whom I worked and trained) I experienced much help and openness; it was only when approaching those who did not know me that I was treated more warily (at worst, surveys would not be filled in, interviews not granted, and requests and queries turned down or ignored). Naturally, it could be argued that what I interpreted as suspicion of my outsider status might have had its cause in one of many variables. But since how I construed my role (as predominantly a researcher or as a member of the profession) seemed to influence people's reactions to me, the conclusion emerged that where I was placed (by others and by myself) had a significant impact upon how I was received.

A Final Note on Names

To protect the informants of this research I keep their names and the institutes to which they belong confidential. I take this measure because many of the informants I interviewed made disclosures that at the worst might compromise their relationships with seniors and colleagues, or jeopardise their positions in the community. Naturally, if this were a species of investigative journalism such 'exposing' (of seniors at least) would be a legitimate task, but as my objectives are academic and anthropological, that is, as I primarily work to understand the reasons for such comments and what they tell us about the community, I believe such discretion does not affect the deeper aims of my project. Also, if respecting anonymity protects informants, by promising them confidentiality I also gave them licence to speak on matters more easily revealed from the safe ground of anonymity. As I now find myself in the position of honouring my early pledges, I revert to pseudonyms where necessary.

As for the names of various psychotherapeutic institutes, I only mention these when not speaking from the standpoint of an ethnographer. On other occasions when referring to historical data I use the names of the institutes freely. In other words, I do not reveal the names of my places of fieldwork, whereas when using historic-

ual factors as to the rise of psychotherapy a complex affair. Nevertheless, when chartering the 'why' and 'how' of the ascending therapeutic culture in Britain a number of themes present themselves for serious consideration. Some of these themes have been discussed by earlier commentators on this expansion. Theorists such as C. Lasch (1979); E. Gellner (1985); P. Berger (1965); R. Sennett (1976) and F. Furedi (2004) have emphasised the decline of religion, the decline of tradition, and the decline of the political sensibility as contributing factors to psychotherapy's expansion. As I shall focus more closely upon these theories in chapter eight, noting how their authors differ in where they precisely locate the social causes of this expansion, here I shall only concern myself with what all such theorists accept: that such expansion has undoubtedly occurred. It is from this starting point that I shall trace an expansion which has entailed a number of highly significant consequences for the practice and training of individual practitioners.

THE BIRTH AND EXPANSION OF BRITISH PSYCHOTHERAPY

From the first psychotherapeutic institution in Britain to the founding of the most recent institute in the present day, one characteristic stands out in the history of psychotherapy—its meteoric growth during the twentieth century. The genesis of this expansion we could locate as early as 1910 when the first group of analysts who were in part responding to the mounting success of psychoanalysis in America, began to actively establish psychoanalytic institutions outside of Vienna (Freud 1986 [1914]: 102). This early movement comprised a number of young physicians and psychologists who gathered around the charismatic figure of Freud with the intention of learning and practising the new medical craft. This company of minds, not happy to leave the movement there, worked to assure the group's continuity and the succession of its leadership. The Nuremberg congress was held in March 1910 to achieve this. It was here where the IPA (International Psychoanalytic Association) was first formed with the purpose of both safeguarding and proliferating what had been so far achieved (Freud 1986 [1914]: 103): K. Abraham was entrusted the chair of the Berlin group, Alfred Adler, the chair of the Vienna group, while Carl Jung oversaw the Zurich

group. A year later the Munich group was set up by Dr L. Seif and in the same year the first American group was formed under the chairmanship of A. A. Brill. In 1913 two further groups were established: Budapest formed a cell under the leadership of Sandor Ferenczi, while in England the first group was formed by Freud's closest ally and tireless apologist, Ernest Jones. The founding of the British Psychoanalytic Society in London in 1913, containing eight members in total, marked the inauguration of the first psychotherapeutic institution in Britain.

After this first British institute was established there was little institutional expansion within psychotherapy until post-war Britain. As M. Jacobs has told us:

> Apart from the founding of the Society for Analytical psychologists, the founding of the Tavistock [1920]... and the rise of the Portman clinic in 1939, the only significant developments mid-century were the foundation of the Association of Child Psychotherapists in 1949... and the wider accessibility of training (and indeed of therapy for the wider public) through the foundation of the Association of Psychotherapists. (Jacobs 2000: 456)

In fact by 1936 all the principle psychotherapeutic organisations were in place: the British Psychoanalytic Society (1913) (later called the Institute of Psychoanalysis); the Tavistock Clinic (1920), and the Analytical Club (1936)—now called the Society for Analytical Psychology.

During the pre-First World War period, and to a lesser extent through the inter-war years, that psychotherapy's expansion remained modest was something largely welcomed within British psychiatry. Many hostilities within medical psychiatry to the new 'talking cure' were deeply entrenched; partly because at that time medical education still instilled a sceptical empiricism that kept watch on what it felt to be ungrounded methods and their proliferation, and partly because these psychiatrists preferred the physicalist leaning of traditional psychiatry that tried to effect cure through direct bodily intervention (Holmes 2000: 389).[19]

It was not until the First World-War that the initial step to bridge the division between psychiatry and psychoanalytic therapy was taken. The war was the most significant factor in launching this rapprochement as publicly funded psychotherapy was developed in an effort to treat victims of shell-shock and war fatigue. Many outpatient services were opened by middle class intellectuals who offered treatment for neuroses, while psychotic disorders were treated in the larger hospitals (Pines 1991). In London the Tavistock clinic and the Cassel Hospital were among the first institutions to offer the new psychotherapeutic treatment, setting up services in 1920 and 1919 respectively. At this time psychotherapy began to leave its imprint on psychiatry in another way as the use of psychodynamic group therapy in military hospitals obliged many psychiatrists to become skilled in the new psychodynamic techniques.

If during these initial years dynamic therapy only made modest inroads into psychiatry, outside of medicine psychotherapy was gaining growing favour in the public imagination. By the 1920s Freud had joined the likes of Einstein and other contemporary scientists by being portrayed in the US and UK daily papers and weekly reviews as a charismatic scientist who was revolutionising our understanding of human nature (Forrester 1994: 183). That Freud assumed this enigmatic role is supported by many retrospective studies that detail the early expansion and growing popularity of psychoanalysis. These studies, as Forrester tells us, show that during the 20s and 30s Freud took on iconic status. Henri Ellenberger's (1970) study broadly records the Euro/American expansion, while Rapp's (1988) exploration of the same expansion in 1920s Britain offers a more situated analysis of the mounting fascination with all things Freudian. Another important study by Gabbard and Gabbard (1987) documents how psychotherapists were portrayed by Hollywood from the 1930s to the 1980s, emphasising how from the early 1930s interest in psychotherapy proliferated in the middle-classes. The rise of therapy in cinema, as Forrester puts it, constituted 'one dream industry feeding off another'—a mutual exchange that served the expansion of psychotherapy very well (Forrester 1994: 183).

The status of psychoanalytic therapy was also improved by the kind of cultural icons who gave it their endorsement. In England in

the 20s and 30s many notable literary and scholarly figures ex-
tolled the uncanny attraction of the talking cure. Bertrand Russell,
T.S. Eliot and Thomas Mann were just some of the admiring few,
while W. H. Auden in his *In Memoriam Sigmund Freud* elevated him
to a kind of modern Moses:

> so many long-forgotten objects
> revealed by his undiscouraged shining
> are returned to us made precious again;
> games we had thought we much drop as we grew up,
> little noises we dared not laugh at,
> faces we made when no one was looking
> (Auden 1950: 59)

Other studies chartering the rise of psychotherapy show that by
the mid-century the therapy's allure was endemic. Eva Moskowitz
(1990) in her book *In Therapy We Trust: America's Obsession with Self-
Fulfilment* shows that it was at this time when the popularity of
psychoanalys really took root in the US. While N. Rose's (1990)
study, which traces a like development in the UK, shows that after
the Second World War the therapeutic ethos had gained influence
with policy-makers and business managers who were keen on con-
verting the application of therapy into economic reward.

Along with these more popular endorsements, there also followed approval from many quarters of the academic community.
To focus on American anthropology, for example, the culture and
personality school headed by such well-known figures as Ruth Benedict (1934), Linton and Kardiner (1939) and Margaret Mead
(1943), embraced psychoanalytic assumptions and argued that
every culture has a distinctive pattern of child-rearing which produces a distinctive personality type—one consistent with that culture. Despite this kind of cultural analysis being resisted in British
anthropology, psychoanalysis was still being publicised in Britain
by anthropologists from W. H. R. Rivers to the current S. Heald
and D. Parkin (1994).

POST-SECOND WORLD WAR EXPANSION

As popular acceptance of psychotherapy increased after the First
World War, by the end of the Second World War psychiatry's characteristic hostility towards psychoanalysis was loosening in certain
quarters. This was partly influenced by the growing acceptance of
dynamic therapy in American psychiatry,[20] not to mention that
after the two world wars, as Lousada reminds us, 'the disturbance,
guilt, and the experience of such immense destructiveness left psychiatrists with much to think about' (Lousada 2000: 471). If pre-
Second World War British psychiatry was in the main hostile to dynamic therapy, then in the post-war climate and through the 1950s
its institutional fortunes were to change. By the early 1960s con-
sultant and psychotherapy posts had been established in a few
psychiatric departments, and junior psychiatrists, along with training in the traditional diagnostic methods, were being routinely introduced to psychoanalytic techniques.[21] During the next decade
there was a steady increase in psychotherapy departments
throughout the UK, with key centres being established in Notting-
ham, Oxford, Manchester, Birmingham, and Newcastle—these
joining the slightly more established units of Edinburgh, Bristol,
and London.[22]

The acceptance of the therapeutic was thus expanding through
the 60s and 70s both inside and outside established institutions.
This can be seen from an assessment of the statistics compiled on
therapeutic attendance around this time, statistics which, although
not focusing on dynamic therapies in particular, nevertheless show
that demand for some kind of talking cure was growing at a rapid
rate. To start with the American case, Donna Lafromboise stated
that by the 1960s 14 per cent of the American public had received
some form of therapy at least once in their lives, while by 1995
nearly half the population had experienced some form of therapeutic intervention. And it is estimated that by the turn of the century this figure will have increased to 80 per cent.[23]

The impact on British society was also significant. As Furedi
points out, since the 1980s (when counselling became one of Britain's little growth industries) the number of people practising the
talking cure and receiving treatment has rapidly grown. For example, just as the amount of registered therapists has dramatically

increased in recent years (e.g. the UKCP Register of Psychotherapists grew from 3,500 in 1997 to 5,500 in 1999—see table 1), so too has the amount of therapy hours being conducted in Britain. For instance, an independent research carried out by Counselling, Advice, Mediation, Psychotherapy, Advocacy Guidance (CAMP) concluded that the number of therapeutic encounters taking place each month in Britain was in the region of 1,231,000, a far cry from the handful of analytic hours being yearly practised by the early analysts (Furedi 2004: 9).

	c. 1960 (Halmos, 1978)	c. 1976 (Halmos, 1978)	c. 1999 (Jacobs, 2000)	c. 2005 (Various sources)
Psychotherapists and Psychoanalysts	400	903	6,900	7,800
Clinical Psychologists (including CBT practitioners)	150	1,500	3,004	4,340
Professional Counsellors		800	1,700	5,000[24]
Total	550	2,203	11,604	16,149

Table 1. Comparative numbers of psychotherapists, counsellors and psychologists[25]

The expansion of the therapeutic was reflected in the proliferation of new kinds of psychotherapy being contrived. As Grunbaum (1984) noted, in 1959 a study was published listing thirty-six different kinds of therapy; while a later work by Wilby (1977) reports no fewer than 200 conceptually different psychotherapies. Current informants in the profession put the number of therapies in existence around the 400 mark. Despite the fact that only a minority of these 'therapies' enjoyed institutional support, their proliferation evidences the growing need to accommodate the increasing interest in therapeutic intervention.

The growth in the years after World War Two brought a vogue for do-it-yourself therapy. As Roy Porter notes, 'pop Freudianism, exemplified in the works of Eric Berne's (1964) *The Games People*

Play... helped people in their quest for self-understanding' (Porter 1996: 388). Other books such as Eric Fromm's (1955 [1942]) *Fear of Freedom*, Karen Horney's (1942) *Self Analysis*, and more recently Scott Peck's (1978) *The Road Less Travelled* seemed to offer new and exciting ways of understanding old dilemmas: 'Old fashioned religious, moral, and material principles were replaced by psychological categories', says Porter, 'the single example of this was the reception of psychoanalysis' (Porter 1996: 396)

The growing trend within post-war Britain to recast social or religious problems in psychological terms, a trend often resisted in the social sciences and particularly by Marxist theorists, was spotted as early as 1949. At this time the director of clinical research at Crichton Royal Hospital, Willy Mayer-Gross, noted that 'during the last 30 years the interest in psychiatry has shifted from the major psychoses, statistically relatively rare occurrences, to milder and borderline cases, the minor deviations from the normal average' (quoted in Porter 1996: 360). Surveys that originally focused on 'abnormal' populations when tabulating mental disorder began to include what had not hitherto been regarded as pathological: 'Psychiatric attention was thereby being extended to "milder" and "borderline" cases, and mental abnormality began to be seen as part of normal variability' (Porter, 1996: 360). The threshold of what people defined as illness dropped further in the coming decades, increasing the overall volume of psychological complaints (Shorter, 1997: 289). With the expansion of the therapeutic, problems that might have previously been considered economic, social, or moral in kind were gradually interpreted psychologically, usually in terms of illness, neuroses, or other injurious psychological problems. Social theorists such as Littlewood and Lipsedge (1987 [1982]), and Furedi (2004: 6) partly locate the higher rates of depression not in an actual rise in pathology, but in our tendency to over-diagnose the phenomena.[26] Our cultural imagination has been socialised to reconfigure ever more experience as 'traumatic' and then to trace the aetiology of current mental states back to these traumatic and psychological origins.[27]

The trend towards 'medicalisation' or 'psychologisation' of discontent was promoted by the interests of the pharmacological companies. As suffering was ever more reconfigured in psychological terms, causes of distress were increasingly located within the person, and what better device to alter the very bones of subjectivity than psychotropic intervention. As the successes of drug therapy began to be publicised and as requests for prescriptions soared, it dawned on pharmacological companies that here lay the future. As one commentator claimed, in the scramble to corner the market these companies would distort psychiatry's diagnostic sense and increase the number of illness categories: 'A given disorder might have been scarcely noticed until a drug company claimed to have a remedy for it, after which it became an epidemic' (Shorter 1997: 319). The availability of treatments, both psychotherapeutic and pharmacological, led to an increase in the recognition of 'problems' that might benefit from these new treatments. This proliferation of problems naturally created a market for therapeutic services, which in turn endowed these services with ever more importance and power.

Therapy expanded in ways that Freud perhaps would not have approved of, because its expansion in Britain was not confined to the rise of the dynamic therapy of psychoanalysis. By the 1970s the talking cure that was once practised in a few scattered private consultancies, now permeated British institutions at many levels in some altered guise—universities, prisons, military institutions, out-patient units, schools, big business and corporate industry, had all to varying degrees institutionalised some version of psychotherapy or counselling. That many of these 'new' psychotherapies were not authentically psychodynamic many conservative psychotherapists would continually lament, but as expansion unfurled relentlessly, it seemed that neither their voices were heard nor their protests heeded. After the 1970s new psychotherapies gradually infiltrated that province once monopolised by the dynamic psychotherapist: the domain of private practice. Soon integrative therapists, counsellors, and clinical psychologists started establishing private consultancies which today far exceed in numbers the private clinics of psychodynamic practitioners.[28] The growth of contending therapies also had many consequences for the more established institutions. One such implication was that new tensions and relationships were steadily forming between the growing number of trainings; trainings that came to order themselves into a complex training network. This complex network I shall now de-

scribe, largely because it is the turbulent context in which each individual institute must manoeuvre.

CENTRE AND THE PERIPHERY—THE PROLIFERATION OF THERAPEUTIC TRAININGS

Accompanying this 'triumph of the therapeutic', as Philip Rieff
(1966) would call it, from the 1960s onward there came a dramatic
increase in the number of psychotherapeutic training schools being
founded in Britain. As the number of these training schools gradually multiplied, a complex network of trainings began to emerge.
Each training school, or training 'institute', as I shall refer to them
here, whilst naturally related to wider social institutions, now also
found itself related to neighbouring training institutes. Thus no
single institute could be said to reside in *de facto* isolation.

As the network of trainings expanded in the 1970s and 1980s,
individual institutes began to order themselves into their respective psychotherapeutic *traditions* (e.g. psychodynamic, behavioural,
or humanistic traditions). Boundaries began to form between these
traditions, the breaching of which became a serious matter. These
boundaries were soon protected by one of two national psychotherapeutic accrediting bodies—the UKCP (United Kingdom
Council for Psychotherapy) founded in 1989, and the BPC (The
British Psychoanalytic Council, once called The British Confederation of Psychotherapists) founded in 1992. Thus any one training
institute through its relationship to a particular *tradition* was linked
to the authority of a wider accrediting body. A diagrammatic representation might look like the figure on the facing page.[29]

All the institutes, traditions, and both accrediting bodies are in
turn related though dynamics of consensus or conflict not only to
each other, but to wider social pressures residing beyond the
boundaries of this training network.

Clarifying this assemblage of psychotherapeutic factions will be
helped by identifying any structural patterns that could be said to
exist between them. Not only will describing this structure help illuminate any shrouded order inhering in what on the surface appears a disorder of discrete institutions, but by exposing this hidden order we may reveal how it precisely affects the individual
training institute, and in turn the individual trainee.

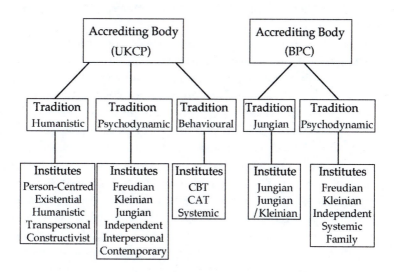

THE GENEALOGICAL STRUCTURE

One way of clarifying this structure is to notice that the proliferation of psychotherapeutic trainings in Britain follows a historical
trajectory that bears the mark of each new school founded at each
historical point in time. To understand this concretely we might
picture an upturned pyramid with the wide base representing the
myriad schools in the present, and the bottom point the birth of the
first training school in the past. From point to base unfolds an ever-
expanding genealogical structure, which documents the naissance
of every disparate school and training (see appendix two). Each of
these trainings has its particular history and can claim ascendancy
from either one or more founding individuals who, in the first
place, would have themselves passed through a given training,
and in the second, would certainly possess more or less recognised
individual prestige. As with any member of a kinship system, if I
may speak analogously, a given institute might trace it roots (via its
founding members) from a previous institution whilst simultaneously providing roots for some newer descendent organisation,
whether this 'descent' is approved by the mother institute or not.
Each institute, then, sits spider-like at the centre of its own web of

links and relations, always functioning in reference to its adjoining parts.

Another important feature of this genealogical structure is that between its constituent institutes we find relations of authority and status, a continual jostling for power, and a hierarchical ordering not always characterised by harmonious accord. For instance, more established training institutions such as the Institute of Psychoanalysis (IPA) or the British Association of Psychotherapists (BAP)—namely, those usually claiming the most illustrious founder-figures or current members, tend to have more say in how the particular 'tradition' to which it belongs functions and proceeds—in this case the psychoanalytic tradition. On the other hand, newer institutions which champion more novel therapeutic techniques, which belong to younger traditions (e.g. humanistic or integrative traditions), and which claim less illustrious figures as their founder-members, might have to struggle more arduously for status in the genealogical structure.

All such institutes whether fledgling or well-known have the opportunity to appeal beyond themselves for the ratification conferred by social institutions possessing higher and more established authority. These authoritative institutions might be either more high-prestige training institutes or traditions within the genealogical structure, or they may be non-psychotherapeutic institutions (e.g. medical, political, or academic institutions) sitting beyond the fringes of the genealogical bounds. This is to say, the struggle to acquire 'symbolic capital' of the kind that grants distinctive status need not be fruitless for fledging institutions if only they can align themselves to an accepted and authoritative institution, whether or not this lies inside the genealogical system.

THE INSTITUTE OF PSYCHOANALYSIS—A CASE IN POINT

Within this network of trainings, or what I have referred to here more analytically as the *genealogical structure*, the Institute of Psychoanalysis is a key centre in terms of power and prestige, for it was the first and only British institute to be founded by Sigmund Freud. It is the oldest, largest, and best-known institute in Britain having for many the most venerable symbols and individual associations attached to it. Such is the mystique of this institute within the profession that only its graduates call themselves 'psychoana-lysts' despite there being no legal bindings prohibiting anyone from calling himself a psychoanalyst. This institute then is a sym-bol that within the genealogical structure holds special prestige. Dynamic therapists trained at institutions other than the Institute of Psychoanalysis must alternatively take up the title, as I men-tioned earlier, of 'psychodynamic' or 'psychoanalytic' psychother-apist, a title which, for many within the profession, lacks the for-midable overtones of the label 'psychoanalyst'. Thus for the major-ity of psychotherapists, especially those within the psychodynamic tradition, this Institute is an authoritative centre, one often ap-pealed to for both affiliation and endorsement. From this powerful centre proceed ever more peripheral institutes often experiencing decreasing levels of status. For example, a general consensus with-in the psychotherapeutic community seems to be that after the In-stitute of Psychoanalysis, there follow in prestige the psychoanalyt-ic trainings within the accrediting body the British Psychoanalytic Council (BPC). Next in the hierarchy come the psychodynamic trainings within the accrediting body of the United Kingdom Council for Psychotherapy (UKCP); following these, the more hu-manistic and integrative trainings within the UKCP; below these come 'alternative' traditions within the UKCP; and finally come the manifold counselling trainings that are regulated by the British Association of Counselling and Psychotherapy (BACP).[30]

The hierarchy of the genealogical structure appears thus:

1. Psychoanalysts in the BPC
2. Psychodynamic or psychoanalytic psychotherapists in the BPC.
3. Psychodynamic psychotherapists in the UKCP.
4. Humanistic or integrative psychotherapists in the UKCP.
5. Other psychotherapists in the UKCP.
6. Counsellors in the BACP.

The traditions nearing the bottom of the list are often those that are newer in conception (see Table 2) and lack the status that comes with having a long tradition of authority behind them. It cannot be said that many institutes belonging to these traditions rest happily with their relatively low status (and indeed many would vigorously dispute the structure I have outlined above). And by observing their manoeuvrings their search for legitimacy can easily be inferred. One such manoeuvre is to acquire status by appropriating symbols from traditions with higher prestige. An example of this can be seen in the British Association for Counsellors' decision to alter its name in September 2000 to the 'British Association for Counselling and Psychotherapy'—apparently including the term 'psychotherapy' within the heading, a term with more symbolic capital than 'counselling', improves the standing of its member institutes in the eyes of the public.[31]

	c. 1950	c. 1980	c. 2005
Cognitive Behavioural	0	2	30
Humanistic / Integrative	0	9	22
Psychodynamic / Psychoanalytic	3	21	44

Table 2. The Proliferation of Three Traditions and their Composite Institutes in the Genealogical Structure[32]

Another device peripheral institutes employ to gain recognition is to attempt aligning themselves with institutes of higher prestige. This presupposes that the prestige one group might experience is often rooted in its proximity to more prestigious centres. This has been attempted by two institutions in Britain, themselves possessing high status but who are at present appealing for higher status still from the International Psychoanalytic Association.[33] If this acceptance is conferred then these training institutes will be permitted by the International Psychoanalytic Association to call their graduates 'psychoanalysts.'

As the central groups enjoy ownership of powerful symbols, the boundaries of these central groups often become sites of contestation. These high-status institutions fight to maintain the legitimacy of their values, symbols, and standards. There is a constant threat that if these symbols are appropriated by alien institutions and become therefore 'overused', the power they possess will be diluted. This dilution may have a negative impact on those institutions which at present enjoy the rewards—economic, professional —of such symbolic ownership. Evidence of the fight to both protect and appropriate dominant symbolic media is scattered throughout the history of British psychotherapy. A brief assessment of the rise of the UKCP and the BPC, the two major accrediting bodies for psychotherapy in Britain, can attest to this.

THE UKCP VERSUS THE BPC—A CASE IN POINT

The United Kingdom Council for Psychotherapy was inaugurated in 1989.[34] The birth of this organisation was largely due to the publication of the Foster Report of 1971. That Report was the outcome of a government-commissioned investigation which recommended that the psychotherapeutic community open a national register in order to regulate and document professional activity. In 1989 the UKCP was founded for this very purpose and now registers all trainings and practitioners that fulfil its training and practice standards. Until the founding of the UKCP, psychotherapy trainings were almost completely unmonitored, most trainings being private ventures run by a largely volunteer staff and dependent on fees from their trainees for survival. Any institution might set itself up as a training centre without being subject to official scrutiny as to its ethical and training standards.[35] Until the founding of the UKCP, if a training establishment either housed or proved to produce competent therapists engaged in publication and sound practice, it could win some recognition from neighbouring institutes and often some institutional affiliation, which in turn elevated the value of the diplomas it conferred. Once the UKCP was founded, this body attained the right to confer legitimacy on training institutes by granting them registration. The new UKCP register also held the names of all psychotherapists who had attained professional status by passing through one of the trainings it ratified.[36]

From 1989 to 1992 the UKCP was the sole registrar for all psychotherapists in the United Kingdom, and also registered all trainings from the most illustrious (the Institute of Psychoanalysis) to the smallest just newly opened. After 1992, however, the UKCP's role as the principle regulating body was usurped by a collection of the most established psychodynamic trainings within the UKCP. Following the lead of the Institute of Psychoanalysis many established trainings decided to break off to form an independent accrediting body, the BCP (British Confederation of Psychotherapists) now called the BPC (British Psychoanalytic Council). This new body, at that time comprising only four training institutes, nevertheless took with it what were regarded as the most prestigious trainings in the United Kingdom, including the Institute of Psychoanalysis (founded under Freud in 1913), the British Association of Psychotherapists (founded in 1951), The Society of Analytical Psychology (founded under Carl Jung in 1936), and the Tavistock Clinic. The cause of the split seems to have been the reluctance of the UKCP to allow the Institute of Psychoanalysis to have a veto over all decisions made by the UKCP committee. When asking the Chair of the BPC (at the time of writing) as to the reason for this split, she responded:

> The Institute of Psychoanalysis is over 90 years old, so this and the other institutes that went with it are very established training societies which when put in the UKCP found themselves alongside some trainings that were ill-considered and still at their early stages. In a sense the BPC was set up to distinguish the established psychodynamic trainings from these other institutes. (Interview 2004)

By not permitting the Institute of Psychoanalysis to veto any decision in the UKCP, power was stripped from this authoritative centre. And because power lies with whoever manages to define the situation, the oldest institute decided to break away. As the BPC Chair further explains:

> We struggled with the UKCP wanting to include everybody, we felt that you actually had to learn to *exclude* organisations—we felt that they had to reach to the standard that we have set and until they could do so they weren't to be included... the UKCP wanted to level down to a common denominator what are in reality unequal groups. (Interview 2004, italics added)

The desire to have this inequality respected by the committee of the BPC was justified, as one senior psychoanalyst in the BPC argued, since,

> the institutes that separated were elite institutes, and
> beyond in training and reputation other trainings in
> the UKCP... the shared label 'UKCP registered therap-
> ist' does not recognise these differences—it served
> them, but I don't think the same can be said for us.
> (Psychoanalyst 2004)

As can be seen from my interview with the Chair of the BPC,
many in this accrediting body outwardly defended their separation
from the UKCP as a move to protect standards and legitimate hierarchies. Other practitioners, on the other hand, more sceptical as to
the real politics of the separation, argued that behind these public
explanations actually sat concerns for 'power, patronage, and economics' (Young 1996: 2). However we decide to interpret what was
behind this separation, one fact stands out: this act of segregation
initiated by the dominant centres served to safeguard their ownership of dominant symbols and their right to legislate their view of
what constitutes 'correct training and practice'. From the perspective of many within the BPC, the history of a given training institute, the kind of psychotherapy it endorses, the kind of practitioners associated with it, as well as the standards of training it expects
(e.g. whether it demands once, twice, or five times weekly analysis
for trainees), are matters deciding its standing in relation to other
trainings. Within the BPC there is a prevalent belief that good practitioners are more likely to come from good trainings, and good
trainings are those that appeal to the values of the dominant centre.
By not having a veto on the machinations at the UKCP, the leading
psychodynamic organisations felt they were literally handing over
their power to define correct training and practice (i.e. the kind of
training and practice conducted in their organisations), a power
which in the hands of another might be used to their detriment.

DIACHRONIC AND SYNCHRONIC APPEALS FOR LEGITIMACY

To turn now from assessing the struggles between the UKCP and
the BPC, when looking at the wrangling between various institutes
and traditions it is interesting to observe that the struggle for status
appears to take place mainly on two fronts: status can be gathered

either *diachronically*, via appealing for prestige from an illustrious past (i.e. from a consecrated history), or *synchronically*, through appropriating symbolic media from dominant present-day centres either inside or outside the genealogical structure. In many respects the more established institutes, which are mainly psychodynamic and those within the BPC, at present appear to gather status 'diachronically' by appeals to their various founding members, traditions, and their previous associations with more established cultural institutions such as the centres of academe and especially medicine. Institutional histories are thus contrived in such a way as to 'naturalise' the hegemony of BPC institutions.[37]

Newer psychotherapies that are without history enough to appeal diachronically for their legitimacy, including those within the humanistic and integrative traditions, largely appeal synchronically for status. For example, as these newer groups have struggled to find acceptance from dominant centres within the genealogical structure, in recent years many have redirected their efforts to winning prestige and legitimacy from alternative centres outside this structure—i.e. establishing alliances with local universities who confer degrees on successful candidates. Such graduates receive not only the usual professional diploma on graduation but also have the opportunity to further acquire masters and in some cases doctoral degrees.[38]

We cannot explain the desire of these newer groups to seek acceptance away from the dominant centres only in terms of the unwillingness of the dominant centres to grant it, since many of these new units oppose the very premises of these central groups and only profess to share their values and symbols to a small extent.[39] It could be said that the growing ability of these newer units to form alliances with centres outside of the genealogical structure has emboldened their opposition of the traditional centres as they are no longer entirely dependent on these for recognition. This emboldening has led some units to harbour beliefs that they are the depositaries of the proper values of the real tradition as the central group has somehow been led astray. These new units manipulate old symbols in different ways—for example, they may call upon tried and tested Freudian principles to illustrate the need for new institutional trainings.[40] Thus they may attempt to develop new interpretations of existing symbols and norms so as to strive for a change in the very basis of the institutional order. This struggle for institutional legitimacy fosters what Max Weber called 'anti-groups' within the genealogical structure itself: groups which create tensions between themselves and the dominant centres.

SEGMENTARY PATTERNING OF THE GENEALOGICAL STRUCTURE

If at moments we might have glimpsed through my representation of the genealogical structure what anthropologists call a 'segmentary patterning', let me now open up this viewpoint to explain how this patterning seems to work. Training institutes are continually forming alliances with other institutes that at other times they might have opposed. For instance, the hot-headed wrangling that once characterised relations between Jungian and Freudian institutes (i.e. the Institute of Psychoanalysis and the Society for Analytical Psychology) has today receded to allow an amicable alliance under the umbrella of the BPC. In fact beneath the canopy of the BPC now lie a myriad of psychodynamic schools that at one point resided in angry relationship.[41] Unravelling the problem of this change, this softening of enduring rivalries, I believe is assisted by noting that all segmentary alliances imply the proximity of a greater external danger. For nothing better resolves the enmity of old adversaries than a new, shared, and nearing threat. If the segmentary interpretation is applicable in this instance the next question we must ask is what form or forms can this threat be said to take.

From our discussion we can infer that a threat is posed to the higher psychodynamic centres by those lower down in the genealogical structure. As the BPC / UKCP split illustrates, many psychodynamic institutions have closed ranks to protect ownership of key symbols that have always assured their dominant position, a position which, as sociologists of the professions might argue, secures definite economic, professional, and employment rewards. But this threat from below cannot alone explain this sudden 'coming together' of once disparate and rival schools, for in the first place, one could argue that this threat from below is not yet strong enough to override such perennial divisions, and in the second, that this merging can trace its origins to a time before the rise of the 'peripheral' and 'anti-groups' in the genealogical structure. For the whole answer to the question as to why new alliances are being formed between old foes, we must look beyond the genealogical structure to the wider social scene in which the structure is embedded—that is, we must look to extra-psychotherapeutic institutions whose alterations have consequently challenged the authority of the psychodynamic.

THE THREAT TO THE PSYCHODYNAMIC

Although with the expansion of the therapeutic during the twentieth century the psychodynamic tradition experienced much institutional growth, this expansion was not accompanied by either an increase in this tradition's status or a solidification of its early hegemony. In fact, despite having located the psychoanalytic institutes at the head of the genealogical structure, it is important to note that these particular 'centres' hold onto their privileged position with increasing difficulty. This becomes more understandable as soon as we look beyond the genealogical structure itself in order to observe the wider public perceptions of psychoanalytic therapy. By this method we will recognise that since the 1970s the psychodynamic has come under increasing threat due to a number of shifting factors, which I shall now enumerate—the first being the fall of the psychodynamic within psychiatry.

THE RESCINDING OF PSYCHIATRIC APPROVAL

A centre outside of the genealogical structure to which psychoanalytic therapy has always appealed for legitimacy is the psychiatric establishment. The main founders of dynamic psychotherapy, S. Freud, C. G. Jung, and A. Adler, were all psychiatrists themselves and it was through them that the practice came to bear the unmistakeable imprint of the physician's consulting room—a fact evident not only in the terminology of psychodynamics but also in the framework of its theory. Dynamic therapy, then, despite its struggle for acceptance from psychiatry during the early twentieth century in Britain, had nevertheless a place in psychiatry from its outset. If early on those approving of psychodynamics were few, from the First World War onwards, and as we have seen, this number was to increase. With this growing acceptance came the rewards of being favoured by medical science. Laymen who trusted in the authority of medicine would also trust the practices it en-

dorsed—psychoanalytic therapy was growing strong from its association with medicine. As Julian Lousada tells us:

> [this association gave psychoanalysis] the tremendous
> advantage of being close to, even if not exactly being
> at the heart of the [psychiatric] establishment... The
> development of psychoanalytic psychotherapy has
> throughout this century grown then, at least in part
> under the protection of an influential faction within
> psychiatry... In my view it is not just the independence
> of British society and the psychotherapy organizations
> or the freedom associated with private practice that
> created the capacity for the growth... but rather the
> protection and inclusion that was offered by psychi-
> atry that enabled such rich development, both organ-
> izationally and intellectually, to take place. (Lousada
> 2000: 471)

This powerful centre not only provided a roof under which practitioners could safely develop their craft, but was also an authoritative ally under whose patronage, in the eyes of the layman at least,
the sanction of medical science was conferred. This strengthening
association between psychoanalysis and psychiatry was growing
even stronger in the United States. Between the end of the Second
World War and the beginning of the 1970s psychoanalysis became
dominant in American psychiatry (Luhrmann 2001: 203-38). As
Bertram Brown (director of North America's National Institute of
Mental Heath) tells us: during this period 'it was nearly impossible
for a non-psychoanalyst to become chairman of a department or
professor of psychiatry' (Brown 1976: 492). As early as 1952 dynamic therapists were heavily represented in the American Psychiatric Association and by the early 1960s they held key positions on
its membership panel, and, more crucially, on its diagnostic committee (p.299). This second detail is important as this committee
decided how and in what way pathology was to be defined. These
definitions, made concrete in the *Diagnostic and Statistical Manual*,
were thus heavily under the influence of the psychoanalytic thinking of the day. This proved to further consolidate the hold of dy-

namic therapy in American psychiatry throughout the 1950s and 1960s. As Shorter says:

> The DSM-II reflected this [psychodynamic] sway. Six of the ten members of the drafting committee were analysts or belonged to sympathetic organizations. The nomenclature mirrored this predominance: Psychoneurotic problems were no longer called 'reactions' but 'neuroses.' The sturdy Freudian term 'hysteria' appeared, replacing 'conversion reaction' and 'dissociative reaction'. (Shorter 1997: 299)

British psychiatry during these years was freer of psychoanalytic influence than its American counterpart. However, when psychiatric opinion began to turn against dynamic therapy, although British psychodynamics had less distance to fall, it felt the impact nonetheless. From the late 1970s onward psychoanalytic psychotherapy across both sides of the Atlantic was to find itself ever more peripheral to medical psychiatry. This meant that a key centre to which psychoanalytic therapy had always appealed for legitimacy began to rescind its approval. A few factors can account for this change: first was the mounting criticism both inside and outside of psychiatry as to the scientific status of psychoanalysis. This was compounded by psychiatry's need to prove itself scientifically to other departments of medicine, which by implication led psychiatry to dissociate itself from 'unverified practices.' There was also the rise of new therapies that appeared to have a stronger evidence base, and that also seemed to better fit the structures of modern medical institutions. And finally, there was the rise of organic psychiatry in the 1980s with its championing of psychotropic over therapeutic intervention.

If we start with the criticisms levelled against the scientific respectability of psychoanalysis we find in the 1950s a series of studies which, when being fully acknowledged by the psychiatric community in the 1970s, were to irrevocably wound the psychodynamic cause. Rather than arguing the case for or against the efficacy of psychoanalytic psychotherapy, these studies pitted psychoanalysis against other 'therapies' to conclude that in terms of successful therapeutic outcomes psychoanalysis produced no better results than did behaviourist, humanistic, or existential alternatives. In fact, in the majority of cases, as Han Eysenck the director of psychology at the Maudsely Hospital argued, psychoanalysis appeared to have lower success rates than its newer counterparts. For example, Eysenck's (1952: 321) study found that only 44 percent of psychodynamic patients improved by the end of their analysis while other therapies could boast improvement rates of 64 percent. While this general conclusion was highly questionable to many psychoanalysts, for many psychiatrists it was seen to be supported by other studies—e.g. Fred Fiedler's (1950) influential investigation which found, firstly, that experienced therapists of different modalities actually behaved more similarly in a technical sense than did therapists from the same modalities who had different levels of experience, and, secondly, that of the several very different sorts of therapy assessed all seemed to work equally well. This second finding, along with Eysenck's, by challenging the claimed supremacy of dynamic therapy had a considerable impact on the field of psychiatry as a whole. As one informant mentioned, it was generally regarded in the hospital corridors as the 'equivalence paradox'. This paradox meant that 'results' (whatever 'results' might be felt to be) for various approaches to psychotherapy were equivalent in spite of the avowed theoretical and technical differences between therapies. Elsewhere the equivalence paradox was supported by researchers such as Nagel and Hook (1964); Luborsky and Luborsky (1975); Farrell (1981); and Williams and Spitzer (1984)[42]—all of which asked for the supremacy of psychoanalytic psychotherapy to be re-appraised by mental health professionals.

   That these and other findings made many scholars, among them anthropologists, claim that if psychoanalysis worked it was not for the reasons that analysts stated, is a matter I shall take up again in chapter two.[43] For now, however, what is relevant about these research findings is that for those who accorded them any kind of authority (and many in psychiatry did), the claim that psychoanalysis was the premiere therapy was now severely undermined. These detractors reasoned that if the dynamic therapists were correct in thinking they had got it right, surely they would enjoy higher outcome rates than did therapists offering 'alternative' approaches. Many psychoanalysts responded to this, as Professor Peter Fonagy mentioned to me in interview,

by arguing against the value of evidence-based research. These therapists turned their backs on this research as on an enemy, which led to the unfortunate
consequence of their becoming increasingly anti-em-
pirical, an attitude that in a climate demanding evidence-based practice has jeopardised the position of
psychodynamic on the British wards. (Interview 2004)

If these studies sought to humble psychoanalytic therapy via
academic wounding, then others were less forgiving and moved in
for the kill. Key intellectuals launched strong attacks on the scientific standing of psychoanalysis, while old critiques, once
thought long-buried by the psychotherapeutic community, resurfaced to remind readers of the questionable nature of its design.
Karl Popper argued that as psychoanalysis was 'non-testable' it
was therefore non-scientific. Adolf Grunbaum (1984) criticised
Popper's conclusion and went forward to show that psychoanalysis could be tested, proceeded to test it, only to conclude it was
false. Ludwig Wittgenstein (1988 [1946-7]) launched searching
questions regarding the nature of Freud's understanding of the
symbolic, while Ernest Gellner (1985) exposed the dynamics by
which psychodynamics rendered itself beyond criticism. Newer
and more popularist studies exposing the underside of the profession were also published in abundance: Richard Webster's (1995)
Why Freud Was Wrong re-analysed the symptomatology in Freud's
early case studies and argued that he misdiagnosed as psychic
pathology many organic diseases; J. M. Masson (1984), an apostate
psychoanalyst, argued that Freud deliberately obscured the importance of childhood sexual abuse, representing patient's complaints as manifestations of a 'false memory disorder'; while
Thomas Szasz (1979), the iconoclast practitioner from the anti-psychiatry movement, compared dynamic therapy to a species of spiritual healing thus undermining its pretensions to scientific credibil-
ity. And within psychiatry itself, anthropologists such as Roland
Littlewood (1982; 1992; 1999) in Britain, and Arthur Kleinman
(1988) in the United States, argued that much psychodynamic practice was culturally biased, urging for it to become more culturally-
reflexive.

These criticisms compounded a general unease within British psychiatry as to the merits of the psychodynamic. An unease which took practical effect when by the 1980s other therapeutic options surfaced that were more congruent with the requirements of the NHS. A psychoanalyst and NHS Director of psychotherapy services mentioned to me in interview:

> What we now call the BPC-trained dynamic therapists have since the 1980s steadily lost ground in psychiatry. What seems to have happened is that tension has grown within psychiatry between those who have had BPC training and those who do not... the non-BPC-trained psychotherapists would characterise those trained there, especially at the Institute of Psychoanalysis, as elitist, out of touch, too specialised, and operating a model that is not applicable to the NHS... There is a cultural and organisational move away from valuing psychodynamic approaches and this is furthered by the rising prominence of CBT [cognitive behavioural therapy] which fits well with evidenced-based intervention and satisfies the political pressure on managers to cut waiting times. This can be done by offering short-term therapy, which CBT therapy is all about, unlike dynamic therapy which is a more long-term option. (Interview 2004)

If the above director partly locates the demise of the psychodynamic in the rise of contending therapies such as the more evidenced-based, less-time consuming, and less-costly CBT, other commentators have rather emphasised the rise of psychotropic intervention as the most significant factor in ousting dynamic psychotherapy from the wards.

Within British and American psychiatry psycho-pharmacology had been growing since the mid-century. In the 1950s drugs such as Miltown and Equanil were promoted as the new wonder palliatives and when launched met the highest public demand of any drug hitherto marketed in the United States. After Miltown and Equanil came Librium (chlordiazepoxide), which in the 1960s became the number one prescription drug in the United States and

Britain. After Librium in 1969 came the birth of Valium (diazepam), which, until the British-created Prozac could be prescribed in the 1990s, was the most successful drug in pharmaceutical history.[44] Equanil, Librium, Valium, and then Prozac, each in their successive turn, demonstrated record levels of patient demand.

The change in climate towards pharmacological psychiatry was reflected in how new versions of the *Diagnostic Statistical Manual* were conceived and drawn up. 'Just as previous DSM task forces had been weighted in favour of psychoanalysis,' Porter claims, 'this one [the DSM III (1980)] was weighted against it and towards biological psychiatry' (Shorter 1997: 301). As Shorter continues, the new DSM III pleased those biologically inclined clinicians who were disaffected with the old psychodynamics and who wanted a diagnostic system based on 'symptom analysis' rather than on non-testable dynamic theories about underlying causes. The new DSM III organised symptoms into discrete descriptive categories (e.g. bio-polar disorder, Cataplexy, and Affective Spectrum Disorder); these categories could be matched with particular drugs that would mitigate the distress they described. As the central architect of the DSM III, Robert Spitzer, later said:

> With its intellectual roots in St. Louis instead of Vienna, and with its intellectual inspiration derived from Kraepelm, not Freud, the task force was viewed from the outset as unsympathetic to the interests of those whose theory and practice derived from the psychoanalytic tradition. (Spitzer and Bayer 1985: 188)

Eysenck mirrored this sentiment back in Britain at the Maudsley Hospital:

> All sciences have to pass through an ordeal by quackery... Chemistry had to slough off the fetters of alchemy. The brain sciences had to disengage themselves from the tenets of phrenology... Psychology and psychiatry, too, will have to abandon the pseudo-science of psychoanalysis... and undertake the arduous task of transforming their discipline into a genuine science. (Eysenck 1952: 207)

Many psychiatrists ill at ease with the 'biopsychosocial model' heralded the new orientation as a victory for science—with the new diagnostic method safeguarded by Spitzer's taskforce, many felt that biological psychiatry was to at last have its day.

> The appearance of DSM-III was thus an event of capital importance not just for American but for world psychiatry, a turning of the page on psychodynamics, a redirection of the discipline toward a scientific course, a re-embrace of the positivistic principles of the nineteenth century, a denial of the anti-psychiatric doctrine of the myth of psychiatric illness. (Shorter, 1997: 302)

The mastering of Freud, Foucault, Laing, Lacan, and other anti-psychiatry and psychodynamic works, was being replaced in psychiatric residencies by a studious memorising of the DSM III. To many psychiatrists the veil of science that had blown unattached for so long seemed at last to drape the shoulders of the Spitzer revolution. With this the ultimate therapeutic aim had largely altered from 'curing' patients through therapeutic intervention to 'lifting symptoms' through judicious prescription. For the psychoanalytic psychotherapists both within and outside the hospital wards this elision towards pharmacology offered a costly slight. Not only was employment for lay therapists within the NHS made a more difficult prospect, but a centre upon which psychoanalysis had always relied for endorsement had removed its approval. Commenting on today's relationship in Britain between dynamic therapy and psychiatry, Julian Lousada, Chair of adult psychotherapy treatment at the Tavistock Clinic (a powerful centre within the genealogical structure), stated:

> It is precisely this relationship that has become more tenuous over the last period. Not only has the authority of psychiatry been undermined, but so too have some of its capacity, and perhaps its willingness to promote the development of its younger precocious sibling. This protection [from psychiatry], is I would

suggest, much weaker and, consequently, we find
ourselves more and more on our own, and more and
more dependent upon our own resources to survive in
a competitive and increasingly crowded market place.
(Lousada 2000: 472)

CONCLUDING CHAPTER ONE

The expansion of therapy through the twentieth century has not
been tantamount to the growing dominance of psychodynamic
psychotherapy. On the contrary this growth has brought with it a
contending sea of traditions all of which appear to jostle for key
positions in the market. This expansion cannot therefore be seen as
having made psychoanalytic psychotherapy more secure, since not
only have cognitive behavioural therapies moved into the NHS,
taking up central posts once held by the dynamic therapists, but
fledgling schools within the genealogical structure, offering new
and affordable 'integrative' and 'humanist' psychotherapies, have
started to pose a threat to psychoanalytic hegemony from 'below.'
These alternatives, by appealing to powerful centres such as academe, are steadily gaining symbolic status and currency. The counselling profession, which is ever more embedding itself within key
social institutions, and the new 'alternative' psychotherapeutic traditions, which are gradually encroaching upon the private market,
are all benefiting from alliances with extra-psychotherapeutic institutions by accruing the status these confer.

The plight of the traditional psychoanalytic therapist has been
further compounded by the key centres of medicine and science removing their endorsement. This removal has been prompted by
many factors: by the evidence-based research findings which question the supremacy and efficacy of psychoanalysis, by the pharmacological revolution that has offered an alternative form of intervention, and finally by the increasing number of authoritative critiques as to the integrity of the profession. All these factors have
engendered widespread scepticism as to the standing of the psychodynamic. And so although the dynamic therapists still enjoy relative high status in the genealogical structure, this position is increasingly threatened insofar as medicine and academe continue to

remove their approval. As the head of adult therapy at the Tavis-tock claims:

> It is true that psychoanalytic psychotherapy appears
> to be swimming against the tide, and it seems to me
> we should not underestimate the difficulties that we,
> as a community, now face. (Lousada 2000: 467)

Questions concerning the relative merits and demerits of the demise of the psychodynamic, although interesting and important, must remain for our purposes subsidiary to questions as to what bearing these changes are having not only upon the psychodynam-ic community, but more specifically upon that traditional steward of psychodynamic thought and practice—the training institute.

If the psychodynamic institute today increasingly finds its syn-chronic appeal for legitimacy undermined, then the diachronic ap-peal takes on especial importance as a means by which legitimacy is conferred. The effect that this strategic conservatism may have on the training of the psychotherapists is something I now intend to survey. Therefore let us now put aside our assessment of the macro-dynamics between the training institutes and the wider world, so that we may focus more closely upon the micro-dynam-ics within the individual training institute itself.

CHAPTER TWO
THE THERAPEUTIC ENCOUNTER

In the previous chapter I provided a broad historical overview of the macro-dynamics within the genealogical structure, and between this structure and certain wider socio-historical factors and forces bearing upon it. With this socio-historical introduction in place, I shall now turn my attention to the individual training institute, and, more specifically, to the first stage of psychodynamic socialisation: pre-training therapy. Alongside describing ethnographically this first stage of training, I shall argue that it inculcates in trainees 'foundational dispositions' upon which a later professional 'habitus' is built. I shall draw upon existing anthropological theories of healing to illustrate how this might take place. Before I undertake this ethnographic task, let me begin by outlining the stages of psychoanalytic training through which all trainees must past, and of which 'pre-training therapy' constitutes the first stage.

Psychotherapeutic training involves many styles of learning, each being thought to contribute to the total education of the practitioner. These differing styles render trainees subject to a number of educational devices which are each thought to facilitate candidates' full professional development. The following styles of learning are applied across trainings and constitute the 'core methods' of any analytic training.[45] These methods are not all simultaneously applied at the start of training, but are added stage by stage to the trainees' education as they gradually progress through the institute.

1. Personal therapy (pre-training beginning year 0). This commences before trainees enter the institute and accompanies the trainee throughout their training career.
2. Theoretical seminars (beginning year 1). These introduce candidates to the essentials of psychoanalytic theory. They can also involve writing assignments and delivering clinical presentations.
3. Private Practice (beginning year 2). All trainees after having spent time in theoretical seminars are expected to take on two 'training patients'. One must usually be seen for 18 months and the other for two years.
4. Clinical seminars (beginning year 1 or 2). The objective of these seminars is to link theory and practice. Patients' problems are considered in relation to core theoretical themes and clinical techniques.
5. Child observation and experiential groups (beginning year 1 or 2). Certain trainings, in addition to the core demands, require trainees to observe mother/child interactions (usually for two hours per week) for a period of six months or one year. These observations are thought to provide data to illustrate developmental theory.

In all, psychodynamic training takes place over a period of at least four years, although many trainees take five, six or more years to complete the graduation requirements. Training is also officially recognised to take place on a part-time basis, although the tag 'part-time' does not quite capture the amount of 'contact time' required of each trainee—that is, the weekly amount of time spent seeing patients, attending personal therapy, theoretical/clinical seminars, and private supervision. Since the amount of contact time alters according to the stage of training which the trainee has reached, not all trainings can offer an exact figure for the time trainees spend in training commitments. On average, however, trainings estimate that candidates could expect 15-25 hours of contact time per week.

These temporal arrangements of training institutes are often more coherent and less chaotic than the spatial arrangements into which these styles of learning fit. For instance, psychotherapy training is rarely undertaken within a bounded institute. Rather, learning takes place in a number of different locations. While seminars and clinical supervision usually take place in the institute, personal therapy, private supervision, and seeing patients are activities invariably occurring in different settings: in private clinics, hospitals, and/or individual homes. In this respect training institutes differ considerably from the 'total institutions' described by Goffman (1961). 'Total institutes' are enclosed psychical spaces in which all 're-socialisation' takes place. Rather, training institutes have very loose spatial boundaries compared with the tight temporal organisation in terms of which they are structured. That this form of organisation influences in subtle ways trainee socialisation is a fact I shall further explore in chapter three. For now, however, let me remain with the task at hand and describe the first stage of training—pre-training therapy.

PRE-TRAINING THERAPY

All psychoanalytic trainings request that every candidate first undertake at least one year of individual psychotherapy before entering theoretical and clinical seminars at the institute. Institutes differ only in the number of weekly therapeutic sessions they expect their candidates to attend. The Institute of Psychoanalysis, for instance, requires applicants to attend five sessions per week, while all other psychoanalytic trainings in the BPC generally ask for three sessions weekly. In fact, the number of sessions requested by an institute appears to increase in proportion to the institute's standing in the genealogical system:[46]

1. Psychoanalysts in the BPC (5 sessions per week).
2. Psychodynamic psychotherapists in the BPC (3 sessions per week).
3. Psychodynamic psychotherapists in the UKCP (2 or 3 sessions per week).
4. Humanistic or integrative psychotherapists in the UKCP (1 session per week or an equivalent introductory course).
5. Other psychotherapists in the UKCP (1 session per week or an equivalent introductory course).

If all candidates have experienced psychotherapy before crossing the threshold into formal training, then the large majority of trainees have undergone more therapy than the entrance pre-requisites necessitate. Most trainees have experienced on average eighteen months of therapy before commencing training,[47] while it is not rare to find trainees with three, four or even five years of pre-training therapeutic experience. As the pre-training analysis constitutes the first stage of becoming a therapist it is surprising how few candidates enter analysis only for the purpose of taking this first step. As I shall look at trainee motivations for entering therapy more closely in chapter eight, here I shall make only one important preliminary note—namely, it is mostly the case that psychotherapeutic trainees initially enter psychotherapy to help themselves, and then only after this experience elect to train to help others. This altruistic motive is one of two key motivations stated by trainees again and again to explain why they decided to enter training. The other is that formal training would further the process of self-exploration they started in their private therapy.[48]

Official training rationales as to why pre-training therapy (and personal therapy generally) is essential to becoming a therapist, differ in emphasis from institute to institute, although Abram and Morgan did identify a general purpose in their official guide to psychoanalytic trainings.

> [Therapy offers trainees] a chance to begin to explore the sensitivities and pathologies that have brought a person to seek analytic training in the first place. The principle is that nobody should, as a psychotherapist, put a patient through a process that they themselves have not been through. (Abram and Morgan-Jones 2001: 59)

This understanding is premised upon Freud's belief that the best way to learn psychoanalysis is to become a patient oneself. In his introductory lectures he emphasises:

> [although] it is true that psychoanalysis cannot easily be learnt and there are not many people who have learnt it properly... there is a practical method none

the less. One learns psychoanalysis on oneself, by
studying one's own personality... One advances much
further if one is analysed by a practiced analyst and
experiences the effects of analysis on one's own self,
making use of the opportunity of picking up the
subtler technique of the process from one's analyst.
(Freud 1975 [1917]: 44)

Carl Gustav Jung, who was arguably the first in Freud's circle
to request every trainee to undergo personal therapy, justified this
in the following way:

the physician must overcome these resistances [to being analysed] in himself, for who can educate others
while himself uneducated? Who can enlighten his fel-
lows while still in the dark about himself, and who
can purify if he is himself unclean?....The step from
educating others to self-education is demanded of the
doctor in this stage of transformation. (Jung 1995
[1933]: 59)

As well as making obligatory the pre-training analysis, institutes insist that the kind of therapy taught on their programs and
the kind of pre-training psychotherapy candidates undertake are of
the same modality. This can prove an inconvenience for psychoanalytic applicants whose personal therapy was undertaken in a
different modality. In this instance, no matter how much time and
money previously spent in non-analytic psychotherapy, if they are
to enter an analytic training they must still undergo the requisite
year of analytic therapy. Having this 'fit' is important to the institutes, as one head of training commented:

We like to know that our trainees are already semi-
prepared for what is to come. They need to have some
understanding of their transferences before attending
seminars and seeing patients—we need to know that
they have at least moved some direction towards
thinking dynamically... having submitted to analysis

will help this. (Head of Psychotherapeutic Training, 2004)

Another head of a psychodynamic training stated:

> to have passed through a year of therapy and still want to move onward is evidence to us that this candidate is eager and interested. Not all people can bear the relentless self-scrutiny of psychotherapy, *especially analytic psychotherapy*. The first necessity of being a therapist is that you can bear this constant looking at the self; without this attitude they cannot expect to ever know another. (Head of Psychotherapeutic Training 2005, italics added)

Interestingly, when I asked trainers as to why pre-trainee therapy is important, most emphasised how it prepares students to 'fit' with the existing institutional system rather than how it provides trainees with an opportunity to decide whether this fit is possible. This distinction appears not so pedantic when we notice that historically most schools have seen pre-training therapy as way of 'vetting' applicants—testing whether the candidate is suitable to attend seminars in the institute. In the psychoanalytic training of the 1950s and 60s, for instance, such 'institutional vetting' was widespread: therapists decided on the basis of their therapy with prospective trainees whether these trainees could proceed into the institute. The problems with this system have been subsequently and extensively discussed in psychoanalytic literature (e.g. Heimann 1954; Meltzer 1986; Cremerius 1990; Kernberg 1986). These writers were concerned that this 'vetting' often stopped trainees from displaying any marked 'pathology' out of fear that their therapists might consider it too excessive and thus bar their movement forward. This fear, the critics argued, would sabotage any sincere involvement on the part of the trainee. Today in the psychoanalytic institutes I investigated this institutional vetting had largely disappeared; most institutes have now opted for 'open' over 'closed' trainings. 'Closed' trainings are those in which one's therapist is a member of one's training institute and therefore has an intimate say in whether one qualifies. 'Open' trainings are alternatively those in which one's 'training analyst' is not a member of one's institute and thus has no examining role within it (Cremerius 1990: 124). In the 'open' system therapists thus rarely report back to the institute on whether a candidate appears suitable for training (or for progression through the institute). They are simply there to offer the psychotherapy that is integral to the training experience. If most international psychoanalytic institutes in the IPA (International Psychoanalytic Association) still opt for a closed system, nearly all other psychoanalytic trainings in Britain have embraced the 'open' alternative[49]—turning pre-training therapy from an institutional test of suitability, to a private test for the trainee as to whether the world of psychotherapy is one for them.

Saying that this 'open' system now predominates in British psychotherapeutic institutes, is not to say that all 'vetting' has ceased. Rather the old 'institutional vetting' has been replaced by a form whose significance is rarely acknowledged by the institutes themselves: by making pre-training therapy obligatory, institutes ensure that all trainees who enter their programs are disposed favourably to the psychoanalytic paradigm or process. This is to say, since it is difficult to imagine any patient who has suffered a negative therapeutic experience electing to train in the therapeutic tradition, trainees are by necessity those whose experiences of analytic therapy have been positive.

During my research I encountered only two trainees whose pre-training therapy had been a largely negative experience (I shall talk of these experiences in chapters four and five), and there was only a very small minority who expressed even mild discontent with their pre-training therapy. Furthermore when such discontent was expressed its cause was usually located in the therapist's personal inabilities than in any problem with the psychoanalytic paradigm itself—thus the therapist was to blame not the therapy. Also for this minority, discontent was often offset by positive experiences gained elsewhere: either from personal reading, personal practice, or a previous positive therapeutic experience. Notwithstanding these qualifications, then, trainees enter the institute with an upbeat and confident attitude towards the practices that they eventually hope to master.

Candidates' cheerful dispositions at the point of entering the institute were highlighted to me in many private moments when trainees admitted the redemptive nature of what transpired in analysis: 'Entering therapy was a kind of homecoming for me', one student reflected, 'here at last I was part of a process that I had for a long time read about... I was very eager and excited to be a part of it all'. Another commented, 'it was my personal experience of therapy that led me to train... my process went so well that my therapist suggested I consider training.' Finally, 'it was my experience of psychotherapy that convinced me of its value... as it helped me so much I knew it could help others; (laughing) you know it wasn't long before I persuaded my husband to enter analysis.' Comments such as these are very representative, and were often uttered with real gratitude for the therapists who made their experience special. Thus if the particularities of pre-training therapy differ from candidate to candidate, one feature invariably shared is that the experience was predominantly informative and thus positive.

Although training institutes no longer explicitly vet their candidates, then, a form of covert vetting still takes place: *by insisting that all trainees first submit to a pre-training analysis, only the keen enter the institute, since those suffering disagreeable preliminary experiences are unlikely to proceed.* Consequently, institutes open their doors mainly to the most enthusiastic candidates; to those whose experiences rather confirm than challenge the efficacy of the model in question, candidates, it may be added, for whom the process of socialisation has already begun. Thus the pre-training therapy ensures among other things that those who enter the institute possess *a strong disposition of partiality* towards therapy so far as they have personal experience of its efficacy.

ANTHROPOLOGICAL RESEARCH ON THERAPEUTIC HEALING

As well as helping to ensure that only those favourably disposed to therapy enter the training institute, pre-training therapy obliges trainees to be 'patients' before their professional socialisation begins. This second fact means that existing anthropological research on how psychotherapy 'heals' and 'affects patients' can help us unravel the pre-training experience of trainees. Before I closely describe the general psychotherapeutic encounter, then, it would be helpful to first survey this literature in order to assess exactly what it may teach us about the experience of the psychotherapeutic candidate.

This research builds upon a general conclusion, outlined in the previous chapter, that 'outcome research' into psychotherapy has reached: that psychoanalytic psychotherapy is often no more successful than neighbouring therapies in alleviating many forms of mental distress.[50] This has led many researchers to conclude that therapeutic success cannot therefore be explained in terms of the 'correct-theory-correctly-applied' hypothesis (i.e. analysis works because its theories are true), since successful results are obtained by modalities whose theories radically contradict each other. These conclusions have led many anthropologists, as Arthur Kleinman tells us,

> [to become therefore] uncomfortable with the tendency of mental health professionals to elevate the Western paradigm of [analytic] psychotherapy into a comparative grid that can be used to study indigenous healing systems worldwide. (Klienman 1991: 114)[51]

Rather, psychotherapy (whether analytic, cognitive behavioural, humanistic etc.) should be understood as:

> merely one [more] indigenous form of symbolic healing, i.e. a therapy based on words, myth, and ritual. (Kleinman, 1991: 114)[52]

Thus instead of using psychoanalytic concepts to explain why indigenous healing works (e.g. the shaman heals only because he is really permitting 'catharsis'; or the witchdoctor helps through 'suggestion'), we should approach each system on its own terms, rather than explaining one system through the concepts of another. Furthermore we should work to identify common features which all healing systems share, and which could possibly account for why they all seem to work in varying degrees.

Kleinman has identified such common features by drawing a distinction between 'process' and 'structure' (1991[1988]: 136). He argues that psychotherapists who reject the idea that a therapy works because its theory is correct, tend to explain therapeutic success in terms of 'processes' (e.g. the therapist possessed good personal qualities; he or she offered social learning, catharsis, confession, or conditioning, as well as a good therapeutic alliance),[53] while many anthropologists and sociologists explain psychotherapy's efficacy in terms of the symbolic structures in which these processes are lodged—namely, the wider social and symbolic structures in which therapeutic practices are embedded.

Let me explain further. Anthropologists such as Dow (1986), Kleinman (1988), Calestro (1972) Prince (1980) and Johnson (1988) have emphasised the centrality of the therapist's 'myth' in facilitating healing. They understand by 'myth' a system of interlinking symbols and theoretical ideas that on composite provide a frame of orientation through which the origin and nature of the patient's problem can be framed and understood.[54] Healing transpires when patients become attached to this mythic system and learn to articulate their 'private' world in its terms. The myth, however, must also be linked to wider systems of meaning, or in other words, and as Kleinman (1991 [1988]: 131) has added, it must provide a 'symbolic bridge' between personal experience and the wider socio-cultural world. This bridge ensures that by understanding themselves in terms of the myth, patients are integrated into wider society— private experience is given public orientation and through this the straying individual is reconciled with and incorporated within the social whole. Dow (1986) labelled this system 'mythic' because for him and others it was not essential whether this explanatory system was objectively true. What mattered was whether it held experiential truth for its users, since it was from the act of 'believing' itself that its efficacy was gained.[55]

The key features that these anthropologists have identified as accounting for why widely dissimilar therapies (indigenous and otherwise) seem to work can be summarised thus:

1. The therapeutic process links patients with a system of symbols (a mythic world) that order and make explicable their subjective reality.

2. Attachment to this system 'bridges' patients with wider systems of cultural meaning as the 'mythic world' is consonant with this wider meaning.
3. Such re-orientation back into the dominant idiom serves not only to reinforce and maintain this idiom, and the existing social order it supports, but also reaffirm the patient's sense of belonging and adaptation.

My purpose at present is not to dispute these theories. In fact, as I shall argue in later chapters, apart from two areas where their application to psychotherapeutic healing appears untenable, they may greatly help us in making sense of how psychoanalytic dispositions become instilled in trainees. Rather, my purpose is to elevate to equal importance in therapeutic healing what we might call the cultivation of a 'psychotherapeutic imagination'; an aspect of the therapeutic process to which these studies have ascribed only minimal authority.[56]

In my following description of the psychotherapeutic encounter, as well as tracing the therapeutic process through which every trainee must pass, I shall make the case that the patient's cultivation of a 'therapeutic imagination' plays a greater part in assisting their transformation than either existing anthropological or psychotherapeutic studies allow for. As to what I actually mean by the 'therapeutic imagination' will I hope become clearer as the chapter proceeds. For now, however, I shall simply define the psychoanalytic encounter as an 'imaginative process'. This process entails a conversion to a new mode of seeing the world, which may or may not include a concomitant conversion to or re-affirmation of a conceptual/symbolic world.[57]

THE THERAPEUTIC ENCOUNTER

When surveying the practice of psychoanalytic psychotherapy many details that may appear inconsequential to an outsider actually have great significance for the psychotherapist. The organisation of the setting and the space, the length of the sessions, as well as the implicit boundaries enforced to delimit the actions, thoughts, and feelings of both therapist and patient, are considered crucial by any trained practitioner. It is invariably the case that knowledge of the significance of these features is initially possessed only by the therapist, while the patient, unless previously self-tutored in the craft of psychotherapy, enters the room largely oblivious to their importance.

Just as certain understandings of the psychotherapeutic process remain hidden to the patient, there are ways of interpreting the therapeutic encounter anthropologically that transcend the official understandings which are taught in theoretical seminars, which are discussed in clinical supervision, or which are vouchsafed to trainees in therapeutic sessions. Before illuminating aspects of the therapeutic encounter that are largely bypassed by practitioners, let me first describe what many psychotherapists understand to be the essential features of therapeutic encounter.[58]

THE THERAPEUTIC FRAME

Any discussion of the therapeutic encounter could start at no better place than with a description of what is known professionally as the psychotherapeutic frame.[59] The term 'therapeutic frame' is a metaphor used in the profession to describe the various boundaries circumscribing the temporal, spatial, and interpersonal dimensions of the encounter. Extending the metaphor we see the therapeutic encounter as a structured happening 'separated' from the quotidian background of daily life. Within the frame's bounds exists an arena delineated as both 'charged' and 'significant' in which standard rules of social engagement are replaced by the modes of interaction governed by the therapeutic ethos. Before we can look at this ethos in greater depth, let me first describe each of these boundaries in their turn.

THE TEMPORAL BOUNDARY

The temporal boundary is something now consecrated in psychoanalytic tradition. This boundary finds its expression in the 'fifty-minute hour'. Early descriptions of the rationale for this boundary emphasise its practical worth: keeping sessions to fifty minutes allows therapists to make appointments on the hour, to spend ten minutes between each patient to collect their thoughts, to deal with telephone messages, have a cup of coffee, or to scribble some notes —all of which are necessary activities in a day where a series of patients are seen (Storr 1979: 11). While these practical reasons are still today offered as explanations, over the years other more analytical reasons have been added as rationales: Every transgression of the temporal frame may yield important information about the patient's condition. By arriving late, for instance, a patient might be expressing ambivalence towards the therapist or the process of therapy itself. They might be 'acting out' angry feelings that the patient is unable to express through words and directly to his therapist.[60] Patients who arrive very early, on the other hand, or who resist leaving the session at the appointed time, might be expressing a longing for more attention or care, an indication, especially in patients who down-play the suffering of their lives, that they experience the world 'out there' as more difficult than they openly admit. Whatever the reasons for a patient's transgression of the temporal boundary, and these are always particular to the individual case, therapists urge there is always a motive dwelling behind the surface fact [61]—as all actions in therapy are metaphors for inner feelings, thoughts and states.

If the temporal boundary, when transgressed, provides clues to the patient's unarticulated feeling and thoughts, it is also designed to promote the patient's sense that the consulting room is a safe place. Providing a secure context is considered therapeutically important, since it is only when the patient feels relatively free of anxiety that the disclosure of private feelings and thoughts can begin to flow. The trainee is taught to provide 'containment' for the patient—namely, a space that is as far as possible impenetrable by outside incursion, whether these are audible (outside noise), physical (a stranger entering the room), or relational (inappropriate advances from the side of the therapist). Therapy transpires in a type of closeted 'cell' whose bounds are designed to focus the minds of both on unravelling the patient's problems.

The temporal boundary, as well as delineating the length of sessions, must also fix the occasions on which these sessions take place. Patients are asked to commit to a particular time and place for each appointment. Once a pattern is established supervisors ask, except on the most unavoidable occasions, that neither therapist nor patient break the arrangement agreed upon. It is taught that establishing a pattern not only makes it easier for the patient to make the sessions part of their weekly round, but that it also endows the space with security. As one supervisor said to a group of first year trainees:

> If a patient is always being moved about [in terms of time and space], he will become disgruntled, distracted, and in the session will waste a good deal of energy trying to settle in all these new environments... we have to settle a patient so that he can for that hour concentrate wholly on what is going on in his own mind, rather than what is going on outside, continuity encourages this. (Psychodynamic Supervisor 2004)

Knowledge of when a patient will be attending the session also enables the therapist to control variables such as noise levels. If the therapist knows exactly when a session will take place, he or she can make adequate preparations by warning others not to disturb, and by ensuring that proximate spaces (outside corridors, adjacent rooms) are free of excessive sounds. If a patient can hear muttering beyond the walls of the consulting room, then she might fear that her talk is audible too—a fear that might inhibit a freedom of expression considered vital if therapy is to succeed.[62]

THE SPATIAL BOUNDARY

The temporal circumscription of the analytical space is complemented by the planning of the physical setting, the organisation of which is also heavily guarded by the therapist's rules and rationales. Here too therapists believe that the meaning of all objects and physical arrangements within the frame must be considered in respect of how they might either support or impede the analytical process. The kind of objects included in the consulting room, for instance, is always a matter for concern. Novice therapists are advised to furnish their practices in ways not too revealing of their personal lives. This means that when therapists practice from their own home (which is today more the norm than the exception[63]) all spaces leading to the room itself must also be free of overly personal items. Thus, although leaders encourage novices to hang pictures and dress the room in a way that invites comfort and relaxation, these pictures and furnishings must preserve the anonymity of the practitioner. As Storr tells us, a bookshelf, for instance, containing only psychotherapeutic literature is preferred to one which expresses more idiosyncratic taste. Confronting therapeutic books, it is said, is less surprising and more reassuring than confronting literature suggesting say, a strong ideological, political or religious faith. If some such preference is thoughtlessly displayed this might arouse discomfort in those patients whose private beliefs appear to contradict the therapist's, thus disposing the patient to remain silent on certain topics he or she might need to discuss.[64]

Displaying family pictures is also discouraged. The reason here being that as important clues about the patient's inner world are communicated to the therapist through the patient's fantasies about how their therapist's life is spent, anything too revealing and thus discouraging of these fantasies must be avoided. For example, a patient's fantasy that her therapist is either single, or lonely, or in need of relationship may point to an erotic transference, which, although not harmful if worked with correctly, may become so if left unanalysed. Furthermore, it is often the case that after a sustained period of therapy the patient develops strong feelings of attachment for the therapist. The birth of this attachment often heralds that a crucial phase of therapy has begun, especially if this is the first significant attachment of the patient's adult life.[65] During such times it is important for patients to believe that they are 'special', just as it was once important for the child to feel such things—pictures displaying the other 'special' people in the therapist's life might undermine this fantasy which is often necessary to facilitate healing at certain points.

Just as there is an appropriate time to foster sentiments of attachment for healing effect, there is also a time to move this attachment onto a more mature plane. At this point a therapist might actively use pictures to emphasise the reality of his or her life—at such times the subtle inclusion of a family photo on the mantle piece might be the very jolt the patient needs to initiate his natural separation from the therapist.[66]

The judicious use of material objects for therapeutic effect is not as uncommon in psychoanalytic therapy as is widely supposed.[67] For instance, to display or not to display a box of tissues was a matter I observed being keenly debated in training seminars. In short, the presence of a box of tissues is a loaded statement. Does it communicate that the patient is expected to be emotional? Is such emotionality wanted? Does the box of tissues arouse feelings of inadequacy in the patient who is unable to be emotionally aroused? The reasoning driving these questions again follows from the psychodynamic principle that all objects, actions, and expressions within the analytic frame must be read as metaphors about the unsaid or the unacknowledged. The 'issue of the tissue' was brought to my attention when a final year student confessed the following in a clinical seminar. The confession aroused considerable debate.

> I had a patient who had been abused at the age of 11 by an older neighbour. This woman, who was now 31, had spent most of her adult life as a journalist exposing sex-offenders, adulterists, and the like. She was desperately angry and unhappy with her life and actually hated this work, but more than this she had for many years lived in total anger with men; as partners she selected men who treated her badly, at work she exposed men who had treated others badly—this selecting seemed to justify to herself the validity of her rage. It was obvious to me that this woman had not grieved for the abuse that she had undergone. She had remained hard and angry and while I understood her anger I knew she had to grieve if she were to thaw.
>
> After a long time in one session she described how, after a court case she had witnessed in which a sex offender was convicted, she wept in the toilets out of sight. As she recalled this event tears came to her eyes. She fought and fought to hold them back till at last she broke down... 'I am sorry,' she said, 'I am so sorry for crying'... From this session on I ensured that I placed the tissues directly in front of her, as a statement saying you needn't be sorry for crying here, to say, yes, you can and perhaps must be sad and cry, be something other than angry. (Final Year Student 2005)

In the therapeutic encounter the objects used might be graded in terms of importance. The box of tissues is an object that can take on high importance at the opportune moment. However, it is still of peripheral consequence when compared to the couch or chair upon which the patient rests. The seating arrangements of both therapist and patient are pivotal matters in the psychotherapeutic craft. Innumerable reasons are given as to why there should or should not be a couch, or alternatively face to face seating.

As with the rationale for the fifty-minute hour, the majority of early justifications for using the couch are mostly pragmatic. As Storr (1979: 17) says, Freud's use of the couch was a hangover from his early attempts experimenting with hypnosis. In the early 1890s Freud had been influenced by the hypnosis techniques then used by Charcot and Bernheim, whose clinics he had attended in Paris. Bringing this technique back to Vienna, Freud and his colleague Breuer discovered that disturbing symptoms could be abolished if through hypnosis the patient could be persuaded to both recall and re-experience memories associated with the onset of the symptomatology. Patients were asked to lie down while the analyst conducted the hypnosis from a position behind them out of sight. When Freud eventually abandoned hypnosis for the technique of free-association, he nevertheless retained the couch. This was partly because he did not like being stared at for eight hours a day, and partly because he found that patients were more able to relax and free-associate when lying in a comfortable position.

Since Freud's early rationale the reasons for the couch have become more numerous and elaborate. For instance, many teachers insist that lying recumbent before the analyst lulls the patient closer to a kind of 'dreaming state'. This state is favoured since, as when the conscious mind retreats during the deeps of sleep, it is thought to weaken the partition dividing the ego and id, thus allowing unconscious material to more easily flow through. A second rationale holds that sitting behind the couch frees the therapist from the inspecting gaze of the patient. This enables the therapist to expend energy otherwise used in concealing subjective reactions, in wholehearted concentration on the patient's material. A final reason, consistent with the previous two, is that having the therapist out of the patient's view facilitates the transference. The patient who cannot see the therapist is more likely to develop a rich fantasy life in respect of the therapist—something that can then be analysed.

For most therapists of the psychoanalytic orientation this final reason is the most crucial, since transference is the single most important factor in therapy. Transference refers to, in its widest sense, the attitude the patient harbours for the therapist.[68] This attitude is analysed by the therapist to help the patient understand their past and present relationships to others. Illustrating the transference at play, one psychotherapist says:

> I was asked to see a girl of twenty-two who had made a suicidal attempt, and to assess whether or not she was suitable for psychotherapy. She was fluent verbally, and was telling me about some of her difficulties in relationship with other people when she suddenly broke off. 'Can't you say something?' she asked. 'I'm doing all the talking, and you are just sitting there listening. I can't bear your silence.'
>
> I said something to the effect that, as she was talking freely, there was no need for me to interrupt her, and then went on.
>
> 'I wonder what you were reading into the silence?'
>
> 'If you don't talk, I don't know what you are thinking of me.'
>
> 'What do you imagine that I might be thinking?'
>
> 'I think you might be finding me boring, or that you are criticising me.'
>
> 'It sounds to me as if you always approach people with negative assumptions; as if you never expect people to find you interesting or likeable.'
>
> She agreed that this was indeed the case. This particular girl had lost her mother when she was very young, and had never managed to get on with her father. She had not had enough love in early childhood to acquire any sense of being lovable or even likeable. We went on to discuss how, if one does not like oneself, one is apt to make the assumption that no-one else will like one either, and thus approach other people with suspicion and hostility. (Storr 1979: 72)

The negative parental attitude this patient had 'introjected' at an early age she had yet to shed or challenge. Owing to this, this patient, it is thought, expects to encounter in all present persons the original parental attitude. This understanding of the transference is premised on the belief that we do not experience people in any objective sense, but that we rather transfer what we have experienced in the past onto them in the present. So far as this patient internalised her parents' perception, she considers this perception as warranted and justified—she feels that the parents perceived what was actually there: a child who was largely unlovable. She thus expects others to see her as unlovable, and with this belief she approaches others with suspicion; a fact impairing her ability to make relationships with others. The therapist's task is to analyse the transference and to provide a 'corrective relationship'. By these means the therapist exposes the roots of this internalised sense of self, shows where it is inaccurate, and indicates why it is inappropriate to this stage of her life. If the child had experienced nothing but love at home then perhaps her reactions would have been different—that is, her transferences would have been more positive, but, given that children tend to generalise from parental relationships to relationships at large, her reactions, as this therapist concludes, were perfectly understandable.

The excerpt above, which I have used to illustrate an instance of transference, describes an encounter where the couch is *not* employed, for initial assessments are always conducted face to face. This is to say, transference can be evoked in face to face encounters, a fact which supports those therapists unhappy with the use of the couch. A general rule that I have found which unravels why a given therapist may opt for the chair over the couch is to note how 'interpersonal' the therapist's theoretical orientation is. The more 'interpersonal' their approach the more likely the chair will be used, while therapists holding to a more orthodox analytical orientation invariably elect to use the couch.[69] Therapists who reside midway between these, the 'analytical' and 'interpersonal' extremes, are more free with the use of the seating arrangement, often moving the patient strategically from chair to couch depending upon the patient's need at a given phase of therapy.

In many respects this use of the couch, as is the case with the use of all objects, reflects the link that many anthropologists have explored between cosmology and the use of social space and objects (Seeger 1981; Riviere 1995; Ewart 2000)—that is, people use and arrange physical space and material objects in ways consistent with their beliefs. In psychotherapy the link between spatial/material and cosmological organisation is apparent to the extent that an expert in psychotherapy might be able to infer with some success from a given consulting room the broad kind of practice transpiring within it. In my own experience of inspecting countless practices I soon became acquainted with common features that would frequently appear in the rooms of practitioners who shared the same orientation. Jungian consulting rooms would often display religious objects of Pagan and Eastern origin: Persian rugs, Buddhist and Hindu icons, pictures and objects of Nordic, Oriental, and African origin; while psychoanalytic rooms would be invariably more Spartan, impersonal, and conspicuously free of religious iconography, mainly for reasons of encouraging the transference as already discussed above. Needless to say, the rooms of 'integrative' psychotherapists always presented me with a greater challenge, but even here it was possible to infer from material objects and spatial arrangements what might be included in the therapist's dominant clinical beliefs.

THE RELATIONAL BOUNDARY

Having so far identified the temporal and spatial boundaries framing the psychotherapeutic encounter, the final boundary that I shall discuss is that which circumscribes the actions and behaviour of the practitioner. From an anthropological standpoint the rules governing how the therapist should behave mirror in many respects what Victor Turner (1967) has called the 'performative demands'—namely, a cultural repertoire of appropriate actions, reactions, and interactions that constrain any form of ritual behaviour. In the therapeutic scene certain modes of relating permitted in daily life have no place; the negation of these everyday modes serves to delimit the space as extra-ordinary against the background of ordinary life. The therapist's very professionalism is closely studied ensuring the performance of a specific set of relational behaviours that are consistent with the theory. Thus the therapist's stance is considered to be the most important therapeutic tool, since by its means the general encounter is led in a prescribed direction.

The first essential characteristic of the psychoanalytic posture that the therapist is taught is professionally known as 'abstinence.' This term was originally used by Freud to refer specifically to the fact that the 'analytical technique requires of the physician that he should deny to the patient who is craving for love the satisfaction she demands'.[70] The rationale behind this rule, a rule embodied in the characteristic *formal* posture of the therapist, as with all other dynamic rationales has altered and expanded over time until today we can identify at least three justifications that are commonly emphasised in training.

The formal posture is firstly designed to underscore the different roles that patient and practitioner are expected to play. The therapist's reluctance to speak beyond either prompting the patient to self-disclose or else offering various interpretations creates an environment in which the patient is coerced to fill the silence. The patient's role is thus to indulge a steady flow of honest self-disclosure, while the therapist's is to sit as a participant observer, inspecting the confessions for clues about the patient's unconscious dynamics. The formality forces both parties to honour the work typical of their respective roles, which reverberate at quite different frequencies.

The formal posture is also designed to stop therapists from either overly gratifying or indulging their own or their patient's emotional needs. Beyond offering 'empathic attunement', which includes conferring respect, warmth and kindly goodwill, the therapist's emotional offerings are sparse. For instance, any emotional involvement that would lead the relationship down the familiar routes of friendship or romantic attachment is widely discouraged. The formal posture, studiously maintained, reminds any patient who desires intimacy beyond what the professional contract allows that the therapist is simply not available to provide for the needs the patient must learn to fulfil elsewhere. Therapists do not see themselves as 'substitutes' for intimate relationships, but as means by which patients can come to understand why there is little intimacy in their own lives and what steps they must take to alter this. Indeed if any romantic attachment should form on either side, trainees are told that it should be openly discussed: if the therapist

senses it in the patient then the patient's fantasies should be analysed for transference clues; if it alternatively surfaces in the therapist then this is to be discussed in supervision where a course of
action respectful to the patient can be mutually decided upon.

Another rule circumscribing the therapist's action is the prohibition against self-disclosure. While certain humanistic therapists
use self-disclosure as a clinical technique (it is regarded as a way of
deepening the relationship[71]), analytic psychotherapists still commonly avoid it. As one seminar leader emphasised:

> Some people interpret the analyst's unwillingness to
> answer the patient's questions as evidence of coldness
> or the desire to maintain a power differential. But
> these interpretations miss why it is essential for the
> patient that we do not do so. For example if a patient
> on returning from holiday asks whether you missed
> him while he was away, it is best you put this ques-
> tion back to him [i.e. rather than answer the question
> ask him his fantasies about what you think]... In their
> fantasies there may be important transference clues
> which you will miss if you let your anxiety about not
> answering questions lead you into doing so. Answer-
> ing questions sabotages the transference at worst and
> at best only encourages the patient to continue asking
> things, which is no good...because this is likely to lead
> the exchange into a kind of conversation; if this hap-
> pens you are no longer conducting therapy. (Seminar
> Supervisor 2004)

As well as illustrating why it is important for dynamic therapists to avoid self-disclosure (i.e. self-disclosure sabotages the patient's transference) this quotation is also interesting as it addresses
at its outset a common charge levelled against dynamic therapists:
that therapists are regularly unfeeling, cold, and remote. In my experience these charges often disgruntle therapists essentially because these critiques, many protest, not only betray an inadequate
grasp of the rationale behind the therapist's formality (i.e. it encourages the transference), but also fail to notice the healing benefits this posture can engender (making use of the transference).

Therapists also defend this posture on the grounds that the *appearance* of coldness deceives as to the therapist's real emotional engagement. One female therapist comments:

> You know sometimes the things you hear as a therapist touch you deeply. Of course I don't express this emotion to any significant degree in the session, but there have been some occasions between sessions when reacting to what I have just heard I have sat there in tears. What I do express in the session is my sympathy with my patient's distress; it is important that they see this, but it is also important that in the session they see my strength. You know patients often test you, they speak of suicide and things, to see if you will panic... it is often reassuring for them to see that you don't—which is basically a way of saying you are not afraid of what they are afraid of, perhaps your trust them and know something they don't know— emotion in this instance must be kept back. (Female Psychotherapist 2005)

It is important to note that this statement was made by a therapist who has embraced the more 'interpersonal' pole of psychodynamics. As with the distinction between the interpersonal therapists, who often prefer the chair, and the analytical therapists, who often prefer the couch, in terms of the relational stances analytic and interpersonal therapists take there is also a difference not so much in how these therapists *appear* to the patient, but in the level to which each therapist might use his or her subjective reactions in service of exploring the patient's internal world. In order to understand the origins of this difference, and what this difference involves, we must first historically survey for a moment the therapist's attitude towards what is known as the 'counter-transference'.

THE RELATIONAL BOUNDARY AND COUNTER-TRANSFERENCE

Throughout the early decades of psychoanalysis there was a reluctant acknowledgement of the therapist's 'counter-transference' reactions (i.e. the 'feelings' that the therapist experiences in respect of the patient, whether they be of love, hate, disgust or care). In this period it was the patient's *transference* rather than the therapist's *counter-transference* that was used as a means of understanding. Indeed, on the rare occasion when the counter-transference was admitted it was seen as a corrosive and disturbing element in therapy, since it was the very factor that undermined the idea that the practitioner was an 'objective' observer. So long as the therapist had emotional responses to his patient these responses threatened a 'clear' understanding of the patient's inner world. In this sense, then, counter-transference was basically perceived as a nuisance, something to be eliminated, or was simply seen as evidence that the therapist's own analysis had been incomplete. Although there is little time here to speculate on the origins of this unease, it may suffice to say that counter-transference was the phenomenon *par excellence* that challenged the notion that the therapist could attain complete objectivity. Admitting the presence of counter-transference naturally meant conceding that the therapist was subject to strong incursions of subjectivity that rendered his stance unscientific. The existence of counter-transference then, so far as it threatened the scientific respectability of psychoanalysis, a respectability which as we have seen in the last chapter was something dearly sought in psychoanalytical circles, was a phenomena little tolerated by the early analysts.

It is not until World War Two and post-war psychoanalysis, a period when the scientific pretensions of psychoanalysis were in abeyance, that the harnessing of counter-transference as a therapeutic device gained credence in certain psychodynamic quarters. It is only during this period that the idea that counter-transference might be used in service of understanding the patient begins to dawn on the psychodynamic scene. Psychoanalysts such as Donald Winnicott (1947), Margaret Little (1950) and Paula Heimann (1949-50) all wrote articles drawing attention to how exploring the counter-transference can assist therapists in unravelling the patient's experience. Other thinkers such as Klein argued that the counter-transference should not be understood only as the therapist's *reaction* to the patient, but also as the therapist *embodying* that which patients were unable to consciously experience in the session and in their waking lives. The idea surfaced that the therapist could feel in the sessions emotions that were 'put into' him by the patient. It was argued that these 'projected' feelings should be analysed as they offered clues as to what the patient was really feeling. If these articles troubled the more conservative psychoanalysts, their ideas were soon picked up by more progressive thinkers. Melanie Klein (1952) was one such progressive, defining the phenomenon by which 'disowned' feelings are put into therapists as 'projective identification'.[72] One analyst illustrates how projective identification is understood and dealt with in the session:

> When I feel very helpless and uncertain in the session [for example] and cannot recognize this as a manifestation of my own emotional history and problems, I may offer to the patient the possibility that he is feeling very helpless and uncertain, but that this is an unbearable feeling for him to experience... I might then suggest to the patient that he is unconsciously making me feel what he himself cannot experience, and that he hopes unconsciously that I can hold this feeling for him and give it words. (Psychoanalyst 2005)

The therapist, then, experiences that which the patient is not yet strong enough to consciously feel. By 'taking on' the patient's experience, and by further labelling and thus ordering that which the patient is not yet able to handle, therapists believe that they are helping their patients. The more able the therapist is to assimilate the patient's experience and make sense of it, the safer the patient will feel in gradually 'owning' and experiencing these emotions, which is the first step to moving out of the sphere of their influence.

This new emphasis on making therapists pay heed to their own subjective experiences ran concomitantly with a new understanding about how the therapist should listen or 'attend' to their patients. If the early analysts aspired after unemotional objectivity, therapists today are increasingly inclined to 'attune' to their patient's emotional atmosphere—viz. feel themselves into the patient's subjectivity for the purpose of understanding. It is interesting at this point to notice that the shift from an analytic to a participatory stance also occurred at the same time in anthropological fieldwork methodology. Just as many early 'veranda' anthropologists conducted fieldwork from a more 'observational' than 'participatory' position, so the early analysts preferred a more distanced stance. Arguably the first conscious methodological shift in fieldwork was taken by Evans-Pritchard (1976 [1937]) in his ethnography of witchcraft in Azande. Here Evans-Pritchard made the methodological point that he learnt about the inherent logic of witchcraft not solely by 'observing' it, but by becoming immersed in it, by applying its rationale to the analysis of his own life: 'I learnt the idiom of their thought and applied notions of witchcraft as spontaneously as themselves in situations where the concept was relevant' (1976 [1937]: 19). This more participatory stance, this 'leaning from the inside' the analytic therapists were acknowledging as a tool for learning around the same time: patients were studied not only in the manner of a natural scientist dispassionately inferring conclusions from collected data, but also by means of becoming submerged in their emotional atmosphere; by 'getting under his skin' as Tanya Lurhmann has put it (1989). The psychoanalyst Erich Fromm explains this method succinctly:

> One might prefer the definition of the analyst's role as that of an *'observant participant'*, rather than that of a participant observer. But even the expression 'participant' does not quite express what is meant here; to 'participate' is still to be outside. The knowledge of another person requires being inside of him, to *be* him. The analyst understands the patient only inasmuch as he experiences; otherwise he will have only intellectual knowledge *about* the patient, but will never really know what the patient experiences, nor will he be able to convey to him that *he shares and understands his (the patient's) experience.* (Fromm, 1960: 122, italics added)

If Fromm talks here about experiencing the patient not only cognitively but emotionally, following Thomas Csordas' (2002: 241) work on 'somatic modes of attention', we may point out that the patient is also experienced somatically. By aspiring to feel themselves *into* the patient's subjectivity, therapists inadvertently experience to some degree the physical concomitants of the patient's emotionality. These somatic impressions the therapist then uses as clues to indicate what the patient is not explicitly feeling. If the patient is fearful but not overtly expressing this, then the analyst, if properly attuning, might feel a fearful unease within his or her own body, a rushing palpitation of the heart; or if there is unspent, unacknowledged grief in the patient, then the analyst's body will feel its leaden weight also. Between patient and therapist there is believed to reside a kind of hermetic dialogue in which unconscious messages are transmitted to the attuned therapist either emotionally, cognitively, or somatically.

In summarising our discussion of the relational boundary, then, in the therapeutic encounter two kinds of subjective engagement are encouraged. Firstly, through the counter-transference: the therapist's subjectivity is scrutinised for knowledge about the patient's unconscious; and secondly, through 'emotional attuning': the therapist gains knowledge of the patient by feeling himself into the patient's subjectivity. The rules delineating the relational stance of the therapist therefore force the practitioner into an idiosyncratic healing posture. What I have identified as the rules of abstinence (which engenders formality), of non-self-disclosure (which facilitates the transference) and of subjective involvement (which facilitates understanding), define the modes of relating within the therapeutic space. Such modes then oblige the encounter in certain directions so as to encourage the transference which can be analysed for the patient's benefit.

In sum, from the psychoanalytic perspective the bounded psychotherapeutic frame not only delimits the spatial and temporal dimensions of the encounter, but also the relational. The rule taught in seminars that one must carefully 'maintain the boundaries' is legitimated by a collection of rationales and justifications, all of which advance the idea that protecting the frame promotes the efficacy of the sessions. Thus within the frame the rules of conventional 'perceiving' and 'relating' are suspended. Practitioners approach all transpiring therein as they would quite literally a dream: as in a dream, everything within therapeutic space has its manifest and latent meanings. Manifest meaning, as is seen in the first layer of a dream, is the literal act, expression, object, or gesture: the brush of the hair, the flippant remark, the momentary pout of the lips, *as it appears*; while the latent meaning is the veiled truth that these acts intimate; it is the shrouded message revealed through interpretation, the underlying cache waiting to be tapped. 'Freudianism in practice sharpened the distinction between the sacred and the profane' Gellner emphasised, 'for people "under analysis", reality isn't quite real... the external world acquires a shadowy quality, a kind of *suris*, of suspended emotional animation'(Gellner 1985: xxxvii). This *suris* renders the primary secondary, the surface potentially profound, and the ostensible a kind of shadow-play behind which fathomable meanings dance. That this bounded area asks both the practitioner and the patient to imagine all transpiring therein as significant, leads us to a number of important anthropological conclusions which in the next section I shall consider.

THERAPEUTIC ENCOUNTER AS RITUAL ENCOUNTER?

The spatial / temporal / relational circumscription of the therapeutic frame, reminds the anthropologist of the boundaries enclosing much ritual activity. Indeed Victor Turner's understanding of ritual is particularly useful for highlighting the ritual aspects of psychotherapy since it extends itself to include 'secular rituals' as they appear in politics, law, and advertising. Turner first spoke of 'secular rituals' at a conference he organised along with Max Gluckman and Sally F. Moore in Burg Wartenstein, Austria (Roberts 2003 [1988]: 7). The starting point of this conference, which was entitled 'secular rituals considered', was that the study of ritual had been wrongly confined to the 'religious' and 'magical' aspects of culture. This was partly because anthropologists had traditionally associated ritual activity with religious activity (Turner 1977: 3). Returning to Durkheim's (1957 [1915]: 38) definition of the sacred as being essentially something 'set apart', these anthropologists alternatively argued that in societies made more secular by processes of modernisation and industrialisation a cloaked 'sacredness' still lived on within the 'set apart' dimensions of actual life. These more prosaic 'set-apart' spaces, Jack Goody (1977) now argued, became the new ritual sites, as they displayed all the features of ritual which anthropologists were only prone to observe in religious contexts. Indeed Turner's famous definition of ritual as 'prescribed formal behaviour for occasions not given over to technological routine, having reference to beliefs and in mystical beings or powers' (Turner 1967: 19), Jack Goody now thought perfectly applicable to 'secular rituals'—as long as the phrase 'having reference to... mystical beings' was omitted.

Turner's definition has indeed been used to illuminate the ritual aspects of the therapeutic encounter, albeit in very specific therapeutic situations.[73] The 'set apart' nature of ritual has been the starting point from which these studies embark: the therapeutic frame not only separates the therapeutic encounter from the everyday, but also creates a space within which the evocation of invisible agents regularly occurs (e.g. parent imagos, unconscious introjections), and within which a charged emotional and liminal (transformative) atmosphere is generated (Selvini-Paazzoli et al., 1977; van der Hart 1993; Whiting 2003 [1988]).

To these ritual aspects of the therapeutic encounter it is clear others could be added. Following Skorupski's study Symbol and Theory (1979: 164), the rules guiding the therapist's behaviour oblige a kind of ceremonial formality characteristic of the behaviour occurring in all ritual encounters. Formality in psychotherapy not only manoeuvres both participants into prescribed social positions, but also endows the social occasion with a legitimating gravitas—a heightened ambiance of seriousness and respect which bestows on the enclosed space a ceremonial depth (a fact again accentuating its 'set-apartness'). This allows us to identify another common feature of ritual occurring within the therapeutic space, a feature emphasised by Scheff (1979): this heightened atmosphere provides ritual containment for people with strong emotions—just as in formal funeral rites where emotions are carefully channelled, in the psychotherapeutic encounter participants find safety in knowing that they can experience deep feelings but with some circumscribed limits and therapeutic support—violent emotions are permitted yet also contained by the therapist; patients can feel excessive emotion without fear of being overwhelmed.[74]

Another comparable feature is discerned by applying Houseman's and Severi's (1998: 271) insight that within any ritual space a series of transformations both 'immediate' and 'eventual' occur —'immediate' so far as the ritual space forces both parties entering the encounter to instantly transform their identities: of one, to practitioner; of the other, to patient. While 'eventual' transformations occur through what they call a 'cumulative series of inclusions'—

that is, the characteristics of one identity (in this case the therapist standing for health, wisdom and effectiveness) are gradually absorbed within the other identity (as patients slowly improve they acquire qualities peculiar to the therapist). As within the therapeutic space both these ritual transformations occur, the therapeutic encounter displays certain features and happenings that Houseman and Severi see as integral to all ritual.

In sum, while such comparisons illuminate aspects of therapy not considered in the psychotherapeutic trainings that I have observed, there are nevertheless a number of methodological problems that undermine any confident comparison of ritual and therapeutic forms. As important as an assessment of these difficulties may be, because discussing them would take us beyond our immediate concerns, I would prefer to move forward into the next chapter to highlight one dominant trope in terms of which the therapeutic encounter can be understood—the dominant trope of irony.

CHAPTER THREE
IRONY IN THE THERAPEUTIC ENCOUNTER

An area of interest that has been increasingly growing in anthropology is that concerned with cultural understandings,
manifestations and uses of irony (Crapanzano 2000, Fernandez and
Huber 2001; Losche 2001). That this interest has extended itself to
encompass the therapeutic encounter appears fitting given that in
the bounded therapeutic space, as we have seen, many appear-
ances are interpreted as other than what they seem. Paul Antze, in
a recent book edited by himself and Michael Lambek (2004), is the
first to investigate irony in the psychotherapeutic encounter by
identifying two distinct but complementary 'ironic' interpretative
strategies employed by practitioners. The first he calls 'rhetorical
irony'. This is where therapists interpret the ways in which patients often use their symptoms strategically to secure desired
ends. For instance, a child who has learnt that by feigning illness
she can arouse her parents' sympathy, if in her later life has forgot-
ten this strategy, may well still employ it unawares to exact care
and attention in times of need. In such cases, as Freud illustrated in
his case study of Dora (1979 [1909]), the therapist interprets the
symptoms as veiled pleas for attention, pleas from which will be
inferred clues as to the patient's character structure.

The second interpretative strategy Antze calls 'dramatic irony'.
Via this device patients are shown that they are under the sway of
childish impulses that they neither fully acknowledge nor understand. This kind of 'Sophoclean' strategy, as Lambek refers to it, ex-

84

poses to patients that 'fate creeps inevitably upon its protagonists despite their earnest endeavours to avoid it' (Lambek, 2004: 5). Through these interpretations patients learn that their conscious explanations for their actions actually hide motivations unpalatable to their waking minds: where love and care were *consciously thought* as motivations, there is rather revealed dependency; and where compassion was thought to dominate, there is unearthed unhealthy attachment. This strategy presupposes that unconscious motivations are often obscured by the conscious mind. Pedantry might be rationalised as thoroughness, indolence as carefree living, and the inability to commit as a taste for adventure. What consciousness represented one way, through therapy might be flipped and perceived in another till the conscious vision of oneself lies submerged under a new vision assembled through analysis. In short, these ironic interpretations lead therapists to read into their patients' lives insights gathered by way of *reversals*.

Extending Antze's analysis, in the main body of this chapter I would like to expose other ironic strategies that operate in the therapeutic encounter; those which reverse common ideas of logic, agency, and finally, of suffering. Through discussing these reversals and thereby deepening our understanding of this first stage of training, I intend to achieve two further aims. Firstly, I shall argue that therapy resembles less a form of symbolic healing (where a 'mythic world' is appropriated) than an 'imaginal' process where a 'psychoanalytic imagination' is developed. Secondly, I shall further explain certain core psychodynamic ideas (e.g. of personhood and individual functioning). This latter aim is essential, since psychodynamic ideas are used in the institute to legitimate certain core devices of training. Thus we must master these ideas if in later chapters we are to make sense of why institutional devices exert a powerful influence over trainees.

THREE IRONIC REVERSALS IN THE THERAPEUTIC ENCOUNTER

One widespread reversal utilised in the psychotherapeutic encounter is that of inverting common logic to provide patients with insights into their inner contradictions. In order to better understand this point let me make use of Fromm's distinction between paradoxical and Aristotelian logic (1960: 101). To speak in the broadest terms, the kind of logical thinking nurtured in most Western educational contexts follows a basic Aristotelian model which is premised upon the three pivotal laws: the law of *identity* (which states that A is A), of *non-contradiction* (A is not non-A), and of the *excluded middle* (A cannot be A *and* non-A, neither A *nor* non-A).[75] This style of thinking permeates our basic mathematical and scientific forms which hold that the acquisition of knowledge proceeds through both inductive and deductive inferential techniques stemming from either the rationalists' premises (from which conclusions are *deduced*) or else the empiricists' conclusions (reached *inductively* as bases for further deduction).

While this formal logic predominates in Western rationalist thought, the opposite form is that which has been termed *paradoxical logic*. This assumes that A and non-A do not exclude each other as predicates of X. This is the logic applied by Heraclitus and the pre-Socratics (Russell 1996 [1946]: 57), it is the logic of the Zen Koan which attempts to undermine 'intellection' (Suzuki 1960: 48); it is also the complex logic, as Evans-Pritchard has shown, underpinning the Nuer concept of twins where two persons are seen as one unity over and above their physical duality, particularly in ceremonies connected with marriage and death (Evans-Pritchard 1956: 128-9).

In the therapeutic encounter the suspension of conventional Aristotelian logic is frequently required of the therapist. One clear example of this is found in the clinical application of Freud's concept of 'ambivalence': 'By this', says Freud, 'we mean the direction towards the same person of contrary—affectionate and hostile—feelings' (1975 [1917]: 478). As one emotion of a simple pair is more accessible to the ego than its opposite, the therapist's task is to infer from the 'patient's material' (i.e. everything the patient presents in the session—dreams, associations, etc.) the unacknowledged counterpart. Interpreting the presence of ambivalence firstly has the immediate effect of undermining the *conscious* belief that only one of the contraries exists; secondly it has the gradual effect of surreptitiously teaching the patient that he or she works in paradoxical ways. Repulsion and attraction, joy and sadness, love and hate are often shown to be simultaneously experienced for the one object. This understanding, habitually reiterated through interpretations, familiarises patients with the idea that contrary emotions reside in their own breast, albeit at different levels of awareness. As patients develop this kind of imagination, divergent experiences such as feeling melancholy in 'the joy of success' are no longer defensively denied or overlooked, but acknowledged as important data which, if correctly understood, will illuminate hitherto uncovered aspects of their unconscious. Here is a simple example of ambivalence being interpreted in a patient:

[*Talking about her husband's irritation*] 'I burnt the toast this morning; in fact I have done this many times recently... strange.'

'Your husband's toast?'

'Yes, his toast.'

'You look upset about this.'

[*Silence. Hesitance.*] 'I love my husband; I am so silly for getting things wrong.'

'You love him and yet recently you have done many things to upset him: burnt the toast, forgetting to meet him on time, and last week you threw away two of his favourite books.'

[*Becoming tearful.*] 'I know I can't believe I keep doing this, you know is just bad luck, these are all silly mistakes... this is all very unlike me.'

At the appropriate time this therapist might interpret the patient's catalogue of 'mistakes' as a furtive commentary on some such following theme: the ambivalent feelings she harbours for her husband, for whom he represents, for the institution of marriage, or else for the life that living with him requires her to lead, etc. To suggest that the suppressed contrary of a conscious feeling can express itself though a person's action is frequently alarming to those unaccustomed to seeing their clearest emotions—love and anger, joy and hate—as Janus-faced and double-sided. Thus the irony in the logic therapists apply leads patients to contemplate the paradoxical and illogical nature of their own internality; it turns the romantic idea of 'pure' emotion into a consoling penchant of naivety.

The Irony of Agency

The irony of logic, discussed above, is closely allied to the irony of agency. The psychoanalytic understanding of agency has also always flirted with contradiction. On the one hand psychoanalytic theory presupposes determinism, while on the other the very act of therapy implies that freedom from unconscious forces can be attained. (What would be the use of therapy if it could not?) In this sense, and in Roland Littlewood's terms, both naturalistic and personalistic modes of thought obtain in psychoanalytic thinking; naturalistic, since it is believed that there are forces beyond our awareness determining our lives; and personalistic, since such determinism can be disabled to allow greater degrees of self-determination (Littlewood 1999: 410).[76] To unravel how therapists cope with the co-existence of agency and determinism, we must first inspect the mechanistic or naturalistic orientation to which Freud was pledged throughout his career.

Freud's mechanistic understanding of the person was consonant with the predominant physicalistic thinking of his day. By adopting the word 'analysis' as part of his system of psychoanalysis,[77] he was acknowledging that the analytical methods then used in physics and chemistry must be as far as possible applied within the new psychotherapeutic craft (Haynal 1993). Broadly speaking, by treating the psyche mechanistically, Freud was very much following the Enlightenment call to apply the methods of the natural sciences to the understanding of social/historical/psychological phenomena.[78] More specifically he followed academic psychologists such as Wilhelm Wundt and Gustav Fechner in applying this methodology as far as was possible to the investigation of the mind. This can be clearly seen in the influence Fechner's psychophysics had on Freud's work (Schlutz and Schlutz 2000: 377).[79]

Then, as today, the mechanistic idea that the ego is moved by hidden forces implicitly asks any patient entering therapy to first renounce the idea that he or she possesses complete control over themselves. The self-blame a patient might feel at living out a particular compulsion (promiscuity for example), rather than being compounded by the therapist's moral disdain (a disdain that implies the patient freely chooses this compulsion), is undermined so far as the compulsion is seen as an unbidden visitation which must be approached analytically not morally. The patient too is expected to make this leap from the self-blame posture ('I' do these things) to the posture of interested observer (what is it 'within' me that moves me in this direction)—that is, as one therapist put it, 'the patient must internalise the therapist's attitude towards the compulsion'.

This internalisation is achieved by leading the patient to re-nounce the idea that their ego is in control. If this does not occur then the self-accusatory stance remains intact prohibiting a more 'analytical' attitude from emerging. Carl Gustav Jung, although himself not a Freudian practitioner, nevertheless followed Freud's idea that if therapy is to get underway then the ego's belief in its own sovereignty must first be dethroned. In the following example of a session with a female patient, Jung illustrates how therapy was stalled until the point at which the patient finally renounced her belief that her ego was in charge:

> My example concerns a young woman patient, who, in spite of efforts made on both sides, proved to be psychologically inaccessible. The difficulty lay in the fact that she always knew better about everything. Her excellent education had provided her with a weapon ideally suited to this purpose, namely, a highly polished Cartesian rationalism with an impec-cably 'geometrical' idea of reality. After several fruit-less attempts to sweeten her rationalism with a some-what more human understanding, I had to confine myself to the hope that something unexpected and ir-rational would turn up, something which would burst the intellectual retort into which she had sealed her-self. Well, I was sitting opposite her one day, with my back to the window, listening to her flow of rhetoric. She had had an impressive dream the night before, in which someone had given her a golden scarab—a costly piece of jewellery. While she was still telling me this dream, I heard something behind me gently tap-ping on the window. I turned around and saw that it was a fairly large flying insect that was knocking against the windowpane from the outside in the obvi-ous effort to get into the dark room. This seemed to me very strange. I opened the window immediately and caught the insect in the air as it flew in. It was a scarabaeid beetle, or common rose-chafer (Cetonia aurata), whose gold-green colour most nearly re-sembles that of a golden scarab. I handed the beetle to

> my patient with the words, 'Here is your scarab'. The
> experience punctured the desired hole in her rational-
> ism and broke the ice of her intellectual resistance.
> The treatment could now be continued with satisfact-
> ory results.[80]

Although many psychodynamic therapists of the Freudian tradition might smile at the supernatural overtones in this vignette,
many would nonetheless still sympathise with Jung's attempt to
undermine this woman's over-investment in the authority of her
conscious mind. Although in Jung's example, and in opposition to
Freud, the non-conscious determining forces assume a more mystical form, his basic attitude towards his patient's reluctance to
cede control is still essentially Freudian: through interpretation and
a good deal of patience the ego's obduracy must be undermined if
analysis is to proceed.

The psychoanalytic technique of subverting the ego's attachment to control not only influences the content of interpretations
but also their form. Here is a senior supervisor illustrating to a
second year trainee how the manner in which an interpretation is
delivered must surreptitiously convey that something other than
the patient's ego is in command. He comments:

> 'So it seems that your patient is repeating a pattern of
> behaviour, now that we have identified this, how
> would you make the interpretation.'
>   'I would probably say something like "the fact that
> you perform this action over and over suggests to me
> that you are repeating."'
>   'No. Stop there. There is something not right here.'
>   [Looking puzzled] 'I don't understand.'
>   'You said *you* are repeating rather than *there is
> something in you* that compels you to repeat. Notice the
> difference. The first implies that the patient is doing
> something, that the patient is to blame. This is a mis-
> take. We know that he is doing nothing at all but
> rather that there is something in him that is moving
> him. The form of your interpretations needs to com-
> municate this otherwise you send the wrong mes-

sage... he needs to learn that it is something in the unconscious doing these things to him.' (Supervisor
2005)

The slow usurpation of patients' belief in their self-determination by such interpretive strategies has been used by some commentators, as Antze points out (2004:119), to attack the legitimacy
of the psychoanalytic project itself.[81] For example, Adam Phillips
(1995: 6), himself a renegade therapist, draws a distinction between
the 'Enlightenment Freud' and the 'Post-Freudian Freud'. The first
is the expert detective unearthing hidden motives, the Freud he believes the majority of therapists emulate. The second is the rarer
ironic therapist who understands that 'to be an expert on the unconscious is a contradiction in terms' (Antze 2004: 119). The hypothetical "Post-Freudian" embraces the difficult question that if all
persons possess a determining unconscious, then on what grounds
can therapists claim freedom enough from their own distortions to
safely analyse those of their patients?

To meet this response therapists often have recourse to what anthropologists would call their *concept of personhood*; a concept,
which, as I shall show in later chapters, legitimates many training
devices used in the training institute. But to stay away from how
this concept is institutionally *used* for the moment, let us remain
with unravelling the essential meaning of this concept.

Personhood, broadly speaking, is that which is gradually conferred on those who have moved progressively out of the reach of
the unconscious so as to emerge from its influence with more self-
determination. When Freud said in his prophetic style that through
analysis 'where there was id there shall be ego' (Freud 1955 [1920]:
38) he was pointedly referring to this very movement: where there
was once compulsion directing the conscious mind, after the compulsion is overcome the ego will be stronger and possess more conscious awareness, and therefore greater agency.

This idea of personhood subtly answers the charge that the project of analytic therapy is marred with contradiction. It implies that
therapists can legitimately analyse others in so far as their own
therapy has been successful. Insofar as it has been, they may then
help in removing the various distortions and compulsions from
which their patients suffer.

The co-existence of agency and determinism, and the contradiction this presents, is answered by analysts in another way. For example, and as one therapist commented to me:

> as soon as the patient acknowledges that there are hidden forces compelling the ego in given directions, they can let go of a certain responsibility—for now the patient can see that the things which caused these compulsions are responsible so to speak—parents, early deprivation or trauma, etc. (Psychotherapist 2004)

However, such 'acknowledgement' does not imply a complete renunciation of agency and responsibility. Indeed a certain level of agency is maintained. Without this the patient could not be expected to set right the original malady. The same therapist continues:

> although the ego might not be responsible for setting up the compulsion, it is responsible for disarming it. (Psychotherapist 2004)

The ego, while renouncing much of its agency, retains a sufficient degree to enable its undermining of that which determines it; and so all contradiction is evaded: patients, by applying their initial freedom will accrue via analysis the additional freedom attained from breaking the chains of unconscious compulsions and distortions. Therapy is thus conceived as a process whereby progressive freedom from unconscious determinism is gradually acquired, despite the fact that total knowledge can never be attained.[82] Through dynamic therapy, then, unconscious motives are brought to awareness and lose their compulsive force. And as the level of compulsion is reduced, so one's portion of agency and thus one's 'personhood' is gradually increased. In short, personhood is therefore acquired to the extent that individuals reduce the levels of unconscious determinism directing their lives and polluting their perceptions with 'transference'.

Thus personhood, psychodynamically conceived, could be defined as a *quality of consciousness*; a quality which, to the extent that it is obtained, allows a person to perceive and to act with greater freedom from compulsion and distortion. However, as the quantity of this quality is never fully attained, complete person-hood is never fully achieved. *Its possession must always be a matter of degree.*

In sum, the irony of agency in analytic therapy resides in a double reversal. No sooner has the patient's belief in agency been demolished, than belief in its possibility is re-established. On enter-ing the room the patient must first concede that his ego is to some degree enslaved, but after therapy has progressed and the determ-ining dynamics have been to some extent unearthed, understood, and disarmed, a certain freedom at last can be claimed. Thus the first step to greater agency, and thus responsibility, is to first accept the relative lack of both critical qualities.

THE IRONY OF SUFFERING

Having now discussed the reversals of logic and the double re-versal of agency, there is a final point to be made on the irony of suffering. To illustrate this last reversal I shall broadly describe one biomedical approach to pain so as to provide a backdrop against which to highlight the specific contours of the psychodynamic un-derstanding.

One basic fact, which, if more roundly acknowledged, might dispel some tension between pharmacologists and psychoanalytic therapists on psychiatric wards, is that analytic therapists rarely approach or treat pain in the same way bio-medics do. The bio-medical understanding is that pain arises when a nerve or nerve ending is affected from inside or outside of the body by a noxious stimulant; thus pain acts as a kind of signalling device 'drawing at-tention to tissue damage or to physiological malfunction' (Wein-man 1981: 5). Pain viewed in these terms is on occasion seen to in-crease proportionately with the severity of physical malfunction or injury suffered: in such a view extreme pain is an index that dis-ease is at its height.[83]

Using the level of pain as a barometer to discern the degree of disorder, a device which among others might be applied in bio-medicine,[84] is an approach bypassed in the psychodynamic tradi-tion. Suffering here is not regarded as proportionate to the severity of the disorder since intense emotional pain is not perceived as an index that the underlying malady is at its worst. In fact, psychodynamic practice frequently regards emotional suffering as implying that the worst is over, and that the organism has started to awaken and demand reparation.

The irony Freud introduced into his understanding of suffering was one of his more controversial strokes. In many respects it reinserted the Judeo-Christian belief that there is 'merit in suffering' into the medical cannon by stating that a means of attaining greater vitality passes through the experience of suffering itself. To illustrate how Freud justified this reversal theoretically, a discussion of his early understanding of anxiety will help.

Freud believed that the repression of libidinal forces—i.e. mental energy including sexual energy (Rycroft 1968 [1995]: 95)—caused these forces to transmute into 'free-floating' anxiety. This anxiety, rather than being experienced by the individual directly, was screened from conscious awareness only to affect the person obliquely. For instance, symptoms and other defence mechanisms became indirect or disguised expressions of the repressed anxiety which in turn had its roots in the libido. Freud's discussion of obsessional behaviour illustrates how he believed symptoms were often defences against fully experiencing the anxiety they conceal.

> We make a third discovery when we come to patients suffering from obsessional actions, who seem in a remarkable way exempt from anxiety. If we try to hinder their carrying out of their obsessional action—their washing or their ceremonial—or if they themselves venture upon an attempt to give up one of their compulsions, they are forced by the most terrible anxiety to yield to the compulsion. We can see that the anxiety was screened by the obsessional action, and that the latter was only performed in order to avoid the anxiety. In an obsessional neurosis, therefore, anxiety which would otherwise inevitably set in is replaced by the formation of a symptom, and if we turn to hysteria we find a similar relation... It would thus seem not to be wrong in an abstract sense to assert that in general symptoms are only formed to escape an otherwise unavoidable generating of anxiety. If we

adopt this view, anxiety is placed, as it were, in the very centre of our interest in the problems of neurosis. (Freud 1974 [1916-18]: 452)

So long as the defences (in this case obsessional symptoms) remain operative, the underlying anxiety will not be fully experienced. And so the patient entering therapy because of unpleasant symptoms, although suffering from the inconvenience that such symptoms may cause, is still free from the anxiety the symptoms were set up to conceal. If the patient is to improve he or she must eventually experience the anxiety cloaked by the symptom, anxiety which may feel more uncomfortable to the patient than the original symptom. However, what is *experienced* as a worsening by the patient is often *understood* as preferable by the therapist, since to the therapist this momentary worsening might indicate therapeutic progression. Thus unlike in certain conceptions of suffering where the height of pain accords with the height of malfunction, in analytic therapy the height of malfunction is located in the less painful symptom or 'defensiveness' which conceals from awareness the fact that all is not well, that the patient's life flows in a neurotic direction, and that precious psychic resources thus remain unspent.

Consistent with this, and in contradistinction to much biomedical practice, the therapist attempts an *ultimate* rather than an *immediate* mitigation of the patient's suffering. This strategy will often require the patient to first feel worse rather than better, since it is in the anxiety behind the defence where the clues as to the patient's real problems reside. Moreover, once the anxiety emerges in the stead of the removed symptom it should not be alleviated too readily lest it impede the efficacy of the procedure. As Freud wrote:

Cruel though it may sound, we must see to it that the patient's suffering, to a degree that is in some way or other effective, does not come to an end prematurely. (Freud 1955 [1918]: 163)

One analytic supervisor elaborates:

When things get difficult for the patient resist the easy option of reassuring that everything will be fine, this

96 THE MAKING OF PSYCHOTHERAPISTS

often does more damage than good for many reasons.
Firstly, it is not true, in fact we have no way of knowing the levels of anxiety a patient holds until the defences are removed. Secondly, setting up false hope in
the patient might actually act as a temporary defence
to moving forward, and will only result in greater
despair and his loss of confidence in you should
things get worse; finally, the anxiety is often the very
spur to getting well. Nothing more awakens a patient's resources than the fullest experience of their
difficulty. The only reassurance that we are entitled to
give is that whatever happens our help will be constant. (Supervisor 2004)

In many respects the growing hostility between the camps of
pharmacologically and psychodynamically based psychiatry, so effectively explored in Tanya Lurhmann's (2001) anthropological
work *Of Two Minds*, might be in part aggravated by these quite different understandings of suffering. The pharmacologists, applying
to the emotional sphere an approach to pain designed to treat the
physical, feel justified in alleviating symptoms pharmacologically
as they would do most physiological complaints. Psychoanalytic
therapists, alternatively, who do not equate physical with emotional suffering, and who see emotional suffering as containing important clues as to the patient's troubles, are loath to anaesthetise this
pain too soon. They think it a mistake to dull the very experiences
whose understanding can potentially bring the deeper healing.

To the dynamic practitioner, then, prescribing anti-depressants
to anyone but the most severely distressed is often an injudicious
act: it may assume that depression is the result rather than the
cause of brain's chemical imbalance, it may opt to palliate symptoms rather than to rout causes, and finally it may deny to the person the suffering in which it is thought reside the seeds of renewal.
To the pharmacologist, on the other hand, the therapist's 'natural-
ism' might appear confounding. The notion that a doctor will ex-
acerbate suffering intentionally appears somewhat harsh, especially as it seems based on an ungrounded theory about how persons function and heal.[85]

The struggle between these understandings often works itself out in the consulting room, as one therapist remarks:

> Many patients when they come to see a psychotherapist for the first time bring with them an internalised image of how a doctor works. As soon as they realise that their image cannot be mapped onto the therapist they might become uneasy. And if this unease is worsened by deterioration in their state of mind, they might start to panic and throw accusations. Again, the way we must deal with this is to communicate our understanding of their deterioration through interpretation—this helps both parties to remain calm. (Psychotherapists 2005)

At the opportune moment the therapist is taught to offer their thoughts as to why things feel worse. This provides a rationale in terms of which the patient comes to imagine the facts of their suffering differently, that is, psychodynamically. For instance, the therapist treating an agoraphobic might say, 'the reason your anxiety has increased is because your agoraphobia (fear of going outdoors) is now beginning to disappear; and so now you are confronting the *real* fear the obsession concealed, your fear of moving out, growing up, and becoming independent. Your agoraphobia was a kind of metaphor for deeper and related fear'. This interpretation, while not removing the deeper fear, might help make the patient's situation more comprehensible to him, and thus less frightening and more manageable.

From an anthropological point of view, whether or not the interpretation is effective because it communicates an essential 'truth' is not crucial. Since one could account for the therapeutic effect of an interpretation by noting that the *act* of interpreting a subjective state in itself brings relief. Interpreting a thing implies that, by a few experts at least, the thing interpreted is understood and known to be part of human experience. The patient's fantasy that he suffers from an idiosyncratic malady particular to himself, which is a fear frequently encountered in the greatly distressed, can be considerably weakened when an experienced professional greets his symptoms with familiarity. At once the sufferer feels less alone, less condemned, less exiled from the general collective. Moreover, to have one's malady interpreted further implies that those who name it understand it, and, as they are in possession of mysterious professional expertise, further possess the skills to facilitate its healing. Thus the very act of interpretation can be an instant palliative.

In sum, the irony in suffering is contained in the fact that the very person from whom one has sought respite might, for a while at least, bring only the opposite. Like the reversal of agency and logic previously discussed, the reversal of suffering follows unconventional routes by subtly conveying to the patient through interpretation new ways of managing and imagining subjectivity, new ways which often seem to contradict conventional understandings of pain, logicality, responsibility and distress.

THE PSYCHODYNAMIC IMAGINATION

The close description of the general psychodynamic encounter offered here and in the previous chapter reveals that the therapist's posture and interpretative manner facilitates the conditions under which patients come to imagine themselves differently. Conceptualising this encounter as transpiring in a ritual / liminal space (bound temporally, spatially, and relationally) where there is inculcated in patients a specific mode of imagining 'self' and 'other' in subtle ways, diverges from the symbolist conception of psychotherapeutic healing outlined earlier. We will recall that the symbolist maintains that healing is partly won by forging links between personal experience and public symbols whether these symbols are semantic, conceptual, or analogical in kind. According to this view therapy works by helping patients acquire an explanatory system (Kleinman, 1991 [1988]: 132) which, in the case of psychotherapy, comprises conceptual symbols (Helman 1994 [1984]: 278) that form a linguistic structure or 'mythic world' in terms of which a patient's experience is realigned in accordance with dominant symbolic media (Dow 1986: 56).

In contrast to this perspective, an 'imaginal' understanding asks that we consider the patient's acquisition of a new mode of perceiving and imagining 'self' as the more primary happening in analytic therapy so far as therapy leads patients to imagine their inner workings psychodynamically. As Laderman (1986: 293) insists,[86] patients are often unaware of the intricate meanings and concepts that comprise the practitioner's symbolic system. And this is the case in analytic therapy since practitioners *do not articulate to patients the kind of explicit links between 'experience' and 'concept' that symbolist theories assume take place*. With Mechanic (1972) we might say that therapists offer interpretations in language that 'makes sense' to their patients, eschewing jargon to speak in lay terms about their troubles.

This is supported by the distinction between 'meta-analysis' and 'interpretation' which trainee therapists are taught to honour. Meta-analysis refers to the process of instructing patients in the clinical concepts of dynamic therapy, whereas 'interpretation' refers to the act of offering the fruits of decoding patients' subjectivity in terms of such concepts. Practitioners are asked to favour interpretation over meta-analysis, and by implication to privilege an analytic over a didactic stance. What is disclosed in therapy, therefore, is rarely the meaning of conceptual symbols, but the meaning of behaviour interpreted in the light of these symbols.[87]

This distinction prompts the conclusion that the symbolist's perspective does not entirely capture the patient's experience since symbolic meanings are seldom shared in the manner symbolists suppose. This observation, I suggest, leads us to pursue an alternative vision of the therapeutic encounter, one which might better capture its non-symbolic communicative elements. Ursula Sharma (1996: 259-60), an anthropologist rejecting symbolist understanding, argues that much healing is affected through the patient's imagination (e.g. via Alexander techniques of visualisation) and that such techniques are effective so far as they mix individual and cultural imagery into 'effective images' that enable healing, movement, or other desired bodily effects. Thus Sharma locates a source of healing not in the 'manipulation of symbols', but in the active appeal to novel ways of imagining the nature of self and suffering.

Where I differ from Sharma is in a matter of emphasis. While she stresses the link between somatic and imaginal processes (i.e. new ways of imagining evoke new somatic/bodily reactions), I urge the connection between psychic and imaginal processes (e.g. new ways of imagining evoke new 'psychological' reactions), without making any claims as to this association's therapeutic effects.[88] This caveat notwithstanding, Sharma's formulation is useful when applied to the psychodynamic encounter where patients learn to 'read' and 'imagine' their subjectivity in psychodynamic terms. Over the last few decades many influential therapists (Hillman 1983; Schafer 1978; Holmes and Roberts 1999) have come to see the clinician's task as essentially one of narrative construction. While agreeing that the construction of an explanatory biography is essential to psychotherapy, we could add that this narrative is a construction by means of a particular way of imagining past events. This manner is communicated from therapist to patient in a bounded therapeutic frame where interpretations which convey new ways of envisaging subjectivity are habitually transmitted.

What the patient acquires in the therapeutic encounter, then, is less a complete semantic, explanatory framework than a *mode of imagining* through which their past, present, and future subjectivity is ordered and understood. Trainee patients, therefore, on the cusp of entering the institute rarely find themselves, like the guests of Procrustes, in possession of a rigid structure to which they are forced to commit, but rather they possess a mode of seeing through which their subjective worlds are slowly being ordered, understood, and re-imagined.

Because I shall illustrate further the contours of this 'psychodynamic imagination' in the next chapter, here I shall conclude by listing those dispositions which we can now confidently assume trainees possess when at the threshold of entering the training institute.

Concluding Chapters Two and Three

At the outset of chapter two I noted that trainees approach the institute with a *disposition of partiality* towards the psychodynamic paradigm. This is largely guaranteed by a form of 'institutional vetting' which requires all trainees to first submit to dynamic therapy before entering the institute; a vetting which ensures, as informants confirm, that only those participants who are positively disposed to psychodynamic psychotherapy self-select to proceed with formal training. To this first disposition we now add a *disposition towards imagining psychodynamically*, so far as pre-training therapy obliges all trainees to first be patients before entering the institute and thus to learn to imagine themselves though a psychodynamic lens as any patient would. During the course of this discussion I have also taken the opportunity to clarify certain rudiments of psychodynamic thought, since, as we will see, the institutes appeal to this imagination to legitimate certain institutional devices central to the facilitation of the trainees' socialisation.

In closing this chapter one final point remains. Although I have argued that a symbolic approach does not entirely capture patient experience, this is not to say that 'symbolist theory' is wholly inapplicable to assessing the career of the trainee, since one of the most important aspects of any therapist's education is learning to master the conceptual framework integral to clinical practice. I differ from the symbolists only in saying that the mastering of concepts does not transpire in the therapeutic encounter but rather, in the case of the trainee, in the clinical and theoretical seminars during which theoretical explanations and symbols are grafted onto imaginal experience. So while there is agreement with the symbolist's conclusions in an ultimate sense, there is disagreement about the exact object to which they apply: not to the average patient (or patient-trainee) whose experience they were thought to capture, but to those who have taken the extra step of consciously working to translate private experience into public precept.

CHAPTER FOUR

THE SEMINAR ENCOUNTER: THE TRANSMISSION OF
PSYCHODYNAMIC KNOWLEDGE

Having described the basic therapeutic encounter in the last
two chapters, and how this encounter endows trainees or
patients with the disposition to imagine psychodynamically, we
are now in a better position to understand the institutional devices
of socialisation which appeal to this imagination for their legitimacy. In this chapter, then, by finally entering wholeheartedly into
the training institute by describing the next stage of professional
socialisation—seminar education—I will show how in seminars
the psychodynamic imagination becomes deeply affirmed and
wins for itself conceptual dressing.

When describing this second stage of training I shall lay special
emphasis on how the roles between trainees and trainers are structured hierarchically. By making use of Elisabeth Hsu's (1999) concepts concerning how medical knowledge is transmitted to novice
practitioners, I shall further illustrate how this hierarchy is legitim-
atised by the various 'styles of knowing' (secret and personal) that
obtain in the therapeutic community. Moreover, I shall explore
how via the institutional transmission of 'standardised' therapeutic
knowledge (knowledge contained in the 'official' or 'core' therapeutic texts) such knowledge is protected from criticism. In all, by
dwelling on these themes I shall suggest that the educative atmosphere in which psychoanalytical knowledge is transmitted is by
and large more 'affirmative' than 'critical', finally concluding that

this style of 'affirmative' education reflects communal anxieties about the dissolution of the psychoanalytic tradition and about the need to duly protect it.

THE SEMINAR

Theoretical seminars are usually held once weekly at the institute. These are meetings that last for about one and a half hours, where key theoretical ideas are taught and discussed. Typically on any one evening there might be a number of seminars taking place in different rooms, each seminar catering for candidates at different stages of their training. Before the seminars commence there is often a buoyant atmosphere in the halls, where trainees collect to greet each other, laugh, and share light conversation. As the hour approaches for the seminars to begin, the chattering din slowly abates as candidates gradually file into their respective groups. Doors close one by one until at last the hall sits silent.

Finding ourselves now in the seminar room we notice the group is small in size, comprising four to eight trainees and one group leader. We also notice that these meetings are not conducted in a lecture style, where the teacher, standing before neat rows of scribbling students, imparts knowledge from notes or memory with few interruptions. Rather the seating is arranged in circular fashion, this organisation being thought to better invite discussion and the sharing of ideas, and to encourage a deeper group intimacy than the formal lecture arrangement can produce.

Seminars leaders are always themselves trained therapists involved in professional practice, and are often graduates of the institution at which they teach. On occasion these leaders are newly qualified therapists who, aspiring to reach higher positions in their institutes, are travelling the familiar route by which such positions are attained: via the teaching and supervising of students. Institutions generally prefer to hire from their own membership (i.e. their own graduate body) since these therapists are familiar with the customs and traditions of the specific training. When seminar leaders are not graduates, however, they are often selected from 'parent' institutions, usually from those positioned higher up in what I have termed the genealogical structure. For instance, the BAP (British Association of Psychotherapists) and the Lincoln Centre will invariably hire leaders from either their own memberships or from the Institute of Psychoanalysis, the institute which heads the genealogical structure. That institutes prefer to 'hire up' than down was a fact I frequently observed.

As with the therapeutic space discussed in the last chapter, seminars are sites where communal ideas, values, and principles are transmitted, and thus could be envisaged as structurally comparable to ritual spaces through which collective meanings are affirmed and shared. That in these sites only communally accepted ideas are transmitted, in some measure explains why individual seminar leaders rarely design their own courses, but rather teach the established curriculum planned by the training committee (i.e. the senior members of the institute). The following summary of a typical theoretical programme, for instance, will remain the same despite the comings and goings of individual seminar leaders (see appendix three for further summaries):

Year 1
S. Freud; K. Abraham.

Year 2
M. Klein; D. W. Winnicott; Infant and Child Development; H. Kohut; Comparative Clinical Concepts; W. D. Fairbairn; S. Ferenczi; M. Balint; Topics on Clinical Management.

Year 3
Psychoneurosis and Character Disorders; Depression; Narcissistic Disorders; Psychosomatic Disorders; Perversions; Comparative Clinical Concepts Revisited.

Year 4
W. R. Bion; Post-Kleinians; Current Themes in Sexuality; The Analytic Attitude.[89]

The commission made by the training committee to the seminar leader, cogently defines the leader's seminar duties. The leaders I spoke to often saw their role as one of primarily upholding and transmitting the collective views of the institute rather than of using seminar settings to communicate significantly personal views of their own. 'I am here to clarify points of theory and to teach the basic ideas of Freud', one leader commented. 'I see that as my remit'. And another: 'In seminars we have a responsibility to see that our trainees understand the core ideas; seminars are essentially about making sure this happens.' And again: 'my teaching is a clarification of the principles guiding clinical practice'(Interviews 2004).

To employ a Weberian (1963 [1922]: 4) distinction for a moment, the role of the seminar leader as conceived by the training committee approximates more closely to the pole of 'priest' than to that of 'prophet'. Prophets, for Weber, were distinguished by their charismatic promulgation of a personal vision or redeeming idea, while priests were those self-selecting individuals charged with the idea's preservation and dissemination: '[The priest] lays claim to authority by virtue of his service in a sacred tradition, while the prophet's claim is based on personal revelation and charisma' (1963 [1922]: 4).[90] This is not to say that 'priests' share no moments of originality or creative rapture,[91] this may well be, but rather that when donning their institutional role it is the communal rather than their own private vision that they are obliged to transmit.

Weber's idea of the priest is rendered more apposite if we recognise it need not only pertain to the religious sphere, since every kind of set and school, it could be argued, has its celebrants and upholders. In this sense we might speak of priests in philosophy, in politics, in the arts, and in psychotherapy. Often these individuals are very learned, and use their learning to administer the agreed-upon ideas so as to ensure that the communal message is transmitted to the next generation. In other words, the priest's duty is to disseminate 'acquired' not 'revealed' knowledge, and by this means to transmit that which is inherited and collective rather than that which is self-conceived.

The proscription laid out by the training committee defines the seminar leader's role as one of propagating communal rather than idiosyncratic knowledge. In this respect the leader's role demands a 'depersonalisation of interest' from those who embody it—this is to say, where one's personal interest diverges from that of the collective, the collective interest is to be preferred. Personal creativity, then, is only encouraged so far as it serves the collective agenda. One seminar leader explained:

> We are all accountable and must respect that account-ability. In our institute we have a definite therapeutic tradition to teach. It is no good if I diverge from that tradition and follow every whim. ['Are you ever tempted to?'] No, no because I feel these ideas as my own... I enjoy teaching them... and I think that my students enjoy learning them. *We play our respective parts and get what we need from this.* (Seminar leader 2004, italics added)

The role that seminar leaders adopt has implications for the trainees subject to it. As Goffman (1959: 253) has maintained, social roles lose their actuality when removed from their context; they assume reality only in relationship.[92] The imparter exists only so far as there is one who receives, while the receiver's identity 'as receiver' dissolves in the absence of the giver. In Barth's terms (1971) we might say that the 'dominant role', embodied in our case in the seminar leader, must inevitably coerce its relational 'other' into the complementary position if it is to be realised. Speaking of the relational dynamic it creates, Sarah, a second year trainee commented:

> Seminars are strange places, here you are an adult learner but often experiencing what you felt many years ago. There is something in the fact that you are expected to learn and that your questions should be more clarificatory than critical. You kind of learn this early on. ['Do you mind this?'] Well it is fine mostly, I suppose, but there are occasions when you want to challenge something and this can be frustrating, because you don't want to upset things. ['Upset things?'] I mean upset the leaders by questioning too much... (Second Year Trainee 2004)

John said the following:

Yes, yes, seminars are places where you regress. I
mean I am not bothered by this... I kind of like sitting
back and listening. But on occasion when I feel suspi-
cious about something and I feel that the teacher just
wants us to take things on board... I often opt for silence... It is rare to find in adult life a context where
you are not expected to know. Everywhere you are expected to be an expert—at home, at work etc. In life
you kind of have to pass about unknowing like a hot
potato. (Third Year Trainee 2005)

This role asymmetry puts many trainees in an unusual and ambiguous position in respect of their customary status: while in their
private and public lives they might parent a family, head a business, teach at college, or nurse the sick in hospital wards, in the
seminar context they are tacitly required to divest themselves of
any such 'typical' position so as to identify with their current and
relatively lowly (student) standing: 'I feel I have to wear a different
hat when I come to the institute' commented Jack, a second year
trainee and a social worker. 'Here [in this profession] I am actually
way down on the bottom rung looking up... this is how it often
feels at least.' Peter, the thirty-one year-old trainee in his first year,
said: 'Yes there is something frustrating at finding yourself in your
early thirties having to start again. I get frustrated sometimes that
there is such a long way to go... You have kind of got to humble
yourself here, and accept that you know relatively little in comparison to the tutors' (Interviews 2004).

In Peter's experience there is something similar about this act of
stepping from the public world into the relative modesty of
'learner status', to the act of returning to the family setting where
only kin statuses such as parent, child, sibling, and grandparent
matter. When entering both contexts one's usual and often higher
status is left at the door. In the training setting it is the relationship
of teacher and student that matters, this configuration eclipsing
higher status-filled roles that trainees on other occasions will embody. Thus the status Peter enjoyed at work becomes 'latent' in the
seminar—he is now an apprentice and expected to behave as such.
He is not asked to lead, to decide, to direct, or to be overly assert-

ive, but to recognise his inexperience, and, with his humility braced, to listen, to learn, and to assume the posture of unknowing.

On occasion a given student is unwilling to assume this position and tensions arise. As I shall speak of acute examples of such unwillingness in the next chapter on dissent, I shall only mention here weaker versions of opposition. In such instances a trainee's habitual status resists being placed in the 'latent' position and periodically manifests itself in strategic ways, often at liminal moments that sit at the boundaries between the external world and the classroom. These liminal points are numerous: they exist at lunch or in the pub, in the halls or during walks to cars or the local bus or train station. These liminal places often provide opportunities for personal discontent to be voiced. And status is reasserted by means of criticising the structures that engender the imbalances. For instance, Sarah, of whom I spoke earlier, would on these occasions often complain about a given analyst being too stern and intimidating, and would continue to criticise his teaching skills (although in our 'official' interview she was careful to temper her complaints despite my insistence of confidentiality). I observed that these liminal moments allow trainees to momentarily vent frustration without the fear of being overheard by seniors—this is to say, the type of dissent emerging in these liminal spaces is what we might call *strategic dissent*, since it is of a kind that does not jeopardise the trainee's position with respect to authority.

In many essentials it is true to say that the status imbalances between senior and junior professionals have analogues in many professional fields. But in the psychoanalytic community the unique component is found in how this relationship is legitimated by psychoanalytic ideas; ideas endowing the asymmetry with specific intensity and meaning. For instance, this role imbalance is perfectly consistent with, or in Rodney Needham's (1962: xxxvi) terms 'analogical to', the psychodynamic concept of personhood discussed in the previous chapter.[93] As I mentioned there, personhood is not given but achieved, gradually conferred upon those who have moved progressively out of the reach of their unconscious and its distortions, to emerge with clearer perception and more self-determination. As the development of this clarity is believed to be facilitated through personal therapy, it follows that the deeper and more thorough your therapeutic experience the more likely you will possess greater quantities of that elusive quality of personhood. In this sense fully initiated practitioners are generally thought to reside higher upon the spectrum of self-knowledge and development, largely because they have passed through many years of training and personal psychotherapy.[94] This belief, when tacitly subscribed to by both trainee and trainer, accords the latter with a knowledge and perspicuity not yet attained by the novice. It is in this sense that the trainer is believed to possess knowledge that is off-limits or 'secret' to the trainee, since this knowledge is only accessible to those who have been fully initiated.

KNOWLEDGE TRANSMISSION

At this point it would be useful to discuss more closely the kinds of knowledge transmitted to the trainee in the seminar setting (including this 'secret' knowledge), for knowledge, after all, is something all trainees keenly seek. But as knowledge can take many forms and shapes (e.g. 'secret', 'personal', 'experiential' or 'authoritative') it will be useful to identify some of the dominant kinds transmitted in the seminar space. In order to help identify these different kinds, let me relate our discussion to Elisabeth Hsu's (1999) investigation *The Transmission of Chinese Medicine*—a study whose insights, when used to illuminate the therapeutic setting, may yield many profitable observations.

Hsu's study of TCM (traditional Chinese medicine) identified three kinds of knowledge transmitted from the Chinese medical doctor to the apprentice in the course of the latter's education: standardised, personal and secret knowledge. Briefly put, standardised knowledge is that comprehended 'more or less in isolation from medical practice'—it is the standard, formalised, 'textbook' knowledge ratified by a political, professional, or bureaucratic elite. Alternatively 'personal knowledge' is essentially that passed on through personal relationship—here both parties reserve the right to 'accept and reject each other on the grounds of character and personality' (p.102). The apprentice chooses a mentor if he or she believes that a relationship of mutual trust will develop. This is important as 'to what degree and what kind of knowledge... [is] transmitted depends very much on the personalities involved' (p.102). This is to say, if the relationship between doctor and ap-

prentice is strong there is a greater likelihood that a deeper knowledge will be imparted. Finally, 'secret knowledge' is that which is
intentionally concealed from the uninitiated. Not only does this
concealment render more alluring that which is hidden, but it also
'legitimates the right of those who have access to [this] knowledge,
secures their authority, and hinders uncontrolled distribution of
knowledge' (p.52). Secrecy then, both heightens the value of the
knowledge concealed and confers power on the knower. It acts as
an adornment which 'intensifies and enlarges the impression of the
personality by operating as a sort of radiation emanating from it'
(Simmel, cited in Hsu 1999: 339).[95] This intensification serves not
only to draw a boundary between lay persons and practitioners,
but also between apprentices and the fully qualified (p. 56).

Despite the many cultural differences between the practitioner/
apprentice relationships of both therapeutic systems, when these
relationships are structurally compared there emerge a number of
palpable similarities. As I have previously mentioned, the psychotherapeutic leader, whether of a session or a seminar, by virtue of
having the rounder therapeutic experience is believed to possess a
clearer vision of unconscious processes—namely, a developed
sense as to both the hidden sources of distress and the best means
for their alleviation. 'Give it time and you will understand also',
says one supervisor to an inexperienced trainee, 'you can't expect
to really grasp these things [the patient's dynamics] so early on'.[96]
Since the act of 'grasping' is thought to require a certain clinical
perspicuity that can only be developed over time, inexperience
bars entrance to the deeper and 'secret' insight fuller personhood
confers.

As fuller knowledge is necessarily denied to the novice, it becomes a valued and honoured commodity. This endows certain
leaders with a special magnetism, accentuating the abilities they
possess. This fact I observed on many occasions where certain
leaders, being particularly revered, seemed to possess for students
a certain *mana*, so to speak. Of different respected seminar leaders I
heard different trainees recount: 'she has such uncanny insight' or
'her understanding is extremely penetrating', or 'I trust his judgement completely'. When trainees discussed their patients in seminars, astute leaders who are thought able to unravel patients'
problems were seen as individuals who can 'bring sense to dis-

order' or 'save your skin'. Even leaders whose popularity was questionable because they were 'difficult' or 'intimidating' were still ascribed a kind of 'special knowing' which obliged deference from trainees. In all, in many trainees I noticed a strong desire for the personhood not yet attained—a special commodity seeming to bring many benefits in its train (e.g. high status, economic reward, power in relation to the unknowing, a sense of greater expertise and confidence, etc.)

That leaders, then, are thought not simply to possess 'standardised knowledge' (i.e. textbook knowledge available to lay person and learned enquirer alike) brings us to our first point of similarity between TCM and psychotherapy: knowledge for both is not seen as primarily 'book-learned', but rather born of experience, of extended practice, of time spent under the tutorship of the learned. And since trainees have yet to acquire this experience, the knowledge it spawns remains secret to them.[97]

If 'secret knowledge' exists in the therapeutic community, so too does 'personal knowledge'. As Hsu observes in Chinese Medicine, in psychotherapy the most important knowledge is acquired through relationship (i.e. via the training therapy which continues up until graduation). As in TCM, the deeper the relationship the greater the value of the knowledge attained. For instance, the more trust that is established between therapist and patient, the more likely the patient will be able to explore ever deeper layers of their internality. And as such exploration is essential if the therapist is to understand the patient, an understanding essential to aid the patient's progression into full personhood, establishing such trust is critical. The equation being: deep relationship begets deep exploration; exploration facilitates deeper understanding; deeper understanding begets more accurate interpretations, a richer therapeutic alliance, and finally deeper self-knowledge.

A further dimension of 'personal knowledge' made less explicit in Hsu's study, is that for psychotherapists the value of personal knowledge is increased if the therapist with whom one relates can claim a venerable 'line of descent'. This means that as therapeutic knowledge is passed on principally through relationship, the potential exists for any given trainee to have a close affiliation (via their relationship with their therapist or seminar leader) to earlier important figures in the movement's history. For instance, Hartvig

Dahl in Janet Malcolm's (2004 [1983]: 88) *Psychoanalysis: The Impossible Profession* traces his therapeutic lineage via K. Menninger (his analyst) though K. Abraham (Menninger's analyst), who was a respected member of Freud's original circle. As both Menninger and Abraham are venerated figures in psychoanalytic history, Hartvig Dahl can claim a venerable lineage and thus a certain authority—the supposition being that the qualities which led these analysts to high therapeutic competence would have been somehow absorbed by their trainees.[98] As the psychoanalyst Michael Rustin explains, because of this 'aristocratic penchant' in the culture of psychotherapy '"lines of descent" are symbolically established and remain important markers of status' (1985: 153). In psychotherapeutic culture not only is persistence over time thought to lead to deeper knowledge, but the pedigree of such knowledge is also believed to *increase* if the leader from whom it is gathered is of an illustrious lineage. Thus, in psychotherapy not only is personal knowledge deepened through relationship, as Hsu teaches us, but it is also heightened if one's leader is of venerable descent.[99]

The tacit belief, held by both trainees and leaders that full personhood includes a certain 'knowledge status' which remains secret to the novice, has a consequence beyond that of rendering trainees more susceptible to the suggestions of those ensconced in positions above them. In addition this belief protects those who claim to be the only ones who can correctly transmit the craft, since it undermines the idea that psychotherapy can be mastered by reading texts alone (i.e. through acquiring only 'standardised knowledge'). If this were possible then anyone could gain expertise in the psychoanalytic craft without submitting either to personal therapy or to any institutional appraisal.[100] This would undermine not only the believed natural hierarchy between the initiated and the uninitiated, and that between different schools in the genealogical structure, but also between the initiated 'guardians of the tradition' and the uninitiated lay-persons residing beyond its bounds.

So far I have examined the imbalances between senior and junior therapists, and how they are supported by psychoanalytic ideas. These ideas support the existence of 'secret' knowledge (accessed through acquiring personhood) and 'personal' knowledge (acquired through relationships and lineage) to which novices have limited access and lay-persons no access at all. Having said a little about secret and personal knowledge, let me now focus on the transmission of 'standardised knowledge'—i.e. the 'official', text-based, theoretical knowledge imparted in seminars. By inspecting what is included in and excluded from the theoretical canon, I believe we may glimpse what further dispositions institutes hope to inculcate in their trainee practitioners.

THE TEXTS: A BOUNDED ENTITY

The American psychoanalyst, Otto Kernberg, writes:

> Major challenges to psychoanalytic theory and technique occur at the boundary of our professional field, and the avoidance of investment in such boundary pursuits protects not only the purity of psychoanalytic work but also the raising of challenging and potentially subversive questions regarding the limits as well as the applications of psychoanalysis. (Kernberg 1996: 1038)

In the above statement Otto Kernberg parodies a latent attitude he considers to be widely held in training institutions; an attitude determining the kind of knowledge imparted in seminars. A useful way to gain understanding as to the precise kind of standardised knowledge transmitted in seminars is through inspecting the curricula enclosed in appendix three. These curricula are of anthropological interest more for what they exclude than for what they include.

When reviewing the curricula what is most noticeable is that all theorists listed are psychodynamic in orientation. Yet it is also true that most of these theorists have subtly dissimilar understandings of dynamic processes. Thus modern psychodynamic training is in some measure integrative (within psychoanalytic parameters), since after having mastered the essential teachings of Freud, candidates in later years must study alternative views which introduce competing and sometimes contradictory psychoanalytic ideas into their existing conceptual repertoire. At these later stages students are obliged to forge integrations, reconciliations, or establish allegiances; activities that often engender much heat and discussion in seminars. As Patrick, a third year student stated, however, these discussions are conspicuous for not transgressing certain parameters:

> There are things debated and things simply not... there is a whole lot of debate about, perhaps, integrating similarities and differences between theories and points of practice, especially in the final year of training, but I have noticed that we avoid debate about whether there is an unconscious or not, about the empirical basis of inner dynamics... The meta-questions concerning the principles that all approaches share are just put out of our minds. Trainers seem not particularly interested in them. (Third Year Trainee 2005)

Patrick's statement articulates a latent taboo in seminars concerning discussing 'meta-questions'. If this taboo subtly draws bounds around and thus restricts what kind of subjects can be discussed, the process of integration that I observed is restricted in two further senses. Firstly, in the sense that only the integrations of different psychodynamic theories are explored, while there is no exploration of integrations between psychodynamic and non-dynamic therapies. This means that what is taught is mostly disconnected from developments in related therapeutic fields (e.g. in psychoanalytic institutes there are no courses taught on cognitive/behavioural, existential, humanistic or cross-cultural psychotherapy). Indeed, whatever knowledge trainees possess about these therapies I found to be derived from other private or public courses of study.

Integration is restricted in a second sense: seminar teaching does not include the study of outside academic critiques or discussions of the psychoanalytic world-view. Related disciplines of anthropology, sociology, philosophy or even academic psychology are largely ignored, and if referred to at all usually only in so far as their findings support (rather than critique) points of psychodynamic theory. That seminar education is circumscribed in like manner across trainings became clearer to me after reviewing the curricula of numerous institutes whose seminars I could not directly observe (see appendix three). In the eleven institutes I surveyed, when searching for the inclusion of relevant sociological studies of psychoanalysis, for example, I only found two institutes which appeared to include a 'social' perspective. On closer inspection of their curricula, however, I found these modules were concerned with explaining social phenomena psychoanalytically—e.g. applying psychoanalytic ideas to understand family and organisational systems, or reducing social phenomena such as 'collective mentalities' and ritual and religious practice to psychology.[101] They were not concerned with social analyses of the profession itself.

Naturally it would be hazardous to draw too definite conclusions from the study of curricula alone, since the relations between a course description and what is actually taught may be tenuous. However, coupling these data with my own participatory observations encouraged the conclusion that the theoretical education of the psychotherapeutic trainee was a heavily circumscribed affair. In terms of anthropological / sociological knowledge, for instance, trainees are generally not taught to explore the limits of the profession they are entering—that is, they learn neither about the system's relationship with other social institutions, the critical interfaces between psychoanalysis and other intellectual disciplines, nor about the social roots and blind-spots of the psychodynamic model. What is generally not imparted, in other words, is any kind of social, critical or historical awareness of what trainees are participating in, how they are participating in it, and how the plight of the profession influences this participation.

This form of what we might call 'bounded learning' is not particular to the modern institute, but has a long legacy in the history of analytic training. In the early 1960s, for example, the anthropologist G. Gorer wrote an article that included the request that therapists formally supplement psychoanalytic education with anthropological / sociological knowledge:

> A number of contemporary social scientists... have submitted themselves to the discipline of learning about psychoanalysis by systematic study and, often, by undergoing a personal analysis. But with very few exceptions... psychoanalysts have not shown parallel humility; they have not made any systematic study of the literature of contemporary social sciences; nor,

despite the vicissitudes of their lives which have often entailed emigration, have they submitted themselves the systematic study of an unknown society, an experience which has many analogues with a personal analysis in the permanent change of focus which it produces. (Gorer 1962: 189)[102]

Philip Rieff, echoing this sentiment, noted that this institutional reluctance to 'step beyond the bounds' has led the trainings, as he argues,

[to] fail in their pedagogic function because they have no overall conception of what they are trying to do, nor a historical perspective on themselves. Psychoanalysis has developed a pseudo-interpretative attitude toward itself, which is the ultimate barrier to the acquisition of those critical competencies that could help a movement now almost wrecked by its own success. (Rieff 1966: 104-5)

Rieff believed that these 'critical competencies' are only acquired if reflexivity in respect of one's discipline is developed, and if the methodological skills needed to test disciplinary claims are cultivated. Otto Kernberg, speaking in the 1990s, asks whether such critical competencies are encouraged in modern institutes. He answers in the negative, stating that the aim of psychotherapeutic education broadly remains the same:

[it] is not to help students to acquire what is known in order to develop new knowledge, but to acquire well-proven knowledge regarding psychoanalysis to avoid its dilution, distortion, deterioration and misuse. (Kernberg 1996: 1039)

Kernberg's comments support the idea that the transmission of standardised knowledge is of a very particular kind indeed, privileging vocational over academic socialisation, and favouring the instilling of dispositions that promote the conservation rather than the development of psychodynamic ideas.[103] In the light of these observations it becomes difficult to agree with Michel Foucault that the psychoanalytic perspective results in 'a perpetual principle of dissatisfaction, of calling into question, of the human sciences in general' (quoted in Forrester 1994: 186). I would disagree because, in the institutes at least, the manner in which dynamic therapy is transmitted encourages no such 'perpetual dissatisfaction' in respect of its own epistemological status. In seminars the reflexive spirit whirls safely within tightly defined intellectual boundaries—that is, within a particular and accepted frame of reference (Valentine 1996: 179). Thus core psychoanalytic tenets (i.e. the unconscious, defence, resistance, transference, etc.) are taken as axiomatic, and what is doubted is only how they manifest in, or apply to, any given clinical case. In short, what seminars tend to advocate is a modernist confidence in (rather than a reflexive questioning of) the foundational tenets of psychoanalytic belief—this fact is perhaps what led Michael Rustin to characterise psychoanalysis as the 'last modernism', a fact leading Andrew Samuels (perhaps in defiance of the institutes) to call for an era of reform. In his *The Plural Psyche* he writes:

> If our generation's job is not to be restricted to professionalisation and institutionalisation, it is necessary to highlight one thing we can do that the founding parents and brilliant second-generation consolidators cannot. This is to be *reflexive* in relation to depth psychology, to focus on the psychology of psychology, a deliberate navel-gazing, a healthy narcissistic trip to fantastic reaches of our discipline; a post-modern psychological outlook, redolent with the assumption that psychology is not 'natural', but made by psychologists. (Samuels 1989: 216)

A UNION OF INTERESTS

The fact that the majority of students are rarely critical of either the circumscription of the 'theoretical body' or the asymmetry in the relationships between leaders and trainees, suggests a union of interest between novice and practitioner, a shared interest observed in the words of the following trainee:

> I have found my theoretical education invaluable. At present I am having seminars with a well-known Kleinian analyst who is very knowledgeable on trans-ference... we are investigating with him counter-trans-ference which to be honest has puzzled me until this recent series of seminars. Discovering the subtle ways patients can put into you disowned parts of them-selves, has provided me with a whole new set of the-oretical tools... I am beginning to see how easy it is to confuse what it is patients put into you with what is actually your own emotional stuff. As my training moves on I'm warming to the ideas more, coming to appreciate their sophistication... They can account for so much of human behaviour... [I ask: 'Have you be-come more convinced of the worth of these ideas since your training?']. I think so, the more aware of these things you become the clearer you see them happen-ing in the consulting room. (Third Year Trainee 2004)

The comments of Peter, a thirty-one year-old male trainee, on two points at least reveal opinions shared by the majority of the students I befriended and interviewed. These are, firstly, that sem-inars, along with providing opportunity for new knowledge ac-quisition, endow the psychodynamic imagination acquired in per-sonal therapy with conceptual dressing; and secondly, that these are sites where confidence in the psychodynamic paradigm is pro-gressively developed.

In respect of the first point, as I argued in chapter three, it is commonly admitted that while students could *imagine* themselves in psychoanalytic terms before attending seminars, apart from pos-sessing a rudimentary or 'popular' understanding of theory the majority of them remained unfamiliar with the deeper theoretical subtleties. I accounted for this by explaining that pre-training ther-apy is more an imaginative than didactic encounter and so does not provide occasion for deep theoretical learning.[104]

With respect to the second point (that seminars are sites where confidence in the psychoanalytic paradigm is progressively developed) in order to offer some insights into why this is so our first step is to notice that standardised knowledge is communicated linguistically, via texts and conversation; a fact asking us to consider the use of language in the teaching setting and how such usage facilitates the trainees' palpable movement into a speech community over the years of their training.

LANGUAGE IN THE SEMINAR SETTING

A pivotal part of seminar education is the requirement that trainees relate their own or their patients' experiences to the ideas being taught and discussed in seminars. For instance, each seminar usually includes a student presentation on a point of theory being taught that week. The presentation involves relating an abstract idea to an empirical instant—that is, the trainee will draw on their own work with patients, or, if still without a training case, on his or her own experience of therapy, to illustrate points of theory in action. This device is repeated in discussions of case studies, where again ideas are not abstractly considered divorced from empirical facts but are intimately related to the subjective phenomena that emerge in therapeutic sessions. For instance, the therapist's different emotional reactions to patients are linked with different species of 'counter-transference', and by these means trainees come to understand their interpersonal reactions in relation to these concepts. These methods are complemented by the advice given to trainees for whom the ideas discussed have had personal resonance—they are told to 'take their experiences to the couch'—the supposition being that the idea has stimulated a complex not yet 'worked through' by the affected trainee. One seminar leader sees being able to talk through the difficult personal material provoked in seminars as justification enough for personal therapy being a core component of training. She said:

> In the classroom we obviously discuss things which promise to have a deep effect on the students. Because everything is related to the self I have seen this happen with my own students many times. You can actu-

> ally see the cogs turning, the realisation: 'Oh what she
> is talking about goes on in me!' Because the classroom
> is not the appropriate place to talk about these experi-
> ences they need to take them somewhere else... espe-
> cially if their experiences are uncomfortable. (Seminar
> Leader 2004)

By this constant attaching of human experience onto the pegs of
dynamic understanding, a proficiency in the discipline's language
is gradually reached—e.g. the difference between the linguistic
competence of first and final year seminar students dramatically illustrates this point. Where first years are hesitant in their command of terminology, final year students wield jargon with accuracy and confidence that makes seminar conversations at this stage
difficult to follow for the uninitiated. With this slow transition into
a speech community, a kind of colonisation of subjectivity takes
place: piece by piece subjective phenomena are imperceptibly
linked to psychoanalytic precepts, till gradually these fragments
are worked into a comprehensive, holistic, vision of the person. By
this means experience is gradually caught in a web of concepts, the
objectification of which forms a symbolic map which has emotional resonance so far as it is thought to capture the subjective workings of 'self' and 'other'. *The psychodynamic imagination acquired in
pre-training therapy now takes on conceptual dressing—so far as the self
becomes wrapped in symbolic / conceptual meaning.*[105] The psychotherapist Fiona Gardner comments:

> analytic thought, theory and reasoning emerge from
> our subjectivity... Analytical principles emerge from
> the theorising of subjective and specific experiences,
> and remain a sort of story telling... the theoretical
> story telling by others provides a knowledge base
> from where we can assess and integrate our own ex-
> periences. (Gardner 1995: 433)

The anthropological question must side-step the philosophical
concern as to whether the psychodynamic/symbolic map depicts
inner realities, and rather push on to consider that if it is accepted
as doing so, what are the consequences for adherents. It is widely

the case that therapists themselves ascribe high measures of truth to psychoanalytic ideas not least because their professional activities depend on their probability. The mastering of the idea thus holds significance beyond the reward of grasping it for its own sake, for inherent in it is a clue to the enigma of not only the troubled and suffering 'other', but the intricacies and perplexities of 'self'. For trainees, the moments of learning or 'apprehension' transpiring in seminars and in private study are thus less pedestrian events than occasions of often high emotional importance. Ideas successfully understood, embodied, and applied to self or other analysis, often arouse feelings of competence and personal worth, a sense of growing personal and professional mastery. Peter, again, said:

> I really know that I have understood an idea when it has become relevant to my own life, when I can see my own problems through its lens... If I encounter something in my reading or my training that really hits me, I will take it to my therapist and discuss why I have had this reaction, why this idea has moved me... during my training I have become more proactive in my personal therapy often exploring themes in the light of the concepts I am learning. (Third Year Trainee 2004)

Asking another trainee what these concepts mean to her, she commented:

> So much, because you see, they provide the bases for all the work that we do; I mean they are indispensable for making sense of what happens with patients. ['Do they provide the basis for understanding yourself?'] Well yes, because these ideas of course are not only useful for patients, but for us all, we are all patients, all suffering to varying degrees, so we can all benefit from knowledge that can help decrease that suffering. (Third Year Trainee 2004)

An essential aspect of psychotherapeutic education is that it is based on this constant relating of precept to experience.[106] Trainees become comfortable with the veracity of psychodynamic assertions not by testing the imparted ideas via the conducting or perusing of quantitative or qualitative investigations, but by making experiments of themselves, so to speak. In keeping with the aloof attitude most institutes maintain towards research-based practice, ideas largely win approval through a subjective 'self-testing'—namely, examining in therapy and private contemplation whether these ideas resonate with and make sense of private states. As Freud long ago admitted:

> If there is no objective verification of psychoanalysis, and no possibility of demonstrating it, how can one learn psychoanalysis at all, and convince oneself of the truth of its assertions...There are a whole number of very common and generally familiar mental phenomena which, after a little instruction in technique, can be made the subject of analysis on oneself. *In that way one acquires the desired sense of conviction of the reality of the processes described by analysis and the correctness of its views.* (Freud 1975 [1917]: 44, italics added)

Relating experience to precept is the means by which the trainee not only becomes slowly proficient in the theoretical language of psychodynamics, but also increasingly convinced as to the 'correctness of [psychoanalytic] views'. Another fourth year trainee states:

> Finding that there are words and concepts for your experience and that through these there is a way of making sense of oneself is empowering. For me these ideas are so compelling because they are about us [indicating to us both], they are intimately related to us... ['Do you trust these ideas?'] Now it would be a problem for my patients if I didn't; actually, I would even say that the word 'idea' is a bit of a misnomer, for me *they are more like realities.* (Fourth Year Trainee 2005, italics added)

SUMMARISING CHAPTER FOUR

To tie now together the central points of this chapter, this style of learning that I have described as essentially *affirmative* is facilitated by the hierarchical relationship inhering between trainee and leader. A hierarchy legitimated by the idea of personhood, which holds that the fuller person embodies knowledge absent to (and thus secret from) the uninitiated. Moreover, by the judicious selection of seminar leaders and the circumscription of the curricula, tight boundaries are placed around the theoretical body; boundaries discouraging intellectual incursions that might overly challenge and thus promote doubt in the standardised canon. That seminar education thus takes place in an 'affirmative' rather than 'critical' educational atmosphere points—among other things—to community anxiety about the protection of tradition.

CHAPTER FIVE
DEFLECTING DOUBT, MAINTAINING CERTAINTY

The 'affirmative' educational devices outlined in the last chapter are generally not regarded as such by the institutes in question—that is, what might be structurally apparent to the anthropologist might be, ironically, psychologically 'unconscious' to the individual member of the observed institute. This is to say that the trainees' slow progression over their training career into a speech community and into ever greater degrees of conviction as to the merit of the psychodynamic ideas, is often not seen by therapists as an outcome of a specific mode of professional socialisation, but rather as owing to the trainee's creditable progression into perceiving more deeply the 'heart of things'.

Where such progression is deemed to fall short, that is, where the trainee remains sceptical as to the veracity of psychoanalytic ideas, I shall here argue that this is invariably interpreted by the institute as something for which the trainee, rather than the paradigm or the educative process itself is responsible. In order to understand this shift of responsibility from system to self, we must first recognise that although seminar education is designed to promote confidence in the psychoanalytic imagination, this style of learning does not eradicate doubt, for doubt lives on in many trainees in one form or another. If this doubt is not adequately managed and judiciously directed, then it threatens to become a destructive force usurping the 'affirmative project'.

124

In the first part of this chapter I intend to explore how doubt is managed in the institute. I shall do this by describing strategies by which doubt is successfully deflected off the system (the ideas) onto other receptacles; strategies offering routes down which practitioners may channel misgivings away from the 'system' so as to protect it from censure. In the second part of this chapter I shall then illustrate through 3 case studies instances when these strategies are *enacted*—i.e. where trainees' doubt, being unsuccessfully deflected off the system, settles on the paradigm itself. In such instances trainees may 'dissent' from the orthodox position. I shall then show that the way in which institutes have historically dealt with such dissent, and how such dealings have shaped over time the whole structure of the therapeutic community.

STRATEGIES OF DOUBT MANAGEMENT

A now qualified and practising psychotherapist reflects on his training experience:

> I was for many years being trained by R. D. Hinshelwood in group psychotherapy. Several times a year we met with people who were being trained at the Institute of Group Analysis... One evening someone who was trained at the IGA said, rather bluntly, that the transference is to the group [i.e. the individual transfers onto the group unconscious material]. I disputed this and said that it was my experience that the transference is primarily to the therapist. It was soon clear that this was a matter of doctrine [held by members of the IGA], something I had not initially realised. When I did, I suggested that we discuss these differing points of view. This proved not to be possible. The anxiety level in the room shot up, and the meeting ended in disarray. Hinshelwood [the leader] took me aside afterwards and said that doing therapy was not like a philosophy seminar, it was more like learning surgery where 'mistakes' are—or are experienced as—life and death matters. It was not possible to stand back and reflect. I found this an important

> moment in my psychotherapeutic education. Having
> worked as a philosopher and historian for decades be-
> fore training as a psychotherapist, I had not realised
> the urgency with which trainees cling to the 'one right
> way' and find it very difficult to hold ideas up to the
> light and ponder them. (Young 1996a: 124)

As I will explore in chapter eight, certain reasons why trainees
are reluctant to doubt the 'one right way', here I shall show some
of the ways in which this reluctance is institutionally supported.
As I have argued, pre-training therapy largely ensures that those
entering the institute are disposed favourably to the psychoanalytic project. When in the institute these trainees are then subject to
educative devices that further affirm the veracity of psychoanalytic
ideas by circumscribing the transmission of theoretical knowledge.
This style of transmission has implications for how practitioners
account for therapeutic failures, for if the ideas are indubitable
who or what can be held responsible for unsuccessful treatment?
The answer to this is again hinted at in the belief that it is only the
fully developed or 'initiated' person who can wield and understand these ideas with mastery (see chapter four). Failures can thus
be easily located in the shortcomings of the uninitiated—e.g. in the
trainee's 'inexperience', or in the patient's holding to an unshak-
able 'resistance' or 'negative transference'.

To illustrate this point I asked ten trainees about how they accounted for therapeutic encounters that did not go as well as they
had hoped. Out of the ten questioned at random only one admitted
to sometimes doubting the applicability of a *certain* idea to a given
case, while the remaining nine made comments such as: 'I would
look to the relationship and ask what had occurred between us to
sabotage our work'; and another: 'you can never entirely blame the
patient, there is always something you could have done differently'; and further: 'some patients might not be ready for deep analysis, this should always be considered'; and finally: 'a therapist
must always be ready to question what they have missed'. This is
to say, none of the trainees asked held the ideas responsible for
therapeutic 'failure'—the cause of failure was thus located in those
subject to or those using these ideas.[107]

This manner of deflecting doubt from the 'system' to 'self' has its structural precedents. Evans-Pritchard (1937) called this phenomenon 'secondary elaboration' when he observed it in the Azande doctor's protection of the oracle's power: if its divining power was found wanting, the Doctor had many explanations at hand that could place responsibility for failure elsewhere—he could blame the Gods, the climate, or even himself, but never did he doubt the oracle's power. Hsu also observed something similar in Chinese medical practice where it was the word incorrectly pronounced (rather than the word itself) that could be seen as a source of therapeutic failure (Hsu 1999: 52). Likewise, in Luhrmann's study of contemporary witchcraft she found that 'Ritual didn't fail because you used the wrong invocation, but because you didn't use it properly' (Luhrmann 1989: 253). As with these other therapeutic systems, it is a latent belief in psychoanalysis that psychotherapy fails not because the ideas are wrong, but because they are either mistaken (by patients) or misapplied (by practitioners). Blaming users rather than the ideas themselves for lack of success, enables practitioners to preserve the veracity of the system in the face of therapeutic failure.

Doubt is deflected from the system in a second way. As I have tried previously to show, for many practitioners the genealogical structure is a kind of caste system which comprises institutes from the elite to the average to the below average. Robert Young (1996b), himself a psychotherapist critical of this stratification, cites some telling examples of how some of those in the higher reaches of the psychodynamic community (i.e. psychoanalysts and psychoanalytic therapists in the BPC) have in the past supported this hierarchical ordering. He cites one psychoanalyst at the UKCP's annual AGM as commenting 'that all people who were not in the BPC [i.e. UKCP psychotherapists] should be prohibited from calling themselves psychotherapists, because, as he put it, they were "charlatans"' (p. 5). He cites another meeting where there was a heated debate about whether psychoanalysts should have a veto against all decisions made in the UKCP. At a crucial moment a senior analyst stood up to exclaim that refusal to grant this would be like 'allowing the students to set their own exams'—a comment with which most agreed (p. 11). On another occasion at a British conference on the relationship between psychoanalysis and psychotherapy a collection of analysts speaking about their own tradition urged that psychoanalysis was the 'gold standard' while the therapists were 'alloys and baser metals' even 'copper' (p. 14). While these examples illustrate more overt declarations of caste beliefs, they highlight through magnification an attitude held more by some of the elite in respect of lesser trainings. I myself encountered this attitude, often in less obvious forms, on many occasions during fieldwork. When attending an induction day at the Institute for Psychoanalysis, for instance, on three occasions it was made clear to prospective candidates that their training was by far the most sophisticated, and had produced the best practitioners. As one trainer emphasised: 'there are a lot of psychotherapy trainings out there, but this is the most thorough, and of course the most respected' (London 2004).[108]

Hinshelwood, a psychotherapist, here comments on why this caste attitude is so prevalent in British psychotherapy, and as to why it so often includes contempt for 'lesser systems':

> one of the most striking features of the profession [in Britain] is its fragmented state, in which rivalrous groups claim allegiance to different theoretical orientations, and protect themselves by arcane terminologies that restrict the possibility of interchange. Each group prises its own orientation above all others... This intensely felt siege mentality of different groups seems to me a strong indicator of a collective defensiveness in action. It suggests to me that the mutually enhancing correctness of the members of any one group within itself displays the degree of insecurity (rather than denied insecurity) of the members. Insecurity is dealt with in this way by inculcating each other (and new recruits) into a system of mutual confirmation of the group's theoretical ideas...
>
> This internal competitive culture is often very painful. But it is significantly relieved by identifying another group that holds to a "substandard" theoretical framework. Internal stability is thus bought by the projection of defeat and inadequacy into other groups. (Hinshelwood 1985a: 16)

Although Hinshelwood's words were written in 1985 the fragmentation he saw as fuelled by the insecurity community members feel within their own profession, is still very much a feature of the community today. A fragmentation compounded, if his thesis holds, by the growing struggle psychoanalytic therapy faces due to the rise of competing psychotherapies and its own growing marginalisation within the psychiatric profession—a struggle I highlighted in chapter one.

Robert Young (1996) has suggested that Hinshelwood's work recalls Mary Douglas' (1966) work on the anthropology of classificatory systems. Douglas asserted that the evaluation of objects (whether material objects, persons or institutions) always takes place within a given cultural framework: e.g. whether a thing is deemed 'good' or 'bad' depends on whether it conforms to the given social order. Where it transgresses, contradicts, or straddles the bounds of the accepted order or 'system of classification'—that is, where its place in the established order is somehow 'unclear', through protection of this order it is dismissed as 'unclean' and once the object is rendered 'unclean' it is then seen as unfit for serious concern or consideration.

Applying Douglas' idea to the psychotherapeutic contexts would lead us to consider that the denigration of competing systems as 'lesser systems' might partly have its origins in the menace these 'systems' pose to those who depreciate them. By dismissing these threatening or contradictory systems as 'lesser', not only do these lesser systems become the receptacles of disowned doubt, but also any genuine claim to authority they might have is effectively dismissed. To doubt that system whose authority, if admitted, would render my own system weak, is to use doubt as a defending shield. If this application holds, the employment of such strategies of doubt management in the psychodynamic community reveals deeper concerns about the protection of tradition, and about the losses community members fear they would incur should communal boundaries be breeched.

Having looked at two strategies of what I called *doubt management* operative in the psychoanalytic institute (i.e. 'secondary elaboration' and the 'disowning of doubt'), let me now try to ground this discussion by describing some occasions on which these strategies were enacted. The following three case studies illustrate instances where trainees' doubt, rather than being successfully deflected off the system, was directed towards either those administering the system or at moments (and especially in the first case) towards the system itself. This resulted in the trainee's active dissent from psychoanalytic leadership.

Before I turn to these cases, however, it is important to note that they illustrate what occurs when trainee doubt and opposition transcends a *tolerated level*. In other words, because different therapists have different degrees of tolerance with respect to trainee defiance, what has been handled in one way by these therapists and institutes might plausibly be handled very differently by others. This is to say, because in the cases that follow the toleration of trainee doubt and dissent might be deemed particularly low, even by other therapists, it stands to reason that other therapists might have managed these cases differently.

The following three case studies, then, are not trying to locate *the point* at which opposition becomes intolerable, for this as I have said will vary from therapist to therapist and from institute to institute. Rather they describe how opposition can be managed when it *passes a tolerable point relative to the given practitioner or institute.* I offer these case-studies in order to show that when opposition passes beyond this point, variously defined, it is invariably seen as dissent and institutionally managed.

A final caveat: to exact from these tales the facts most relevant to our present designs we must look beyond either the personal agendas of their authors or any sentiments they may arouse in ourselves, in order to focus on the task of revealing any structural concordances they might share. This is to say, what I believe to be most important about these vignettes resides behind their anecdotal interest in their deeper structural form.

This first case concerns a twenty-nine year-old trainee, John, whom I met at a series of open seminars conducted at one of London's premier psychotherapeutic departments. What alerted my attention to John were the kinds of critical questions he asked the panel of analysts leading the seminar and the earnestness with which he asked them. After befriending John I discovered some of the origins of his concern: A year before our meeting he had been accepted to train at a prestigious psychoanalytic institute, but since his pre-training analysis had been 'particularly negative' he had decided to put aside his training aspirations. The following events he recounted to me over a series of meetings which ran in tandem with our attendance at the seminars.

In John's early twenties he was in psychotherapy for two years. During this time he developed a keen interested in psychotherapeutic ideas. After this first and as he called it 'useful analysis', he spent many years working as a nurse in the NHS while researching for his PhD. He decided to enter training despite what he referred to as his 'growing healthy suspicion of certain psychotherapeutic claims', simply because his 'interest had never died'.

For the first weeks of his pre-training therapy things proceeded well. 'I played the role of the obliging patient and gave my therapist all the information he desired; I tried to be as honest as I could about my life and life-history despite not having any real need to speak about these things'. Nevertheless he spoke, for, as he said, 'I wanted to give the process a fair chance'.

He also mentioned that had his training institute not required him to attend therapy he would never have gone voluntarily, since he felt 'uncomfortable discussing my innermost at a time when I experienced no need to... I wasn't in crisis'.

After about the third month therapy started to deteriorate for the John. His sense of discomfort in the sessions grew—he felt out of step with his therapist and was reluctant to participate. He also felt that his therapist's interpretations were predictable; this constant referring to the transference, John said, was 'obvious and tiring'. John, it seemed, 'no longer wanted to play the game'.

This feeling went on for about a further six weeks until John finally decided to disclose to his therapist his doubts about whether he really wanted to train, and the fact that he felt contrived in sessions. His therapist's continued response was to interpret John's concerns psychoanalytically—e.g. the therapist detected in John a 'resistance' to the therapeutic process, and urged that they work together to find a solution to this. John again thought these responses were inappropriate for, as he put it, 'how could I accept his interpretations when my problem was that I doubted as true the theory which gave rise to them'. John said that at times he felt like a sceptic arguing with a believer, a sceptic who had all his arguments dismissed simply as 'devil's speak', that is to say, as 'rationalisations' or 'resistance'.

Because John couldn't accept his therapist's diagnosis and interpretations, and because the therapist was unwilling to diverge from his orthodox position, by the fifth month of therapy an inevitable stalemate was reached. This expressed itself in John's increased unwillingness to participate in the sessions. For example, regarding this period he said, 'I would arrive and simply sit there in complete silence, counting the minutes until the end of the session... for me', said John, 'this was an extremely painful protest'. Often the analyst would try to break this silence, sometimes with a little success. But as soon as the therapist had once again engaged John, he returned to what John called 'the analytical game'—a move to which John would again respond by retreating into silence. John felt that until his concerns were met and respected, this dynamic would perpetually remain. Such a pattern continued all the way to the end of analysis some one month later.

Let me close with John's summary of what he felt went wrong. 'I felt my therapist misunderstood my real concerns which were about my growing doubt regarding psychotherapy. This was a real issue for me because let's not forget I was about to start a full training... I had so many questions: was I suited for this profession? Did my growing scepticism indicate I had made the wrong choice? Did my questioning really point to real inadequacies with psychotherapy? These should have been seen as legitimate concerns rather than as excuses for my reluctance to participate.'[109]

ILLUSTRATION TWO

This next illustration is drawn from the psychotherapist Marguerite Valentine's published account of her own pre-training therapeutic experience, supplemented by personal correspondence with her.[110] She said that writing her account was motivated by 'an experience of therapeutic failure, which left me with feelings of having been judged "pathological" or alternatively "unanalysable"'. What follows is derived from her published account:

> I would now like to consider my own experience. Both experiences of therapeutic failure were with Kleinians. When I began I had no idea what 'being a Kleinian' meant. I asked the therapist which school she followed. She replied, 'Kleinian'. No doubt being a Kleinian can mean different things. I therefore offer a particular perspective—that of the patient.
>
> She told me firmly from the start that she 'worked with the couch'. I acquiesced with this as it seemed by her manner non-negotiable. It took some time before I began to have a sense of the kind of relationship which was slowly unfolding. Sometimes she kicked the couch as she crossed her legs. Over the months she developed a certain attitude. It was not analytic, more correctional. I was told, or rather corrected, for holding apparently distorted views and perceptions. There was never any possibility of a dialogue. The atmosphere was punitive. Interpretations were delivered with great certainty.
>
> She was not interested in what I call the 'real event'... The fact that I had a number of troubling and traumatic losses in my childhood seemed a matter of indifference to her. But she was interested in 'phantasies'—an interest seemingly in isolation from any relationship with the external world. She was highly attuned to spotting signs of idealization, grandiosity, envy, hate and competition. Once I told her how much I liked small babies. I was told categorically that I idealized them. When I developed a very painful abs-

cess on my gum and took time off to visit the dentist, I was told I was more in touch with bodily pain than with psychic pain. Furthermore, I was told I was 'teething'.

I eventually and suddenly left after an unpleasant row which she seemed to find exciting. She said triumphantly, 'At last' and at that point I became aware of her frustration with me because, as she had said, I did not 'project anything'.

After this experience, I set out to find a less dogmatic, more empathetic therapist. I was given the name of an Independent analyst. I had hoped an Independent would theoretically be open and have the quality of mind to be responsive and imaginative. 'Independent' seemed a misnomer. She practised as a Kleinian without identifying herself as such, but was 'classical' [Freudian, analytical] in terms of technique. I wanted to come three times a week. She insisted on five times because she said she was an analyst. Again there was no space for discussion. It felt as if I was there for her benefit—a feeling which became stronger, the longer I stayed.

This particular analyst specialised in 'wild analysis'.[111] I often felt shocked by what she said, which felt grossly intuitive. Interpretations were delivered without reference to my thoughts, feelings or context. They made no sense. They were wild, and I found myself processing them hours later, often at night. As my insomnia increased, I eventually told her this. She said I was trying to control and blame her.

I began to question some statements but this seemed to incite her more. Interpretations were delivered as attacks. It was as if her authority and her view of the world were challenged. I was told that I was 'malign' and that I had to 'negate' everything she said. From my point of view, I felt I was fighting for my identity. Once, after struggling to make sense of a particular experience for which I felt a sense of achievement, she said 'I suppose you think you thought that, despite me'. The atmosphere was invariably harsh, combative, and I dreaded each session.

The therapeutic framework was also not protected. Her son once walked into the session. At other times he ran loudly up and down the stairs, slamming doors and dropping things on the floor upstairs above us. She encouraged me to be angry. I thought a more appropriate response would be for her to protect the boundaries. It seemed another crazy situation whereby the external world, past and present, is discounted in favour of assumed phantasies and preoccupations about bodily functions and emissions. The fetishism of the 'here and now' only added to feelings of not being heard, of not being understood, and of not being seen for whom one was. Her theoretical beliefs, values and style dominated, and in this a retraumatization occurred.

ILLUSTRATION THREE

The final tale of woe is offered by Robert Young, who like Marguerite Valentine is now an established psychotherapist with a number of publications to his name. Here I quote him verbatim from his published account, which, unlike the first two accounts cited, which both dwelt on dissent in the therapeutic encounter, deals exclusively with dissent in the institute. Again, my analysis of this event is facilitated by my personal conversations with him:

> Members of my cohort in a highly-regarded post-graduate psychotherapy training stood up to the powers that be [this is to say, as Robert told me, he complained about the students not being given sufficient say in whether the institute left the UKCP—a decision that would have greatly impacted on their professional status].[112] We did this with respect to various matters about training standards and being treated as adults. Without any hint of difficulties before that day, we were told that a majority of us would have to train for longer than we had been led to expect and until

the doubts about our competence were resolved by further supervision... We remonstrated. We had been told that we were their best group ever. I had been given their prize the previous year. We were now being told that a certain supervisor whom we liked and admired was our severest critic. This was stunning. On the evening of the meeting when we had finally managed to get the senior teaching officer to meet with us to try to sort this matter out, someone suggested I phone and ask this allegedly severest critic what he had said. I did, and he replied that he had made criticisms but that if anyone was not being allowed to qualify on time because of anything he had said, he was being used as a scapegoat. When his supposed criticism of the group was repeated in the showdown meeting, I quoted what he had said to me not a half hour earlier. I was removed from the group. (I eventually came to the conclusion that his criticisms were, in part, bound up with his loyalty to the other most highly-regarded training organisation, in which he was an active teacher...)

The Chair... met with me and said that he guaranteed I would qualify if I would agree to leave the seminar and have supervision with someone new for three months until things cooled down. I went to think about it and spoke to the designated new supervisor, whom I came to regard as a benign probation officer. He said that I had not been told the whole truth: the likelihood was that I was going to qualify but not be made a member. This... move was inconsistent with the organisation's own publicity, which stated simply that completing the training led to membership. I was shocked by this deceit and made a bigger fuss, including strong backing from supervisors, who had also been grossly misquoted. The supervisor who took the strongest line (an eminent and very senior training analyst and former director of the Institute's clinic [the Institute of Psychoanalysis], who has since been made head of another prestigious psychotherapy training) was dropped from the programme. Near the end of the probation period my parole officer said that they were in the wrong and that all would be well if I would only be forgiving for a few weeks longer... I kept my counsel; there was a vote in which the mendacious teaching officer tried her utmost to prevent my being made a member, but she was outvoted. In spite of these and a number of other matters where students felt unfairly treated, she remained in office for some time and was able to arrange things so that a like-minded person (and vehemently outspoken opponent of the UKCP) became her successor.[113]

NOTICING PARALLEL THEMES

The common thread running through these cases is the way in which dissent was managed by the analysts and subject leaders. In the first case, John felt that his concerns over entering a profession about which he harboured doubts were dismissed as 'resistances'—namely, as symptomatic expressions of unresolved conflicts. Thus John's concerns were interpreted as saying more about his 'inner world' than about the community he questioned. Likewise, in Marguerite's case her complaints were interpreted as due to 'negative transference': they were seen as issuing from her 'malign' intent, and her desire to 'negate' her therapist. Again, her protests were configured as 'symptoms', as admissions about her subjective reality. Finally, in the case of Robert, his standing up to the training institute was punished by extending the tenure of his instruction—a gesture implying that his defiance was linked to some unconscious hostility that only further training and analysis could fix.

Whether the authorities in each of these cases were right to view these protests as issuing from personal problems is of course a matter to be argued. However, as I shall later suggest, since such management of dissent can elsewhere be identified in the profession, and since some of the most eminent therapists have at one point or another been branded as 'dissenters' only to be later embraced (just as Robert's punishment was later repealed after his

138 THE MAKING OF PSYCHOTHERAPISTS

spirited protest)—it remains a familiar occurrence that protests are cast as symptoms of personal problems. This is to say, in all three instances it is feasible to suggest that the causes of dissent were pathologised, and thus viewed as motivations from which the individuals in question needed to be released: if smooth progression into the psychoanalytic community was to succeed, Marguerite needed to be freed of her 'malignity', John of his 'resistance', and Robert of his insurgence. Thus in each case we witness the device of 'secondary elaboration' being employed; a device placing failure on 'self' rather than 'system'.

A further point of interest is that the devices used to manage dissent in the therapeutic encounter (e.g. between therapist and patient) were also applied to manage dissent in the institute (i.e. between trainee and committee). In other words, the same device was applied in both contexts with equal efficacy. This permeation of the therapeutic ethos into the institutional setting, a phenomenon already noticed in how ideas of personhood support status imbalances between trainees and seniors in the institutes, further reinforces the idea that trainees are in some sense still 'unfinished', and are thus to be equated more with a patient than with a therapist. While on the one hand this equation follows naturally from psychoanalytic beliefs (outlined in chapters two and three), on the other hand, as we have seen, it renders trainees open to the infantalisation and disenfranchisement that abuse of this equation can bring.

In respect of this equation on many occasions I witnessed trainees being treated as patients when outside of the therapeutic encounter: e.g. students arriving late at seminars were asked to consider their motivations for being late, as if lateness was an attempt to break the 'frame' and communicate latent hostility. (This grafting of the therapeutic 'frame' onto the seminar space, renders the patient / trainee hierarchy operative in the trainee / leader encounter.) On another occasion at a training conference that was running twenty minutes late, a senior analyst who was invited to give a seminal paper stopped short twenty minutes before the end of her talk and said that 'the session must always begin and end on time'—which meant the audience were treated as patients.[114] And again, once when trainees complained that the institute had not sufficiently forewarned them that certain key courses would be dropped, it was stated that trainees were obviously not feeling 'adequately held' and that reality sometimes did not conform to expectations.

Applying techniques devised for the therapeutic encounter to the management of trainees in the institutional setting suggests that the internalisation of therapeutic 'dispositions', a process 'completed' in the senior members of the institute, penetrates into the very core of subjectivity and self-identity. In the terminology of Habermas (Eliot 1992: 105), we might say that such dispositions forge an 'inner colonisation' so far as the therapeutic imagination does not confine itself to assessing patients, but to the assessment of extra-therapeutic domains—self, institute, and society.

DISSIDENT RESPONSES TO PATHOLOGISATION

If there are commonalities between how dissent was managed in all three case studies, it is important to note that the dissenters themselves responded to what they felt as the 'pathologisation of their protests' in quite different ways: while John experienced the same treatment to which both Marguerite and Robert were subject, unlike them he elected to discontinue training, or, as he phrased it to me, 'to shelve his desire to become a therapist'. John's protest, then, ended at the point of his leaving therapy and thus never reached wider public attention. For both Marguerite and Robert, alternatively, their defiance did not stop with their aforementioned protests. Rather both completed their training, received accreditation, and then proceeded to legitimate their original protests by publishing their stories.[115]

The different ways in which John on the one hand, and Marguerite and Robert on the other responded to the 'powers that be' could be formalised in a working distinction between 'resigned' and 'active' dissent. *Resigned dissent* is that which offers no further resistance after the initial act of protest or defection. This species of dissent is seen in John's response which fell silent after he left his therapist. *Active dissent* alternatively does not abate after the first insurgent act, but rather extends out over time and space: old grievances are acted upon at a future point, often being drawn into the public domain for debate and discussion. This active dissent was performed by Robert and Marguerite, both of whom later published their troubled accounts. We could add to these forms of 'active' and 'resigned' dissent the *strategic dissent* mentioned in the last chapter (i.e. dissent that expresses itself in safe ways—largely in liminal spaces, and thus does not directly challenge authorities). To put these forms of dissent in a scale of strength—strategic dissent is the weakest form; resigned is a stronger form, while active the strongest form.

While I know of few precedents in psychotherapeutic literature illustrating instances of resigned dissent (by definition this stands to reason), the history of psychotherapy is replete with instances of 'active dissent' to the degree that one could argue that it exists as a defining feature of the therapeutic community. To look at the historical record for confirmation of this assertion, not only did active dissent play an integral role in the inception of psychoanalysis, but it has continued to feature as a common happening throughout the entire course of its institutional development.[116] To start with Freud's original circle of psychoanalysts, from this initial group the active defections were plentiful: Wilhelm Stekel resigned owing to his doctrinal differences with Freud in 1911. While later in the same year for the same reasons Alfred Adler handed back his membership taking with him Bach, Maday, Baron, and Hye. Shortly after this, the dissension having the deepest personal impact upon Freud occurred when Carl Jung resigned from the International Psychoanalytical Society in 1914, again for reasons of doctrinal discord (Jones 1955: 143-171). Subsequent therapists who suffered either momentary ostracism or outright expulsion from the IPA because their views diverged from the orthodox line, include such influential therapists as: Karen Horney, Erich Fromm, Franc Alexander, John Bowlby, W.R.D. Fairbairn, Heinz Kohut, Jacques Lacan, Harry Guntrip, Wilhelm Reich, and Harry Stack Sullivan—all individuals, we might profitably observe, evidently preferring the 'prophetic' to the 'priestly' role.

That many of these individuals managed to institutionalise their defections is also clear: Alfred Adler instituted his dissent by founding the Society of Free Analysis in 1911. Carl Jung's dissent was instituted in a series of schools spread internationally; the British counterpart being the Society of Analytical Psychology established in 1946. Karen Horney, after being stripped of the training analyst status by the IPA in 1941, founded the Association for the

Advancement of Psychoanalysis (AAP) for the dissemination of her ideas.[117] Erich Fromm and Harry Stack Sullivan institutionalised their dissent in the William Alanson White Institute in 1943. Lacan's doctrinal differences found residence in the *Société Francaise de Psychanalyse* in 1952 in Paris.[118] Melaine Klein, after the 'controversial discussions' in London in the early 1940s, found a home for her vision in the Tavistock Clinic (colloquially known as the 'Klein Shrine'), before being reintegrated into the Psychoanalytic Institute's training after the 'Gentleman's agreement' in 1946.

Post-war dissensions have been just as numerous, if not more dramatic, resulting in the opening of entirely new schools of psychotherapy which reject psychoanalytic foundations—this largely accounts for the birth of many *non-psychodynamic psychotherapies*. Of one time psychoanalysts and psychiatrists who have founded such schools we can think of R. D. Laing and his championing of 'Existential therapy'; of Friz Perl's and his 'Gestalt psychotherapy'; of Eric Berne and his 'transactional analysis'; and of Rollo May and his 'humanist psychotherapy'—to name some of the more well-known dissenters from whom have sprung new 'schools' and training institutions.

The fact that these dissenters have often been subject to the same *ad hominem* dismissals as were levelled against Marguerite, Robert, and John suggests that the employment of devices that cast 'protests and symptoms' is no infrequent occurrence. Ernest Jones (1955), for instance, the first and longest President of the British Psychoanalytic Society as well as long-time apologist and friend of Freud, used these devices to explain away the many defections afflicting the early psychoanalytic community. In his seminal biography of Freud's life there is a whole chapter dedicated to the description of the early dissensions. It is useful for my current argument to explore for a moment its main assertions.

He begins his chapter by noting the widely accepted fact that real personal understanding emerges only once the patient's 'resistances' have been removed. 'When the resistances have been overcome', says Jones, 'the subject [patient] has insight into aspects of his personality to which he had previously been blind' (Jones 1955: 142). However, and as Jones then makes clear, because the forces of the mind are dynamic and are thus prone to shift unexpectedly 'it may come about that the insight first gained is not necessarily permanent and may once more be lost... this is equally true for the analyst as for the patient' (p 142). He then proceeds to say that only Freud himself has been able to achieve 'the difficult feat of making a very extensive self-analysis' (p.143), which presumably meant that Freud's insight was the more deeper and permanent. When speaking of the other analysts, on the other hand, he complains that 'none of the other pioneers had had much personal experience of their own unconscious or only in glimpses' (p. 143), a statement which implies that Jones felt their insight to be less permanent. Jones felt the proneness of early therapists to 'relapse' into non-clarity had many unpalatable consequences:

> When an analyst loses insight he had previously had, the recurring wave of resistance that has caused the loss is apt to display itself in the form of pseudo-scientific explanations of the data before him, and this is then dignified with the name of a 'new theory'. Since the source of this is on an unconscious level, it follows that controversy on a purely conscious scientific level is fore-doomed to failure. (p. 142)

Thus Jones hints that the origins of rival psychotherapeutic theories are caused by 'losses of insight', the cause of which the dissenters were unaware since these causes were still unconscious. They were 'unconscious' because these dissenters, unlike Freud, had not 'much experience of their own unconscious'. Jones' comments crescendo in the following passage:

> Those of us who, like myself, remained close to Freud while openly disagreeing with many of his conclusions have been described as timid and docile people who have submitted to the authority of the great Father. It is, however, possible that they should be better described as men who had come to terms with their childhood complexes and so could work in harmony with both an older and younger generation, *whereas the dissidents may include those who still feel obliged to perpetuate the rebelliousness of childhood and to keep*

searching for figures to rebel against. (p. 144, italics added)

It is plain that Jones in these passages is working to dismiss early dissensions as symptoms of unresolved conflicts existing in the detractors. By this means he exempts Freud and the IPA from responsibility for these schisms and places it on those still led by their 'childhood complexes'.[119] The implication is that if these detractors possessed a clearer vision or greater 'personhood' by means of a 'deeper analysis', they would have realised their own folly, and, like Jones, put aside their suspicions and remained in the fold. Thus again we witness here a clear example of 'secondary elaboration' being performed.

It must be remembered that Ernest Jones was the outright leader of British psychoanalysis throughout the first half of the twentieth century; he had supreme power in overseeing how training in the Institute of Psychoanalysis was conducted. And since other psychodynamic institutes followed the example of the British Institute it is plausible that his influence went further. He decided on the curriculum, on who would deliver it, on the trainees who would receive it, and on those who would comprise the training committee and supervisory elite. Jones' power would never have been so extensive had his leadership not received full approval from the IPA, led by Freud himself. This suggests that the attitude Jones' took towards dissidents, rather than communicating a personal proclivity, was representative of orthodox position held by the centre of power in Berlin and Vienna—that is, he spoke as a true priest, not for himself but for his community.

This historical evidence of psychotherapeutic schism illustrates that there is nothing untypical about Marguerite's and Robert's active dissent, nor about the way in which it was managed by the institute. These cases only differ from the historical examples in that their consequences were more modest. Thus these cases have their structural precedents; precedents that inform us as to why the community is in a fractured state today.

While many dissenters, breaking with the orthodoxy, founded schools that often became mirror-images of the bounded orthodoxy which they opposed, other dissenters, once heretical, have been reintegrated back into psychodynamic mainstream. This process of integration is clearly seen where, for instance, Kleinian and Object Relations thinkers such as John Bowlby have been welcomed back onto the curriculum at the Institute of Psychoanalysis. It is also clear where certain psychodynamic trainings in addition to offering seminars on Lacan and Jung, have integrated into their structures different training 'streams'—e.g. within the BAP institute one can train as either a Freudian or Jungian.[120] In this sense contained in heresy reside the seeds of integration.

This pressure to re-integrate once disowned movements has been helped not only by the fear of increasing community fragmentation, but also by the growing sense that long-time psychoanalytic foes must pull together in the face of an ever-growing threat—namely, the growth of non-psychodynamics psychotherapies, and the expansion of pharmacologically-based psychiatry. Schools are thus increasingly finding themselves uniting with movements whom in the past they would have opposed. Jungians, for instance, while arguing for their own school against classical psychoanalysis, when confronting non-dynamic treatments such as CBT or pharmacologically-based psychiatry, might unite with psychoanalysts to serve the broader analytic cause. This segmentary behaviour, as I mentioned in chapter one, has been helped by the foundation of the BPC: an umbrella organisation beneath whose professional canopy once divided psychodynamic units now work together for the one psychodynamic cause.

SUMMARISING CHAPTERS FOUR AND FIVE

I have attempted to show how dissent, once transcending a tolerable level, can be managed by the powers that be—i.e. via methods of 'secondary elaboration' and the 'disowning of doubt'. I have also shown that the use of what I have termed *doubt management* is not confined to the consulting room, but rather can extend out into the training institute by being applied to the management of trainee doubt. Furthermore, as these devices are used to protect communal boundaries and beliefs, one upshot is that dissident schools emerge; schools which today are increasingly ordering themselves in segmentary fashion for strategic ends. From these observations we could claim that there is a strong causal relationship between how doubt is managed in the clinical setting and how the wider community has become structurally ordered. This pivots on the observation that the psychotherapeutic imagination into which trainees are professionally socialised is rarely confined to the therapeutic encounter itself, but comes to order and direct how individuals relate to each other within the institute.

CHAPTER SIX
CLINICAL SUPERVISION

In the two previous chapters I described the 'affirmative' atmosphere in which the inculcation of conservative therapeutic dispositions takes place. By the circumscription of the theoretical body, by the appeal to shared concepts of personhood which legitimate role asymmetries, and by the devices of secondary elaboration, and the successful management of doubt, trainees are institutionally coaxed into embodying a professional habitus which builds upon the foundational dispositions of 'partiality' and 'imagining psychodynamically', discussed in chapters two and three. In offering these comments I have argued that instances of dissent, no matter how infrequent, always presuppose a greater force against which the mutiny is levelled—in this case, an institutional consensus born from a kind of 'social contract' of conformity, peer-fellowship, and a union of aims between novice practitioners and the initiated. I have further argued that such consensus is buttressed by the devices and preferences of psychoanalytic socialisation which finds it difficult to tolerate individual transgressions of institutional boundaries and valued beliefs.

While in the next chapter I intend to further highlight the institutional factors by which this consensual or 'affirmative' atmosphere is nurtured, in this chapter I have two central aims to first achieve: to illuminate the psychoanalytic understanding of aetiology, and to provide an insight into the next stage of training—clinical supervision.

146

As to why I select the topic of aetiology for especial attention this follows from the dominant place aetiological concepts assume in the therapeutic craft. The psychoanalytic understanding of causality constitutes a kind of omega point around which the whole practice of therapy—I believe—revolves, as all therapeutic action is predicated upon key assumptions about causes of distress. I believe by assessing how therapists' assumptions are subtly affirmed in clinical supervision, we will come to learn how a central disposition guiding the therapist's craft is inculcated.

THE ORIGINS OF THE PSYCHODYNAMIC UNDERSTANDING OF AETIOLOGY

Before setting down our case study of clinical supervision, let me first introduce the psychoanalytic conception of causation; this discussion will complement the case study of clinical action soon to follow.

Following the historical methodology of Collingwood (2002 [1940]), Evans-Pritchard (1961) and more recently Mark Hobart (2000), if we wish to expose the foundations of psychoanalytic ideas of causation then it would be useful to explore certain sociocultural influences bearing upon the movement's founding father. Thus we must first ask whether Freud's attitudes, values, and presuppositions were all things upon which the social circumstances of his day left their mark. In order to consider this question more closely let us first try to gain an impression of the surrounding socio-cultural atmosphere of the European intellectual classes in the decades before the First World War—the period during which Freud advanced most of his foundational ideas.

In Central Europe peace had largely reigned since 1871, and the middle classes were increasingly benefiting from developments in industry, trade and science; developments which were securing their social, political and moral hegemony. Universal suffrage and education were being widely instituted, promising an end to the disenfranchisement and inequality of the early nineteenth century; and from these developments (it was thought) would inevitably spring an improved situation for the underprivileged classes. Thus, despite the global inequalities which deeply marred international economic and political relations, a global inequity which appeared remote and abstract to most middle-class Europeans, the fruits of various political, ecclesiastical and economic reforms back home had put many in the middle classes into a state of considerable optimism (Fromm 1974). The era of irrational authority and social injustice was thought in abeyance, being replaced by the rule of law, democracy and the steady march of enlightenment values. In this atmosphere of general hopefulness a political and ideological positivism was taking firm root, consistent as it was with the social experience of the European middle classes.

The fact that Freud himself was a child of such enlightenment optimism I shall argue stands out in his personality. As is illustrated by many close studies of his life, Freud was a conventional man of his day; a man representative of middle-class Vienna who largely accepted the central mores of the society in which he lived.[121] While at face value this representation of Freud's relationship to his social world seems inconsistent with the popular view that Freud was highly at variance with social convention, if we probe deeper we notice that Freud, apart from opposing a strong social taboo on sex, accepted most of his society's dominant values uncritically. We can infer this acquiescence from both his practice and his writing. His positivism and objectivism, his views on the patriarchal family, his dichotomising of the rational/irrational and championing of the former, and his acceptance of the economic values of the middle classes, are all attitudes that betray themselves in his writing and way of life.[122]

An important consideration that these reflections raise is whether Freud's general outlook coloured how he understood the causation of suffering. This is to say, so far as Freud regarded the society from which his patients largely came as healthy (modern bourgeois Vienna), was he therefore more prone to locate the causes of personal distress in his patients' psychology rather than in the society of which he generally approved? An interesting entrée into this question is to recall the reasons why Freud abandoned his theory of childhood 'seduction' (which implied a corrupt social world); replacing it with his theory on childhood 'phantasy' (one shifting the cause of distress to the realm within).

As is well known, Freud originally traced the aetiology of hysteria to actual traumatic events in childhood, usually to the child's seduction by an adult. This was often seduction of a daughter by a father, as is illustrated in the case of Katharina in his Studies of

Hysteria (1977 [1905]). It was believed that if patients could recall cathartically the original abuse then the repression and the symptom would automatically lift. Freud's use of his seduction theory lasted until around 1900 (his letter to Fliess in 1897 heralding its end), at which point he slowly embarked upon a radical reformulation of his aetiological vision. This finally led to the new conclusion, as he tells us,

> ...that the neurotic symptoms were not related directly to actual events but to wishful phantasies, and that as far as the neurosis was concerned psychical reality was of more importance than material reality. (Freud 1977: 34)[123]

In other words, the stories of trauma which his patients confessed were now *not* to be interpreted as descriptions of real events, as had earlier been the case, but as fantasies motivated by their childhood libidinal desires. The various disclosures of his female patients were therefore not to be read as genuine recollections, but as fabricated actions and stories. And while this did not diminish the importance of these memories, it did alter their meaning—for now they spoke of *psychic*, not *social*, happenings.

The question of why Freud abandoned his seduction theory has been the subject of much controversy, but as this debate is only tangential to my current concerns, let me treat it only briefly here. Certain scholars such as Jeffery Masson argued that Freud's revision ignored the considerable clinical evidence, even material from Freud's own patients, that the abuse he repudiated as fantasy was actual and real (Masson 1984: 27). Indeed Masson's claims seem to be supported not only by a thorough reading of the Fliess-Freud letters, edited by Masson (1989 [1985]) himself, but also more widely by later psychiatrists and social researchers who have subsequently revealed that childhood sexual abuse was far more prevalent than Freud supposed.[124]

Masson explains Freud's abandonment of the seduction theory as owing to his reluctance to further outrage the psychiatric community with his findings. And although this explanation may in some measure account for his revision, it seems improbable that it explains it entirely. For in the first place, it appears highly incon-

sistent with Freud's well-known disregard of conventional psychiatric explanations as well as with his evident nonchalance, often in
spite of himself, concerning aggravating the psychiatric community. But more importantly it overlooks Freud's considerable social conservatism which could only have been threatened by what
his own seduction theory implied: as ever more patients came to
him with hysterical symptoms he was forced to conclude that not
only was childhood sexual abuse disturbingly common, but that it
regularly occurred in the most 'respectable' sectors of society. Even
his own father seemed potentially guilty since Freud noticed hysterical symptoms in both his own brother and sister (Storr 1989:
18). In fact, in a letter to Wilhelm Fliess dated September 21st 1897,
Freud clearly admitted that as hysteria was so common it could not
possibly be caused by childhood abuse, since, as he says, 'surely
such widespread perversions against children are not very prob-
able' (Freud 1989: 264). Thus with the growing numbers of patients
came his growing disbelief and doubt, which, rather than settling
on the upright world of Vienna, settled on his own theoretical construct—the seduction theory that he consequently abandoned. In
other words, the consequences of his seduction theory being correct were too much at variance with his social conservatism, which,
apart from opposing the rigid sexual mores of the day, supported
the paternal social structure which he saw as integral to civilised
life.[125]

However we decide to interpret his discarding of the seduction
theory, what is most important to note for our current argument it
is that after its abandonment Freud would habitually assume that
what were reported by patients as real events were actually
products of phantasy—phantasies that pointed to the existence of a
childhood sexual life (hence the birth of his psycho-sexual stages of
development). In fact this shift in orientation was perfectly consistent with another tendency that was clearly pronounced in his early
case studies—namely, Freud's need to help patients return to conformity with their social surroundings, rather than empower them
to criticise or alter the potentially damaging social circumstances to
which they were subject. In this sense Freud advocated adjustment
to, rather than reform of, the social world in which his patients
found themselves.

If we accept that Freud's attitude to the dominant mores of the day influenced his concept of aetiology, then allow me now to illustrate how by implication this orientation influenced all subsequent developments within the field of mainstream psychoanalytic psychotherapy in Britain—setting in train a discourse psychocentric in orientation; one that cast suffering in ever more psychological terms, and one diametrically opposed to the more social vision of human suffering prevalent in much social science today.

DEVELOPMENTS IN THE PSYCHODYNAMIC UNDERSTANDING OF AETIOLOGY

To acknowledge how Freud's psycho-centric orientation influenced later theoretical developments, we must start by discussing the distinction between 'analytical' and 'interpersonal' or 'object-relations' orientations in British psychoanalytic psychotherapy. At the outset of psychoanalysis Freud's therapy was highly 'analytic', with the 'interpersonal' or 'object relations' orientation only emerging in the latter half of the twentieth century. While this new 'interpersonal' approach never constituted an overthrow of the analytic stance (it kept as axiomatic basic analytical ideas), for many analysts it gradually replaced the 'need for pleasure' as the dominant human drive, with the 'need for healthy relationship'. For those who accepted this change not only was the analytic understanding of transference and counter-transference altered, but so too was the analytic understanding of aetiology.

The key difference with the new interpersonal or object relations approach was that it particularly emphasised, as Freud did not, the child's *attachment* to its primary caregiver. Therapists such as Fairbairn, Winnicott, Bowlby, Klein and Balint, all unequivocally saw the origins of much pathology as arising from various kinds of loss of intimacy children had suffered with their parents—especially with their mother. A special interest was therefore taken in the mother/child relationship, as its disruption was believed to damage the child's potential for maturation. Thus for the new object-relations theorists neurosis did not only spring from the repression of disturbing fantasies, but from real deprivations, from *real* events.

With these changes object relations analysts returned to an earlier vision of aetiology that Freud had largely abandoned along with his theory of seduction: they reinstalled a respect for *real* rather than *imagined* events as causes. But instead of seeing the traumatic events as 'sexual abuses', they also saw them as 'relational deprivations' occurring within the first few months and years of the child's life: if the child was denied sufficient 'mothering' or 'mirroring' it would develop a maimed sense of self. This could engender psychological complications in adulthood from 'schizoid' or 'narcissistic' personality traits, to obsessive/compulsive or phobic disorders, etc.

COMMON AETIOLOGICAL THEMES

While both object-relations and Freudian orientations debated how far the causes of suffering were real or imagined, both still unequivocally agreed that early childhood was the key phase of human biography. One subsequent result of this has been that both orientations have instinctively learnt largely to favour *early* rather than present events in their explanations of current suffering. Current troubles are seen as inevitable given the childhood history of the person in question. The present malady has its roots in a personality that was structured in childhood.

Many commentators have argued that this vision has led on occasion to a form of reductionism which has not helped psychoanalysis in the political domain. Andrew Samuels, for instance, has argued that this reductionism has been partly responsible for why government policy makers have largely ignored the insights of therapists:

> In asking the world why it didn't turn up for the first session, we need to acknowledge the seemingly incurable psychotherapeutic reductionism and triumphalism that parallels that of the media. Psychotherapists write articles for newspapers about the phallic symbolism of cruise missiles going down ventilator shafts in Baghdad or they call Mrs Thatcher a restorative container for British greed... What is the point of this? Maybe the world was right not to turn up. (Samuels 2000: 8)

Other theorists have asserted that developmental reductionism inhibits theorising about how the present or more recent continuous social environment affects the person's current functioning (Kleinman 1998, Littlewood & Kareem 1992). By not taking account of these later experiences, others have argued that strictly developmental psychoanalysts have downplayed the role of social factors in the causation of illness. As Peter Fonagy and M. Taget write:

> Although infant research confirms some speculation and informal observation, the developmental argument of a linear evolution from infancy to adulthood cannot be sustained. Human development is far too complex for infantile experiences to have direct links to adult pathology. In fact the extent to which research is available, longitudinal studies of infancy suggest that personality organisation is subject to reorganisation throughout development based on significant positive and negative influences. (2003: 162)

The aforementioned scholars regard much developmental thinking as prone to underestimate how *later* and *current* 'living' styles, which might have been *socially* rather than *developmentally* induced, affect the individual's capacity for healthy living. Furthermore, their work raises the concern that so far as developmental thinking bypasses the question as to what extent the developmental dyad is part of a family system that is itself structured by a wider social system, it underplays how a *socially conditioned* change in the family influences the developmental dyad and through this, the child's development. In this sense, to the degree that the dyad is considered in abstraction from the wider social scene, it omits the relevance of society at a second stage of influence.

To clarify these two points, then, the two broad orientations now widely applied in British psychoanalysis rest upon an understanding of aetiology that is circumscribed both *spatially* and *temporally*. *Spatially*, since the search for causes stops at the boundaries of the family (especially the developmental dyad), overlooking the manner in which different socio-cultural systems can structure and influence these primary ties. Secondly it is circumscribed *temporally*, since events in childhood, rather than later events, are privileged as the main determinants of adult suffering. In short, with these two perspectives at its heart, the psychoanalytic vision of aetiology prevalent in Britain today is largely *psycho-centric* in that it privileges psychological over social causes of suffering. This general perspective, as I have suggested, can partly be traced to Freud's attitude to the social mores of his day, which, by disposing him to regard in modern Vienna few things of reprehensibility, led him to locate the sources of his patients' discontent in their psyches rather than in the general social conditions to which they were forced to adjust.

THE CASE OF ARYA—AETIOLOGY IN THE CLINICAL SEMINAR

With this brief introduction to psychoanalytic aetiology in place, we must now venture forth from the sphere of principles into that of facts. The following empirical discussion provides an instance of what an understanding of causation might entail when applied to the treatment of patients. The case discussed is based on the transcript of an audiotape recording—this was of eight clinical supervision seminars held at a training institute in London. The three seminars presented here are sessions 2, 5 and 7 of this series of 8.[126]

As is standard for clinical supervision, these seminars are intimate affairs, in our case involving only three trainees and one supervisor. Like theoretical seminars they are usually held once weekly at the institute and in the evenings. They differ from the theoretical seminars in terms of the content discussed: each week a different trainee 'brings to the group' the case of a training patient with whom he or she is currently working. These cases are assessed by the supervisor (trainer) who decides on the basis of the trainee's presentation whether he or she is proceeding correctly. Structurally speaking, in terms of the affirmative context and devices employed, clinical supervision and theoretical seminars are comparable, as here too the roles between trainer and trainee are clearly defined, while critical reflection falls less on either the truth or falsity of psychodynamic ideas than on whether they are being correctly applied in practice.

To turn now to the people involved, the Supervisor in question is a middle-aged male psychoanalyst (trained at the Institute of Psychoanalysis in London) whose research interests are cultural issues in the therapeutic encounter. Two of the three trainees are British males (early thirties) in their first year of clinical supervision; while our final trainee, who is the student presenting the case, is a forty-two year-old woman from India, who has previously trained in India in CBT (cognitive behavioural therapy). The patient she discusses is a twenty-one year-old Indian girl (Punjabi), whom I shall call *Arya*.

THE EVENTS LEADING ARYA TO THERAPY

The trainee therapist starts by informing the group that her patient, Arya, came to England one year ago to live with her British-Indian husband (Gujarati, thirty-one years old) whom she had married three months earlier in India. Her problems started four months after she had arrived—her husband became increasingly critical of her domestic mistakes. At this time his possessiveness and jealousy also began to grow. He started to prohibit Arya from going out and from mingling with the rest of his family. Over the next few months the abusive episodes worsened, becoming physical and more frequent. After seven months he was hitting her 'on most days' and becoming very aggressive sexually. For the next few months Arya 'lived in misery' until finally, on an evening when he was particularly abusive, she 'escaped' through a window to stay with an aunt whom she had recently visited. Her husband contacted her two days later to say he had filed for divorce and that she should never return. It was two months after this event that Arya was referred to our trainee therapist by her GP She described herself as feeling depressed, heartbroken, and extremely lonely.

SUPERVISION SESSION ONE

The trainee relays to the group what she felt to be the important themes of her last session with Arya. Three themes in particular stand out. Firstly, Arya's ambivalence for her ex-husband: at the beginning of the session Arya expressed a desperate hope that her husband would take her back, while at the session's end, when asked how she might win him back, Arya's immediate response was: 'No, no, I want a divorce, definitely divorce; I never want to go back, if I do he will be fine for a few days then he will start beating me'.

The second theme concerned Arya's astonishment at the change in her husband's behaviour, from a wooing lover (sending gifts to her from London) to 'the cruel man he became'. Arya said, 'I did ask him why his behaviour changed so much and he said that he was always like this, that he had two sides to him, that he could be soft and angry.'

The third theme concerned how he treated her in public. The trainee quotes Arya: 'My husband would not let me speak to any of his brothers. Once we had to go to his brother's house for a function, he was hurrying me to get ready. And as I came down the stairs his older brother was waiting in the hall. I asked him whether he wanted tea or coffee. Immediately my husband pushed me into the kitchen and shouted at me for speaking to his brother'. At other Gujarati gatherings Arya was told she could not talk to certain women and certainly to no men at all.

THE GROUP'S COMMENTS ON SUPERVISION SESSION ONE

Supervisor: In this session she clearly indicates that she felt cheated and deceived; that he represented himself as one thing and turned into something different. He even accepted that he has two sides to him... What was surprising is that at the beginning of the session she wants a second chance, to go back to him, while at the end she is adamant that she is not going to return. So is it one or the other?

Trainee Therapist: In the previous session she was longing for him to call her back. Also she hoped that the elders would intervene and improve things, that both families would talk and demand a harmonious reconciliation. This was her hope. But then, yes, by the end of this session she wants the separation; she has even had her lawyer request her belongings to be returned.

Supervisor: Do you know what is going to happen financially because I would imagine it plays quite an important part. Will he return whatever she gave to him?

Trainee Therapist: She is not quite sure about that...

Supervisor: Not that you should be concerned about this, it is not the therapist's concern as such, but it is indirectly as I would imagine it would have many implications for what her condition is going to be... One thing that is striking about the session, really, is that the emphasis is on external things; you know you ask a question and she gives you some information about the husband or about the family. But there is really very little emphasis on her experience, on what it feels like for her to be in this situation.

Trainee Therapist: Yes, she repeatedly *says* that she is depressed and feels like crying; yet she says these things in a dissociated way.

Student One: So she was not angry?

Trainee Therapist: No, the anger was not expressed through her body or tone of voice, it was passive anger: 'I am feeling angry, I am angry towards my husband', but nothing else...

Student One: She is talking about being angry, but you sense no anger in the room.

Trainee Therapist: Yes, Yes... [*Silence*]

Student One: I was wondering whether that could have been explored?

Trainee Therapist: Yes, but then I was feeling that there is a cultural element here too. I am uncertain about Punjabi culture, but in the culture I come from as a woman I cannot express my anger very much. As a woman you have to be very soft, and even if you have anger you should learn to hold yourself and not express it. This posed a problem for my own therapy here, actually. When I was going through some difficulty, my therapist expected me to get really angry and made me practice verbalising my anger [*she laughs*] and so I can sympathise with Arya's hesitance [*silence*].

Student Two: Does your issue with anger prevent you from exploring hers?

Trainee Therapist: OK. Good question. I need to think about that. [*Silence.*]

Supervisor: She is clearly indicating that she has felt trapped, not just physically in the sense of being locked in and not being allowed to talk to anybody, but also in the sense that she found herself in a position from which she couldn't quite see a way out. She says more than once that she has done her best to please her husband, and so cannot understand why she has been treated in this way. She feels that whatever she does she will fail.

Trainee Therapist: Two things still surprise me. She doesn't want to go deeper into what motivated her into marrying a man after one glance at a photograph; a man she had not seen and rarely spoken to, that is one thing. The other thing is that she never considers her part in all of this—what *she* has contributed to this situation.

Supervisor: [*Eagerly*] Right, yes.

Student Two: [*In agreement*] I noticed this.

Trainee Therapist: I feel that there is a block somewhere. [*General agreement.*]

Supervisor: I think these are two very valid points. Regarding the first one we could speculate that her wish to get away from India, from her family, or from her parents is very strong indeed to the point that she would almost marry anybody who was offering. It happened to be this man who also seemed to be nice, to write kind letters, to give her nice gifts and so on. Or then again maybe it's due to her wish to come to England, her wish to leave her family, her wish to have children, who knows. Whatever is the case there is something else underneath this specific wish to be married to this man—it is not about *him* in other words. Yes, and the second point, I think it would be fair to assume that she might have played her part, but that is not to justify the way he seems to have behaved, but to try and understand it... so she may have played a part by being too passive, by provoking him, we are not sure.

Trainee Therapist: Yes, Yes.

[*Omission.*]

Supervisor: [*Closing the session.*] At the moment we are given facts 'my uncle did this, my husband did that', but we don't know enough about what it *feels* like for her. It might be possible as you say that anger is not one of those feelings that, culturally speaking, a woman of her age is able to get hold of; but I am sure that she has feelings of one sort or another. If she does not experience it as anger, she might experience it as humiliation or as a feeling of being deceived or whatever. I mean I think one should try to focus a bit more on the current form of words, let's put it that way, rather than on what she *should* do or what he *has* done. These kinds of facts might be of more interest to a social worker, or to a biographer who had to write a story of what happened to her; but this is not the job of a therapist, *which is about trying to understand the internal world and to somehow create the conditions where the subjective experience can be expressed and shared with you, so that it can be understood and interpreted.* [*Turning to a student.*] You wanted to say something?

Student Two: I agree, I mean so far there has been a lot of talk about situations or events happening external to her, but not much talk about her internal reaction to these. I mean it is understandable; I am not blaming her, of course, but all the more reason for someone to draw attention to that fact that there are other ways of approaching these things—she needs to go into herself for answers, so to speak. [*General agreement.*]

A Brief Analysis

At the beginning of the seminar, the group is evidently moved by the description of Arya's circumstances, circumstances which, from another standpoint, would seem to provide explanation enough for her suffering. But instead of discussing whether therapy is appropriate for Arya (to what extent is her pain due to unfortunate circumstance rather than pathology?), the group still works to analyse her inner workings—a search which, after all, therapists see as their remit to undertake. Arya's subjective problems are insinuated with comments such as: 'she only focuses on external events not her reactions to them' (in psychodynamic parlance such behaviour could be expressive of an 'avoidant personality'). One student points out that, 'her anger is passive and not expressed' (a characteristic of the 'schizoid' character).[127] And there were questions that all agreed were important: 'what was her motivation for marrying this man?'—and, 'what did she contribute to this situation?' While these comments and questions overtly declared very little, they implied very much—namely, that a part of Arya might be conspiring against herself (e.g. unconscious motivations or needs perhaps).

Another feature of the seminar is the absence of any technical instruction from the supervisor. Although this is unusual, in this instance it seems understandable: while the nature of Arya's distress still remains unclear, it is difficult to decide upon any curative strategy. The supervisor feels we need to know Arya a little better before a strategy can be decided upon, but there are two impediments to this—Arya's focus on external events (which the supervisor sees as problematic), and the fact that certain behaviours can be accounted for on cultural rather than psychological grounds (e.g. her emotional 'repression' being due to a cultural rather than psychological prohibition). The questions whether other factors too have cultural explanations also inhibits discussion—as one of the group mentioned to me after the session: 'there are many cultural themes here that I do not understand and this makes defining her problems much more complicated'. With these comments in mind, let us turn to our next transcribed seminar.

SEMINAR NUMBER TWO

The first theme discussed is Arya's longing for her husband. Yet she also wants him to return her belongings and passport (symbolic of her desire for independence). This contradiction is unravelled when it becomes clear that more than wanting the belongings themselves, she desires the contact that his returning them will necessitate.

The second theme is trust. Arya said, 'I usually trust people, but no longer; I have learnt a good lesson, I cannot trust anyone on this earth.' The therapist asked Arya whether she can trust her, Arya responds: 'No, no, no, I don't mean you, really you help me; I mean other people like my husband and in-laws. If my husband can betray me, how can I trust others?'

The final theme is about separation, for while Arya is happy to be away from the abuse (sexual, physical, verbal), she still misses her husband and his family: 'There were people like his brothers who were good to me and I loved his family members, because once I got married I treated all his relatives as mine own'. She continues, 'I still remember all the places where things were kept (the dishes and clothes) sometimes these memories are so vivid and comforting—I have to struggle to detach myself from them'.

SEMINAR DISCUSSION

Supervisor: [*Addressing the group.*] Any thoughts?

Student One: What struck me about all this was how she spoke about her husband's good qualities and how she is going to miss him. This contradicts very much the representation she offered a few weeks ago; and also the original representation she gave of his family [*General agreement—Arya had been angry with the family for siding with her husband and not criticising his treatment of her.*]

Trainee Therapist: Yes, she now feels that there are many people she is going to miss. I think there is a sort of fear about letting this family go, no matter how bad they have been.

Supervisor: I suspect there is something else too. I wouldn't want to be on the wrong track, you are more familiar than me with the cultural rules, but I wonder if when a young woman leaves a family to marry, in a sense she rejects her own family, in order to belong to a new one I mean. But now *she* has been rejected from the new family, well, she now doesn't belong anywhere. She doesn't belong in Britain, she doesn't belong in India. She does not belong with her family. She doesn't belong with her in-laws. And at that point (and I am just speculating here), at that point she is entirely on her own.

The other thing is that although she mentioned passports, I take the passport as being a symbol of her identity (it has her name, picture, address etc.) and the fact that she has no access to her passport is disturbing not just because she doesn't have a visa, and is unable to travel, but because she has almost been deprived of her sense of identity, of who she is, by whoever holds her passport. And so she belongs really nowhere; and she is quite desperate. I think a lot of her depression and a lot of her tears are partly to do with that. She needs to find a place where she can settle, where she can be, where she can, so to speak, get her passport back, her identity back. But of course this isn't the whole picture.

Trainee Therapist: Yes, the passport symbolises a lot. [*Pause.*] Another thing that is still a mystery to me is why she would agree to such a radical overhaul of her identity; why this man, why this country?

Supervisor: So she might have been more calculating than you thought?

Trainee Therapist: Yes, yes.

Supervisor: It wasn't just because he was sending her nice presents.

Trainee Therapist: Exactly, and normally if a girl has a problem and the parents are open to receiving her back the girl will return. But she wants to remain in Britain and be independent.

Student One: This is interesting, isn't it?

Trainee Therapist: Yes, because she grew up in a very close and loving environment the parents were very protective, but after marriage she has suffered so much here; but the desire to get back to her parents is not uppermost.

Supervisor: At the moment we don't know why she has no desire to go back, but let us put this aside for right now because there is something else I think we might discuss here: I thought that you were right to notice that when she said that she couldn't trust anybody she meant you as well, her emphatic denial 'no I mean everybody but you', would not convince me. You know she might consciously, but I think somewhere there must be some ambivalence. I mean if she sees herself as being so inept at assessing and judging other people, why wouldn't she be deceived by you? Indeed, you might be giving her a nice place in which to express herself, and nice interpretations and so on, but what is the difference between this and the nice presents her husband gave her? So while I think it was right to point out that she might find it difficult to trust you, I would not have taken her flat denial too literally... I think she could trust you more deeply if you allowed her to see that there is a part of her that actually does not trust you. You become more trustworthy if you make her face the fact that there is a part of her that cannot trust anybody; I mean she has been so massively disappointed and betrayed and so on...

Student One: I wonder how much she has been deceived in her life prior to these recent events?

Supervisor: Quite. We don't really know much about her relationship with her parents for instance—to what extent she feels that they have let her down and betrayed her.

Trainee Therapist: She has an inflated vision of them; they are very nice and gave her everything, etc.

Supervisor: [*Smiling.*] Yes, but...

Trainee Therapist: That she doesn't want to go back to her parents does tell us something.

Student One: One could say that the reason that she isn't going back is because it would be shameful to do so.

Trainee Therapist: Yes, maybe she doesn't want to go back because she does not wish to bring shame to the family, etc. I am not suggesting it is her fault but she might feel it is.

Student Two: But would shame account entirely for her not wanting to return?

Trainee Therapist: Perhaps, maybe, but not entirely.

Supervisor: The suggestion is that she does not really trust her parents, that is why she does not want to go back. We don't really know what was going on in her family.

Student Two: And do we really know how far she consented to the marriage?

Trainee Therapist: Well she told me she wanted the marriage.

Supervisor: But did she give her consent because she felt that she couldn't let her parents down after they had arranged things? The point is we should question the idea of how free her decision really was. In theory she could say yes or no, but in reality did she *really* have a choice?

Student One: And if she didn't have a choice, assuming that, and assuming that her parents knew she would accept it, why did the parents choose a man in England rather than a man down the road —I mean it is a huge distance to send your daughter.

Supervisor: A man from a different background, who lives in a different country, and who turned out to be so inappropriate for her.

Student Two: And why did the parents choose a man in London? This choice is surely significant.

Therapist: You are implying that if the parents choose someone in England for her, then the parents in a sense wanted to get rid of her...

Trainee Therapist: So maybe it is my assumption that she wanted to come to England and marry an Englishman—perhaps I have read too much Austen. [*General amusement.*]

Supervisor: It seems that the truth is very complex; wanting to get away from her family, wanting to come here, wanting to get married, wanting to obey her family's wishes.

Student Two: [*After a protracted silence.*] She seems a very sad young lady.

Supervisor: [*Regretfully.*] It is a very sad story. I am sure not uncommon, but sad, yes.

[*Omission.*]

Supervisor: Look we are coming to the end now, so let's round up. We are not sure at the moment what restraints she has internalised. Rather than discuss this at the moment, let's say that it is probably a mixture of family pressure, external pressures, psychopathology of her own, education, you name it. What would be more useful would be to try in the following sessions to *move her away from the external reality of things*—is she going to get divorced or not, and so on. Rather try to read the whole thing at a more internal level—forget about the external events and try and see and understand her experience of them—this will reveal to us the landscape of her internal world. How does it feel for her to be in this situation now? What part she might or might not have played in finding herself here? How does she feel about you and talking to you about certain things? I think one is very tempted whenever there is a clear series of external events, for instance in the case of people who have been traumatised, abused or tortured, to focus entirely on that and to forget what her own individual personal experience of it was, which I am sure will be very different from person to person. So if the focus can be redirected towards her internal world rather than to the events then perhaps she would really begin to benefit and trust you rather than just say that she trusts you. *You are there for a different purpose other than healing her external life, that is what is special in a sense about what you have to offer her.*

Student One: And do you think that by taking that approach which is therapeutic rather than a social worker's approach you will be getting her to focus on her relationship to these events and to get her to reflect upon herself?

Supervisor: And where she comes from, and how she finds herself in this situation, and what part she has played in it.

Student One: And what part she can play to get out of it. [*General agreement.*]

A BRIEF ANALYSIS

What stands out in this seminar is that while the participants might be framing diagnostic interpretations privately, they have yet to reach a diagnostic consensus. This delay takes place for two reasons. Firstly, the cultural barrier—in many ways Arya's world is unfamiliar (the patients of most therapists are British and middle-class), and that the training therapist is herself Indian obliges more sensitivity. Thus the students and the supervisor seem reluctant to draw conclusions until all the key cultural facts are in (e.g. in the omitted sections there were many questions asked about Arya's values and beliefs, about arranged marriages, etc.)

Secondly, the external events to which Arya has been subject make it difficult for the trainees to look beyond these for an explanation of her suffering. The supervisor senses this, and yet while he acknowledges the impact of external events by saying, 'the depression could be a lot to do with having lost her identity' he still concludes that 'this of course is not the whole picture'. He implies that there might be something else behind these events, some precipitating 'motivation' which possibly helped lead Arya, unbeknown to herself, into this situation. Furthermore, by suggesting that Arya discloses her 'inner experience', the supervisor is in fact requesting the type of data (fantasies, fears, inner contradictions and internal objects) from which a diagnosis of her problem and 'personality structure' can be drawn. Thus what are being sought-for here are very specific kinds of subjective facts. This preference for the personal over the external and collective, anthropologists have argued may well serve to legitimate the application of psychodynamic interpretation and intervention where they might not be required.

For instance, cross-cultural clinicians have argued against gathering data of psychodynamic interest alone, since it privileges 'universal' inner experience over external socio-cultural meanings, symbols, and events. Jadhav, Littlewood, and Raguram (1999), for instance, have critiqued this psycho-centric tendency of psychodynamic practice:

> The process of deliberately filtering off cultural components of patients' narratives to yield symptoms and signs, including defence mechanisms... is considered credible and meritorious [in psychodynamic psychotherapy]. We argue that this relates to an effort on the part of alienated health professionals attempting to approximate their patient's stories as stories to Western therapeutic narratives, to arrive at some sort of goodness-of-fit with the latter. (Jadhav, Littlewood & Raguram 1999: 102)

While these authors are specifically talking here of how therapists recast patients' narratives in therapeutic symbols (a usage overlooking that patients often better respond to understanding their world in its own symbolic terms) their comments have application to the manner in which the psychodynamic concept of aetiology might ignore other aetiological considerations. This is to say, not only might certain indigenous symbolic meanings be filtered away, but so might also certain aetiological perspectives which are irreconcilable with a psycho-centric vision of suffering.

SEMINAR NUMBER THREE

The main theme of this session is that at its end the therapist sets her patient, Arya, some 'homework' (some exercise between the sessions which may help increase the patient's self-esteem). Setting homework is taboo in psychodynamic therapy. The trainee's actions were thus more in accord with the principles of CBT (cognitive behavioural therapy) of which she possessed much knowledge and which encourages that therapists be more didactic than exploratory with their patients. The therapist made this suggestion because she felt Arya's 'self-deprecatory feelings were inhibiting her from taking steps to improve her situation'.

The second theme concerns Arya's reluctance to tell her parents of her unhappiness. Arya says, 'You know I do not share any of my deeper feelings with others. I fear that if I unburden my heart my family will suffer. I do not want them to suffer.'

SEMINAR DISCUSSION

Supervisor: You felt you had to set her some homework?

Trainee Therapist: Yes, I felt I had to ask her to sit and write a list of her good qualities as a kind of re-balancing. I felt that it would be good for me to counter her self-deprecation.

Supervisor: How do you feel about alternatives?

Trainee Therapist: Not giving her homework?

Supervisor: Yes. Look, it seems to me that it is more important to understand why she feels she has no good qualities, than to get her to make list of them. But I do understand—it really depends on which type of framework you see yourself working with. [*The supervisor is aware that this trainee is referring to CBT ideas.*] As a psychoanalyst, I would work in a non-directive way and therefore would not give instruction. Another colleague might say at the end of a session 'we must stop now but we could talk about this next time'? But I would not even do that because that is also giving some kind of instruction. Of course, if there is something that was incredibly important to her and she doesn't return to it, I might interpret her avoidance, but I wouldn't instruct her to come back to it —do you see the difference? I mean, there is nothing intrinsically wrong about getting someone to think about their good qualities and write them down—by doing this you won't damage her or anything like that. It is really all to do with what you see your role as being and what your therapeutic attitude towards your client is. Is it a more directive one? [*The trainee remains silent.*]

Let me put it this way, if someone is very quiet in the session, I don't think it would be the job of the therapist to make them talk, but it would be our job to understand why it is difficult for them to talk. After all, they've travelled here, they've paid their money, they sit in the chair or lie down in order to tell you things, so why can't they? This suggests that there is some kind of problem, some issue, some anxiety about you or the situation or something else. So it is that conflict, that issue, which I would want to explore—I would not tell them that they must talk and that I cannot help them until they do. [*Pause.*] Actually, this analogy is useful because she has a problem with talking. Does she talk much with the aunt she lives with?

Trainee Therapist: Apparently not. And I was concerned why she couldn't say anything to her parents either, although they call her.

Supervisor: But again, we do not know what relationship she has with them so it is difficult to know why she doesn't tell them things. Say, if her parents were quite elderly and fragile it would be different than if they could just take things in their stride. [*Pause.*] But how depressed is she?

Trainee Therapist: She is improving. From my point of view she wants to move forward despite her inclination to move back, and moving around and filling the whole session with her sob story...

Supervisor: [*Interrupting.*] What concerns me here, and I think this is central, is that she doesn't seem to feel that she can get her life back in her own hands and get what she wants; I mean there is something about that which *suggests she doesn't have or cannot quite find the internal resources to improve her situation.* And alright, perhaps she could go to her parents and they might help, some other people might, but it seems to me that, although I wouldn't describe her as a definite suicide risk, I wouldn't rule that out altogether. So some attention should be paid to that because it is an option for her as for anyone at any point in our lives. But she seems to be perhaps a little closer to choosing that option than some of us might be.

Student One: [*Slightly distressed.*] Yes, she feels herself to be very restricted and determined by other things, external things; she experiences herself as very powerless.

Supervisor: Right, yes she feels this, so what would you see the role of the therapist as being then, what could you as a therapist do to help someone like her now? What should you take from that session and look at further?

Trainee Therapist: [*Pause.*] Perhaps her difficulty with sharing her burden with her parents, perhaps with her insisting that she is to blame for the failure in the marriage?—although, after all, she is the one who decided that she couldn't stand it any longer. Perhaps the fact that she feels bad is because she hasn't conformed to what is expected of her, in marriage, work, etc.? But most importantly, I feel that she hasn't got an identity of her own, so she conforms to that identity or the idea or the expectation placed upon her by somebody else.

Supervisor: Right, good. So she has to be what others expect her to be because she doesn't know who she is—that is something. But I am after something else. There is another clue here vital to unravelling what is going on. [*Protracted silence.*] Think of what you did. This is important.

Trainee Therapist: [*Hesitatingly.*] Instructing her?

Supervisor: Exactly! In that is the clue. By instructing her you end up colluding with her belief that she cannot know who she is, so you are going to tell her or give her a task that would allow her know. But by doing this in a sense you become like the husband who gives her instructions to do her sari up—I am exaggerating here, but you see what I am trying to say. As a therapist it is very easy to fit the role that the patient expects you to play. This is very clear for instance when you work with patients who have some sort of perversion, not necessarily a fully flown sexual perversion, but who have a certain *masochistic* tendency to put themselves in situations where they suffer—and as this is familiar to them they almost enjoy it—the familiarity. Well, now, when you have such a patient you will find yourself, whether you like it or not, and however hard you try, being quite sadistic towards them. It might just be in the sense that you arrive a couple of minutes late or that you make them choose the more uncomfortable chair, or that in your voice something will emerge when offering an interpretation, or you interrupt them—something minimal but something nonetheless that will reinforce the *sado-masochistic pattern that they are used to and you find yourself in the sadistic position.*

Or the other way round, the sadistic patient might make you feel passive and persecuted and oppressed. These are clear examples of how in the transference and counter-transference those personality traits or perverse traits or whatever they are, are re-enacted in the therapeutic relationship. And it is important not to allow yourself to fall into the trap, to set the homework so to speak, in order to then be able to reflect on this. So when you find yourself acting sadistically towards a patient, and this is the last thing you wanted to do, *then the patient's masochism becomes palpable, and now you can work on it and understand it, and link it with early events in this patient's life or link it with early experiences—you notice the repetitions they live.*

Student One: So from how our patients make us feel we sense the tone of the patient's personality.

Supervisor: Yes, that is right; we fit their personality and become that which is familiar to them, even if what is familiar is harmful. This is why so many people who have been abused as children end up as abusers themselves, for instance, or end up being abused again as adults. It is as if they only knew that way of relating to other people. This is why they relate this way to the therapist, and a therapist will inevitably fall into making this possible by adopting consciously or unconsciously the complementary attitude. But unlike others, you are in the very privileged position of being able to think about it and use it to understand *the internal world of your patient and the internal objects of your patient,* which also gives you a lot of responsibility. As you all know, the concept of the internal object is an important one and it has to do with the parents we carry inside ourselves—who are quite different from the parents we have had out there; they might be more benign or angrier or more difficult or more neurotic or more generous than the real parents really were. There are often parents who are more harsh and forbidding than the actual parents—so these internal objects govern the self-concept.

Student Two: They are both related and they both communicate to you at the same time...

Supervisor: Yes, yes, so to come back to Arya; her internal parents seem very fragile people who might be very upset or angry or anxious, while actually her real parents might be nothing of the sort. In fact her parents might be quite worried of having a daughter who never talks to them. So why does she think she is protecting them, when in fact she is worrying them more. You see, what we are really concerned with is her fantasies not the reality. And the main part of the therapeutic task is to explore these things, these objects, and to question them, to challenge them, so that hopefully those internal objects will be less persecutory or less depressing or less maddening than they really are. People who already have good internal objects are unlikely to come to us, they don't need it. They are fine, yes of course, people go through loss of marriage, loss of friends, of illness, etc. but if they have sufficient inner resources to deal with it then somehow they cannot get on successfully. But those who cannot need therapy. Do you feel that we understand our patient a little better now, as well as what we can do with her?

A BRIEF ANALYSIS AND CONCLUSION

Before studying further the implications of psychodynamic aetiology in the next chapter, let me draw some preliminary observations from the case-study discussed. This final seminar is to be distinguished from the previous sessions for two important reasons. Firstly, here a partial diagnosis is finally hinted at (i.e. masochism) a diagnosis which later becomes explicit, since the supervisor later suggests that Arya suffers from masochistic traits.[128] This was inferred from the 'relational dynamics' between patient and therapist.[129] The 'sadistic' act of setting homework was seen to be provoked by the patient's need to settle in her familiar masochistic position, a position requiring a sadistic complement to be actualised. This diagnosis was supplemented by the supervisor's suggestion that the patient has poor 'internal objects'. This was thought to explain not only the existence of her masochism, but also why Arya was unable to manage her situation adequately; a situation with which people possessing healthier internal objects would cope better.

The second reason why this session differs from the previous two is due to the group's mood being different. In this session the supervisor is more decisive, more earnest than in previous sessions, perhaps because he feels he has a firmer grasp on what he suspects are Arya's problems. The trainees respond gratefully to this new authority, they appear more engaged, less frustrated, more eager to learn. The mood remains buoyant in the halls once the session has ended where they express their satisfaction: 'we got somewhere today', says one; 'very interesting, great session, he's very good' says another. While the trainee who analysed Arya commented to me later in interview:

> This was a really helpful session; he has given me a lot to work with. After the other sessions I felt slightly unsatisfied, things were not really clear, actually I felt quite confused...
>
> 'So now do you have a better grasp of Arya's problem?'
>
> 'Yes, I was just groping about before, but now I have formulated a clearer objective—I am looking forward to our next session.'

Talking informally to the supervisor the following week, he said:

> 'I would advise [the trainee] to stay with these relational clues, because we now have something that we can work with.'
>
> 'And her external situation?'
>
> 'As therapists we can do nothing about this directly, but we can alter her reactions to it and also the inner tendencies that compel people (unconsciously) to search out disasters. What we need to do now is work to release her from her any compulsion she might have to repeat this situation in the future.'

In sum, as the trainees now feel they possess some kind of general diagnostic insight; they have a clearer understanding of the clinical steps to be taken. If Arya's 'masochism' is in part responsible for her compulsion to seek a sadistic 'other', then the clinical task is now to expose to Arya the roots of this masochism through interpreting the 'material' she presents, and through revealing the relational dynamics she manifests with the therapist. These clinical techniques, which are employed to repair through 'insight' and the 'corrective relationship' early relational deprivations, will also be used to treat the patient's negative 'internal objects' (i.e. her 'internal' parents rather than her real parents'). These internal objects might be the real source of the masochism. These objects sabotage the patient's ability to communicate and deal successfully with trauma. Thus with clearer diagnostic understanding comes the therapist's conviction about how best to proceed clinically. The therapist now knows the aims of her clinical action—action, as I shall further explore in the next chapter, which opts to alter the patient's inner-world rather than the social circumstances in which the person is embedded.

CHAPTER SEVEN
ILLNESS AETIOLOGIES AND THE SUSCEPTIBILITIES OF TRAINING

I opened the last chapter by noting that to fathom the psychodynamic concept of aetiology we must look to the specific sociohistorical conditions out of which it arose. Emphasising how this concept is psycho-centric, I then illustrated through our case study how trainees learn to use such aetiological understanding to guide their clinical interpretations and actions. In this chapter, by contrasting psychodynamic aetiology with aetiologies found in other healing systems studied by anthropologists, I shall not only locate the psychoanalytic conception within a wider scheme of aetiological classification, but also illustrate that the psychoanalytic notion of aetiology constitutes one basis for the practitioner's *conviction* that psychodynamic therapy has something to offer any patient in emotional distress.

My second aim in this chapter is to note that as the theory and practice of psychotherapy is transmitted in the social space of the institute, the covert pressures of this space bend trainees' subjectivities toward a posture of receptiveness. In other words, we will see how such receptiveness is nurtured by the various institutional stressors to which trainees are subject, stressors disposing novices to submit to the guidance and instruction of seniors.

CLASSIFICATION OF ILLNESS AETIOLOGIES

Having in our possession the conceptual and empirical data of the last chapter, we are now in a stronger position to place psychoanalytic aetiology within a wider system of classification. The classificatory system I would like to discuss is not an indigenous nosology (i.e. one created by the therapeutic community), since it is founded on anthropological rather than psychotherapeutic principles. However, as I offer it here to better understand, or more clearly translate, an aetiological outlook that practitioners embodied *as a core disposition*, for the purposes of my central argument its contrivance seems justified.

To understand psychoanalytic aetiology in relation to other aetiological systems let me first review some existing anthropological literature pertinent to this subject. Not only will this enable us to set psychotherapy down within a broader context, but it will also help us to illuminate through contrast and comparison the exact kind of aetiology psychoanalytic therapy embraces.

ANTHROPOLOGICAL & ETHNOMEDICAL STUDIES

In surveying the ethnomedical literature on illness aetiologies one thing immediately arrests our attention: such systems look to orthodoxy (the concepts the practitioner holds) rather than orthopraxy (the practice the practitioner undertakes) for the basis of classification. Since the early work of W. H. R. Rivers (1924) this criterion has served to clarify the aetiological idiosyncrasies of diverse healing systems. However, this 'concept-centred' emphasis has led to a depreciation of praxis or clinical *activity* as an equally useful criterion by which different aetiologies might be classified and ordered.[130] In what follows I hope to show why omitting to take praxis into account constitutes an oversight, one which for our purposes warrants rectification. Before I do this, I shall first look at some concept-centred classifications, paying especial attention to Young's dichotomous classification of 'externalising' and 'internalising' systems.

The first classificatory system I shall discuss is from Seijas (1973), which classified non-Western aetiologies into 'supernatural' and 'non-supernatural'. He explains:

> Supernatural etiological categories refer to those ex-
> planations that place the origin of disease in supra-
> sensible forces, agents, or acts that cannot be directly
> observed [e.g. susto, evil eye, sorcery, spirit intrusion
> etc.]... Non-supernatural explanations of disease are
> those which are based entirely on observable cause-
> and-effect relationships, regardless of whether or not
> the relationship is mistaken because of incomplete or
> faulty observation. (Seijas 1973: 545)

A system similar to Seijas' was earlier offered by Nurge (1958) who, discussing aetiology beliefs in a Philippine village, found a distinction between 'supernatural' and 'natural' causes. The former being caused by spirits and witchcraft etc., the latter by phenomena in the 'natural world'—i.e. changes in climate, diet, and bodily sensations.

A later study offered by Foster and Anderson (1978) takes issue with the work of both Seijas and Nurge on the grounds that they conflate under the category 'supernatural' things quite distinct conceptually. They write:

> [For Seijas and Nurge] The term 'supernatural' refers
> to an order of existence beyond nature or the visible
> and observable universe that includes beings such as
> deities, spirits, ghosts and other nonmaterial entities.
> Witches and sorcerers do not belong to the supernat-
> ural world. Sometimes they draw on the supernatural,
> but their powers are best thought of as magical, con-
> sisting of spells charms, and black magic. To classify
> witches and sorcerers as supernatural—as Seijas and
> Nurge must do—seems to us to do violence to the
> concept. (Foster and Anderson 1978: 54)

Foster and Anderson thus offer an alternative classification based on what they term 'personalistic' and 'naturalistic' explanations. For them, the 'personalistic' system is one in which illness is caused by an external agent who might be either nonhuman (ghost or ancestor), supernatural (deity or God) or else human (a witch or sorcerer). Alternatively in 'naturalistic' systems illness is understood in impersonal, systemic terms. Here illness is a result of either external natural forces, disequilibrium in the body (e.g. between yin and yang), or disequilibrium between body and either the social or natural environment (p. 53).

In a real sense Foster and Anderson's classification, which is offered as an improvement on earlier systems, has been subsumed under a more recent system of classification advanced by Young (1983) who defines all healing systems as either 'internalising' or 'externalising'. Externalising systems are those placing the causes of ill-health outside the person—in precipitating social or metaphysical factors; while internalising systems do not look beyond the body and mind for the causes of distress. To illustrate this difference: a practitioner looking for external causes for a patient's fatigue, will not locate the cause of the fatigue in the patient's body, but will allude to variables outside the body and might ask, for example: whence the sequence of events causing the fatigue?—is there social tension or even some witchcraft at play? (Evans-Pritchard 1934: 70). Alternatively, an internalising practitioner such as a biomedical doctor will follow the chain of causal influences only so far—the fatigue may be traced to anaemia, anaemia to blood loss, blood loss to a bleeding stomach tumour, the stomach tumour to certain carcinogens in the diet. At this point the doctor's inferences will usually stop, since although certain psycho-social factors might have influenced the sufferer's diet, such factors are of little *clinical* relevance to a doctor trained to treat the body alone (Blaxter 1970: 160).[131]

Having now illustrated Young's externalising and internalising system, let me indicate how it subsumes Foster and Anderson's (which in turn replaced Seijas' and Nurge's): 'naturalistic' explanations such as disequilibrium *in* the body could be classed as 'internalising'. On the other hand, the 'naturalistic' explanation of disequilibrium *between* body and environment could be classed as either 'internalising' or 'externalising' (depending on which domain diverges from the socially defined norm). Finally, 'personal-istic' explanations such as witchcraft and spirit possession, because of their external origins, fit neatly into the 'externalising' category.

While Young's classification can thus include the systems so far discussed, it is not without its own limits: i.e. it insufficiently accounts for systems that give equal weight to *both* domains in the aetiology of illness. For instance, Beatrice Whiting's (1950) classic study of the Paiute offers a clear example of a system that is neither exclusively externalising nor internalising. For the Paiute the cause of a given disease can be traced to either the external or internal domain. This led her informants to claim that 'no layman could predict what the doctor's power would tell him' (Whiting 1950: 30). However, she did identify some diagnostic trends: any given disease could be caused by any one of four causal agents. She writes:

> When they [the doctors] determine the cause as failure to obey one's own power, the censure is on the patient's own action [internalising cause]; in ghost sickness, the blame may be based on the deceased's relatives [externalising cause] or on the patient for thinking of them [internalising cause]. In the case of sorcery, the blame is placed on someone else [externalising cause]. (Whiting 1950: 64)

For the Paiute healer, the cause of any disease can be traced to either external or internal events, depending on the person who brings the complaint. From Young's standpoint, and in contradiction to his dichotomy, we must say that the Paiute system uses both types of aetiology.

Young's response would be that his dichotomy is rather a continuum in whose middle ground can be strung systems that are both internalising and externalising, such as the Paiute's (Young 1983: 1205). However, while this concept of the 'continuum' can accommodate such middle systems, Young does not explain exactly the forms such middle systems might take, either conceptually or clinically: do all middle systems trace one disease to one causal domain (either external or internal), as the Paiute do? Or do some acknowledge that *both* causal domains (or possibly more) jointly entail *the one disease*?

In respect of the second question Robin Horton's (1970) study of the Kalabari of the Niger Delta provides an instance of a system which sees both domains involved in the one disease. Kalabari diviners may first treat a disease with herbals in a purely unreligious way. But if this intervention produces few positive results there is believed to be 'something else in the sickness.' The healer will then draw upon wider diagnostic knowledge and relate the disorder to a more comprehensive range of circumstances—often to disturbances in the sick person's social relations. Whilst directing alleviative action at the community (social drama), he or another healer will also offer appeasement to angered spiritual agencies, thereby administering a further type of treatment. As the diviner's remedial action is multi-directed it also assumes multiple aetiologies (Horton 1970: 342-368).[132] Thus individual, natural, social, and metaphysical causes are seen not as mutually exclusive, but as often working together to cause the particular instance of disease or discontent.

The usefulness of Young's distinction would be deepened if it included a supplementary description of the various forms these 'middle systems' can take. At present he neither describes how these middle systems conceptualise aetiology, nor acknowledges that middle systems must inevitably entail clinical action more diffuse than that found in strict internalising or externalising systems. That is, his study does not inquire as to the unique kinds of *clinical action* to which differing middle systems (or the polar systems) give rise. For example, in the internalising system of biomedicine, which assumes that biologic concerns are the more basic or 'real' concerns, remedial action is largely directed at *one domain alone*— the body; whereas in systems such as the Kalabari's, remedial action is *directed at potentially many domains*—at the body, at the relational field, at spiritual agencies, etc.[133] Thus accompanying the multiple forms of aetiology in 'middle systems', we can expect multiple forms of clinical intervention, just as in strict internalising or externalising systems we can expect intervention of a more circumscribed kind. It is this link between orthodoxy and orthopraxis that remains unexplored by Young. Yet as it is precisely this linkage that is crucial for understanding psychotherapy, it seems necessary for my specific purposes to advance a new system of classification that is less a replacement of, than an attempt to supplement, Young's concept-centred model.

To devise this auxiliary model I shall use a different criterion by which to classify aetiological systems, basing it on healers' *clinical actions* rather than on their *causal formulations*. This criterion not only builds a classificatory system upon the ground of instrumentality, but has the added merit of accounting for systems, as Hsu (2004) has shown, that do not follow a Western understanding of causation when making diagnoses (e.g. ancient Chinese systems spoke more of 'synchronous signs' than of 'causation')—systems that by implication would be misrepresented if classified by any of the concept-centred models discussed.[134] By classifying systems according to the domain at which clinical practice is *directed*, we classify in accordance with what all healing systems unequivocally share: a healer who *clinically acts*.

In the light of this instrumental model, for my purposes I shall speak of mono-directive and multi-directive systems as auxiliaries to the externalising and internalising categories[135]: *mono-directive* systems being those that level clinical action at one domain (e.g. the body); *multi-directive* being those that level action at two or more domains (e.g. at body, social relations, spirits etc.). These 'directive' and 'externalising/internalising' systems, I further argue, are compatible, and thus can be unified into a more comprehensive classificatory structure as the following summary will show:

<u>Orthopraxis</u>   <u>Orthodoxy</u>[136]

Mono-directive—Internalising (e.g. Biomedicine—healing via medicine, surgery, etc.)

Mono-directive—Externalising (e.g. Forms of witchcraft—healing via sacrifice)

Multi-directive—Internalising (e.g. Psychiatry—healing via pharmacology [the body] and psychotherapy [the psyche])

Multi-directive—Externalising (e.g. Witchcraft—healing via social drama; prayer, oblation)

Multi-directive—Externalising / Internalising (e.g. Sorcery—healing via medicinal intervention [the body], and via social drama [external])

Although this classification is not exhaustive (i.e. it documents neither 'inconsistent' systems nor healing ideologies underplaying causality) it is an attempt at a classificatory scheme which attends to both concept and action—a scheme, which, as I now intend to show, will help us better understand the practice of psychoanalytic psychotherapy.

PSYCHOANALYTIC AETIOLOGY

Psychoanalytic psychotherapy, like certain forms of biomedical intervention, is a predominantly *mono-directive, internalising system*. It is *internalising* as its conceptual thrust privileges psychology in causal explanations (as theoretical description at the beginning of the last chapter demonstrates). It is *mono-directive* since alleviative action is primarily aimed at removing psychological impediments to health. Beyond altering the 'inner world' of patients, psychotherapeutic intervention has little to say: there is no direct intervention in the patient's social world, there is thus no 'social work', no suggestion or advice—as the facts of our case study illustrate. Rather there is a tendency to coax patients into interpreting their situations psychologically. This is not to say that psychotherapists 'intellectually' ignore other influencing factors (e.g. our supervisor saw Arya's immigration as implicated in her 'loss of identity'); but because the therapist does not stop here, but moves incrementally to consider either precipitating events or else to locate in subjectivity the inability to cope, we can speak of dynamic therapy as privileging a kind of psychological interpretivism which looks beyond the external causes to the internal 'masochism' or 'objects', so to speak.

In this sense the relevance of physical explanations of distress or of what anthropologists such as Comaroff (1985), Kleinman, Das and Lock (1998), and Sharp (1993) have called 'social suffering'[137] are generally downplayed in all but the severest cases.[138] In fact, concepts which trace emotional suffering to social causes (e.g. 'anomie', 'alienation', 'ennui', and 'mal du siècle'[139]) are replaced by concepts consistent with psychodynamic interpretation (e.g. 'depression-affective disorder', 'anxiety disorder' or 'affective symptoms' stemming from 'character disorders'); concepts which

define subjective states in accordance with psychoanalytic interpretative understandings and modes of intervention.

Learning how to regard the patient's presenting issue in psychoanalytic terms, as I have tried to show in our case-study, is at
the heart of what it means to think and act psychoanalytically. In
fact, whether or not therapists make sense of phenomena perhaps
better understood from other interpretative standpoints is not
much considered in training. Therapists are not taught to question
whether they are simply 'recasting' phenomena in psychological
terms, and instead learn that they 'unearth' them: unearth their
roots and their shrouded meaning, which are concealed behind the
brute incidences of life. This psychodynamic imagination, this intellectual strategy, justifies to the therapist the deployment of the
mono-directive / internalising intervention even in what could be
considered from other standpoints as 'problems' not reducible to
psychological causes and thus inadequately met if treated by psychological methods.

By means of inspecting case after case during the tenure of their
training, trainees become expert in reading psyche into any script.
That any patient's narrative has its 'psychological layer' is a conviction bolstered over years of honing one's psychodynamic imagination to read into distress phenomena treatable by psychotherapeutic intervention. Such thinking, rooted in psychoanalytic theory, endows psychotherapeutic strategies with purpose and legitimacy, since it provides a basis to the widespread conviction that
when patients are in any kind of emotional distress therapists have
something vital to offer.

DIAGNOSIS AND CONVICTION

The therapeutic understanding of aetiology, discrete, neat, and
pragmatic, is a pillar of conviction upon which practitioners can
lean for support and confidence; confidence, as one therapist in the
NHS disclosed to me, that is indispensable to successful clinical
practice:

> it is what allows therapists to act; to act in what are of-
> ten stressful and uncertain situations, actually in face
> of unknowing... since we can always help and have

some impact, it is just a matter of finding that specific entrée into the problem we encounter, and making sense of it—after this we can make use of our particular expertise. (NHS Psychotherapist 2005)

To trace something unknown back to something known is gratifying, reassuring, and endows the therapist with confidence and moreover with power. Hesitancy, reservation, and the anxieties of vacillation are largely eliminated by the conviction that one's model can render the mysterious fathomable, the perplexing discernible, the strange familiar and routine. Because the embodied theory is felt as an authoritative guide, and since it therefore offers the practitioner a certain clinical orientation and security, we can understand why belief in its veracity, and consequently its 'applicability', is dearly protected.[140] To illustrate the conviction many therapists have in the applicability of their form of intervention, consider the following words of one senior therapist whom I interviewed during my fieldwork:

> If I ever turn down patients, and I do this very rarely, I never do so because I don't think therapy can help; it is because I think that this particular patient is not suitable for me, or on the rarer occasion that they are not quite ready for it. ['Do you believe therapy has something to offer anyone in emotional distress?'] Therapy is about the belief that there is always something we can do once the patient is ready, even if the patient doesn't know it. (Senior Therapist and Supervisor 2005)

How practitioners develop such a sense of conviction in the relevance of their particular form of intervention, has itself been the subject of much scholarly discussion. Renee Fox (1957), for instance, first identifies three kinds of uncertainty endemic in medical socialisation, before describing how students develop conviction in medicine in spite of these.[141] She starts:

> The first [kind of uncertainty] results from incomplete or imperfect mastery of available knowledge. No one

can have at his command all the skills and all the
knowledge of the lore of medicine. The second depends upon the limitations in current medical knowledge. There are innumerable questions to which no
physician, however well trained, can as yet provide
answers. A third source of uncertainty derives from
the first two. This consists of difficulty in distinguish-
ing between personal ignorance or ineptitude and the
limitations of present medical knowledge. (Fox 1957:
208-9)

Fox (1980) continues in a later paper to describe the conviction
that nevertheless emerges:

Students [despite these uncertainties] gradually
evolved what they referred to as a more 'affirmative
attitude' toward medical uncertainty... in clinical situations, they were more prone to feel and display sufficient 'certitude' to make decisions and reassure patients. (Fox 1980: 7)

Joan Cassell (1987: 242) when discussing Fox's work shows how
other anthropologists have interpreted it differently. Jay Katz
(1984), for instance, noted that the students described by Fox experienced growing certainty in their chosen specialities as their
training continued because medical socialisation was essentially
about routing hesitancy and clinical irresolution. This kind of
'training for certainty', as Sinclair has also shown (1997: 146), is
something students happily embrace. For Katz, certainty was instilled by instructors who criticised any display of vacillation in
students, urging that doubt would impair the student's effectiveness with patients. Katz suggests that the pyramidal nature of
medical training, moving from medical school, to graduate training, to the final goal of specialisation, was instrumental in securing
this confidence. As the students progressed their conviction grew,
since extended socialisation would not only 'foster beliefs in the
superior effectiveness of treatments prescribed by one's own speci-
ality' but would also 'tend to narrow [their] diagnostic vision' (Katz
1984:188, italics added).[142]

This correlation between the development of 'conviction' and the 'narrowing of diagnostic vision' operates not only in biomedicine, but also, as I have argued, in psychoanalytic systems so far as therapists gradually learn to read into any script problems treatable by psychotherapeutic techniques. This raises the question: if in both these systems a mode of practice (e.g. mono-directional) is analogical with a mode of being (e.g. a disposition of conviction) can we suppose this correlation to be a general feature of mono-directional systems? Furthermore, if a general linkage obtains, do other aetiological systems (e.g. multi-directional) also bring their distinctive experiential correlates?—that is, would a practitioner of a diffuse 'middle system' better cope with doubt and uncertainty than those practising in more circumscribed systems?[143]

Important as such questions are, they must remain subsidiary to the more pertinent matter I must now investigate—namely, a factor that both Katz and Fox's work presupposes: the presence of 'susceptibility' in trainee practitioners to move into a posture of conviction.

TRAINING STAGES AND SUSCEPTIBILITIES

As the presence of susceptibility precedes both the 'affirmative attitude' and that which this attitude affirms (i.e. conviction in the merit of the clinical system one employs), in the final part of this chapter I would like to explore not only the different kinds of susceptibility to which trainees are subject throughout the course of their training, but also the institutional conditions that engender such susceptibilities in the psychotherapeutic novice. These institutional conditions, I shall argue, provoke socially induced responses (stresses, inclinations) which in turn render trainees more susceptible to the internalisation of pivotal clinical dispositions, and in this case, to the embodiment of affirmative mono-directive / internalising practice.

In noting the importance of stress in facilitating processes which transform persons, we take our departure from authors such as Anthony Wallace (1961) and his idea of ritual learning, whereby stress is evoked in participants to secure a gradual reorganisation of experience resulting in far-reaching cognitive and emotional changes. Such learning may be found in tribal initiations (La Fontaine 1985; Herdt 1987; Richards 1956; Sarpong 1977), individual conversions to religious movements (Heelas 1996: 35-52), in the 're-structuring of behaviour' that accompanies recruitment to messi-anic cults (Katcher and Katcher 1968), and in the stressful trans-formations persons undergo when becoming a nuclear physicist (Gusterson 1997), a psychiatrist (Luhrmann 2000) or a medical doc-tor (Becker et al 1977; Sinclair 1997). In what follows I shall de-scribe the emotional atmosphere in which supervision of the kind outlined earlier transpires. I shall illustrate that the events of super-vision never occur in an affective vacuum, but are rather shaped by the emotional conditions of training which evoke stresses in train-ees that render them susceptible to conform to and accept the clin-ical instruction on offer. In this sense we follows Becker's observa-tion that:

> Much human conduct is orientated to the immediate
> pressures and social controls originating in the situ-
> ation in which the person is presently acting, and that
> he will organise his behaviour so as to take account of
> and in some way adjust to them. (Becker et al 2002
> [1977]: 442)

As I have already touched on one 'susceptibility' in chapter two —viz. the 'disposition of partiality' which leaves trainees receptive to 'affirmative' educational techniques, to this foundational dispos-ition I now intend to add some new susceptibilities that arise at different stages of training as responses to implicit or explicit insti-tutional stresses and demands. This is not to say that these suscept-ibilities are discrete, faithfully coming and going with the passing of their concomitant stages, but that each stage engenders a domin-ant susceptibility which can be re-experienced in mitigated form at other stages if the conditions of training demand it.

Finally, the susceptibilities described articulate the experience of trainees who fall within the parameters of the 'general experience'—that is, the most commonly shared experience by the majority of trainees I befriended. That this 'common experience' is something one can clearly observe in the training institute means we can speak of it as 'collective' rather than 'individual'. This in turn leads us to suppose that it is preferable to regard it as socially induced by the conditions of the training institute, rather than to see it as a product of individual psychology.

EVALUATIVE APPREHENSION AND FEAR

During the first stage of training candidates are rendered susceptible to the guidance of elders by the fear that they will be judged as unsuitable for the therapeutic profession. The evaluative gaze of the training committee is often experienced as intense and pervasive, mainly because at this stage of training candidates are subject to the continuous assessment of supervisors who are not so much judging trainees' skills as practitioners, but themselves as persons. It is this inability to allow 'high grades' and 'successful results' to speak for their suitability that renders trainees so vulnerable. Trainees quickly learn that they are judged on something more intangible, less easily demonstrable or quantifiable than 'examination performance'—namely, on a vaguer kind of 'aptness' as perceived by evaluating committee.

Whatever constitutes such 'aptness' remains mysterious to many trainees until they are informed about how they are being perceived by their seniors. In the institution I observed, trainees were informed of their progress in one of the two tutorials which they attended yearly. These meetings on the whole tended to focus more on personal issues (the trainee's 'traits' and 'behaviours') than on academic results. Despite the potentially upsetting turns these meetings could take, most trainees I spoke to found these 're-lieving' and 'reassuring' affairs, occasions when pent-up 'fears' and 'reservations' about how they are being perceived were dissipated. 'You never quite know what the trainers are thinking', mentioned one student of psychology training at the institute,

> so there is always a part of you that expects the worst. So far the feedback I have received has been fine, but there is some internal saboteur that still anticipates problems. (First Year Trainee 2004)

This trainee later told me with some reticence that his ruling fear was that the committee would discover that the woman he lived with was not in fact his wife (his therapist who was affiliated to his training institution knew this, and so he was concerned this would be informally communicated). He feared that his position would prejudice them against him. He confessed to me:

> I am 39 years old, and so I am not at ease with my situation... I sometimes think there is a quiet belief about where you should be in life at my age—they might at some level hold my situation against me, this is my fantasy at least. Maybe I am wrong, but you know I fear the response. (Third Year Trainee 2005)

While indeed this fear might well be a product of 'fantasy', we also realise that these fantasies might be easily exacerbated given that assessment falls on the 'trainee as person'.

When asking senior members to characterise the apt candidate they often used terms such as 'responsive' or 'relational'; they appreciated those who were able to adequately 'process' their reactions (understand them), and 'reflect' on their faults. Also those candidates who were highly prized displayed a 'personable' manner in relation to peers and superiors. Showing a 'self-reflective' stance which saw trainees 'willing to doubt their own positions' was also something trainers desired. Because these appellations are vague enough to include under their rubric a wide range of meanings and behaviours, we might form a clearer definition of senior members' preferences through negative definition: attributes less favoured were those that were overly 'questioning', 'critical' or 'defensive', or, as one trainer put it, those that made one 'too confident and sure'. Another trait that was disfavoured was 'over-intellectualism'—candidates 'who use their intellect as a defence'—that is, who employed intellect to repudiate theory that, if accepted as commenting on one's subjectivity, would expose unpalatable truths about oneself. In short, we notice that the rejection of these traits is largely congruent with the vocational rather than academic style of education the 'affirmative' institute adopts. Trainers by and large value attributes complementing the smooth transmission of knowledge that it is the duty of the institute to facilitate.

To question now what sits at the base of evaluation apprehension we could first point out the fear of what a negative evaluation would mean or bring. Many trainees undergo considerable personal and economic sacrifices during the tenure of their training. Most maintain full-time jobs and many have families. Because of these circumstances candidates are often eager to move successfully through their training; and because of the understandable anxiety about the economic and personal losses that any extension of their training would entail, they fear being asked to 'take some time out' or to repeat a year. And while such cases are rare (only about 5% of candidates) the fear of being stalled featured in a disproportionately high number of informants. Trainees expressed the prospect of being held back as 'unthinkable' and 'awful'. Another called it 'something that would be shameful and embarrassing'. This last comment is interesting because it articulates another fear widely held. One trainee explains:

> I would be ashamed because I'd feel judged to the core. People here [fellow trainees] are interested in how you are doing, but most people in your life know that you are training—you know, people are interested, they ask you how it's going and so on. Well to turn round and say well, actually, they've gotten rid of me, I think would be difficult. I mean this is not like a pottery course or something, its about health and suffering and all that; it is about personality—these places have the last word on these things so to be judged negatively by them, well, this would say a lot about me now wouldn't it? (First Year Trainee 2005)

Trainees often perceive trainers as they do their therapists—as endowed with special dexterity to uncover faults of which they themselves are unconscious (a fact consistent with the idea that leaders possess deeper 'secret knowledge' and more 'personhood' than novitiates). The atmosphere these beliefs generate renders trainees more vulnerable to trainers' comments, for this 'asymmetry of knowledge' means the power to define the trainee's subjectivity rests almost exclusively in the hands of the evaluative body. Not that such power is necessarily abused, but that such asymmetry, more implicitly felt than explicitly acknowledged, engenders trepidation to test whether it might be. This dim trepidation fosters a disposition to conform to the image of the trainee they feel is appreciated, since trainees cannot be expected to win at a game in which their opponent controls the rules and the outcome. Jane spoke to me privately of her insecurity:

> You actually do not know whether you are 'mature' enough, or able enough—what is maturity exactly? This makes me feel very uncertain sometimes. I have one leader I just don't agree with, but sometimes I feel he has my life in his hands, and so then I think I should just go along with things. But then I get confused because I just don't know what he is looking for... [*Jane fears he is dissatisfied with her.*] If I knew I could adapt myself and things would improve. (First Year Trainee 2004)[144]

While not exploring the institutional conditions under which 'evaluation apprehension' is furthered, authors such as Frank and Frank (1993 [1961]: 64) do note that this apprehension made students susceptible and 'pliant' to trainers' suggestions. This pliancy exhibited itself, as Charny asserted, through trainees adopting the hidden agenda 'of trying to show off and win approval of the authoritative supervisor' (Charny 1986: 19); something confirmed by Ashurt's observation that trainees' insecurity provoked a need to 'impress the supervisor and be the "favoured child"' (Ashurt 1993: 172). My own observations confirm both the presence of this apprehension, and of attempts to win its mitigation by strategies to secure ratification and 'official' approval of the kind dissolving painful thoughts of being judged unfavourably. To these observations I add that this apprehension might be generated more by trainees' fantasies than by evidence of real abuses, and thus is always a fear of the 'what if', and the 'imagined'.

So far we can tease out three institutional conditions under which these fantasies (and the susceptibility to conform that they engender) are given added vitality. The first concerns the *locus of judgement*. At the early stages of training trainees are judged as persons not practitioners. This places them in a position of 'exposure' and vulnerability, given the existence of the second condition: *ownership of concepts*. The debate about trainee suitability transpires in a discourse of concepts only the evaluators are qualified to employ, but whose authority both parties accept; a factor in turn entailing the third condition: the game favours the leader—namely, trainees are vulnerable to a discourse which can impute destructive unconscious motivations to their ostensibly innocuous acts; they are subject to a discourse within which they are socially positioned as 'novice' and so as 'unqualified' to wield these concepts in their own defence.

The fantasies and anxieties these conditions provoke, coupled with the fear of what negative evaluation will bring, constitute part of the subjective climate making trainees more susceptible to the suggestion and convictions of those ensconced in positions above them.

SUSCEPTIBILITY STEMMING FROM CLINICAL STRESSES

The next palpable set of anxieties to which students are subject arrives after they have passed key, initial thresholds (first year assessment; first series of seminars) and now sit in charged expectation of seeing their first patients. It is at this point that trainees, still being judged as persons, are now also judged as practitioners. With this new ground of evaluation, and with their new responsibility, comes a whole new set of apprehensions.

At this stage a widespread anxiety concerns their readiness to undertake the work of a therapist and whether they will succeed with patients. For many candidates training is not the bridge linking two domains; it is one domain, the institute, while the other resides far-off in the consulting room; there is always a gap, a stark dissimilarity. One prepares you for the other, but isn't the other—a leap must be taken. Alison, a third-year comments:

> Seeing your first patient was for me frightening and stressful—it was truly a 'first' experience. I remember being remarkably nervous; you forget the books and you are suddenly with this person, who might be sad, lonely, despairing, avoidant or whatever. Here's the human drama up close, and she looks at you with wide eyes, expecting guidance. If only they knew that you are thinking—that you had not done this before. (Trainee, London 2005)

Once the leap is taken new fears about one's competence commonly surface. These fears can be compounded, firstly, by the length of therapeutic time often needed before any positive change in the patient occurs (something the novice awaits assiduously); secondly, by the common claims of patients that they feel little improvement or that things are getting worse; and finally, by the uncertainty about the outcome at the end of therapy. A fourth-year student, Morgan, discloses,

> I think that some years ago, without even knowing it, I began to formulate an idealised image of the therapist (competent, mature, etc.). I suppose it was the image of the therapist I'd be by the time I'd start practising. I sort of regret this now because compared to this standard I am so far behind; and I have to say that I am now intimidated by my own creation as well as a tad guilty for not living up to it. (Trainee, London 2005)

The fear of being ill-prepared is linked to the fear of harming or losing patients. In terms of losing patients, the majority of trainees, when asked, awkwardly admitted to feeling anxious about what patients leaving precipitously would entail. As trainees have to treat patients long-term to fulfil assessment criteria, losing a patient after only one year would cancel that training case—this would mean starting from scratch with a new patient and having all that time and work not count. That this plays into concerns about extending training, and that these concerns might influence trainees' clinical work, was something I put to one Dean of Training—she responded:

> I think the problem about how this anxiety affects the training case has not been very deeply explored [by the community]... yes, we do not know how this anxiety might affect practice, especially during the first months. (Dean of Training, London, 2005)

Accompanying these concerns about readiness and fear of failure, are those relating to the patient failing, worsening greatly, or even committing suicide. These are concerns that afflict all therapists to some degree, but especially the novice. New therapists not only fear for the patient, but fear that failure will reflect badly upon them, constituting the definitive judgement on their competence and suitability. One psychotherapist says:

> Therapists who worry that a patient will 'die on them', really suffer. Most likely they are really trying to do their job, with all the thoughtfulness and energy this calls for, but they expend an enormous extra amount of energy worrying that the patient's failure or dread outcome may hurt them—the therapist. This kind of worry can wear a therapist out. (Charny 1996, p. 23)

The following vignette shows in magnified form the kind of worries many trainees entertain. In a space of a few minutes this inexperienced trainee became subject to a series of stresses which play upon most therapists' minds at one time or another:

> I had been seeing a patient for only about five weeks. She was extremely depressed and would often talk of fantasies about jumping from the local quarry... On the sixth session I went out into the waiting area as usual to collect her—but she wasn't there. So I went back to check after five minutes, then after ten, and again after fifteen—she still wasn't there. Well with these passing minutes you can imagine my growing fear. I checked and re-checked the appointment book for a cancellation—there was nothing. I decided to wait a few minutes more before phoning the clinic's manager... but it was while waiting that I became my most disturbed and frightened. I thought I'd lost her, I was so scared. I paced my room thinking—I should have done this or done that, my God! Maybe I should have made that intervention! A better therapist would have—I should have worked harder, or taken the

threats more seriously... I also dreaded how this would reflect on me! Basically I panicked... these minutes have stuck with me; they woke me up to what we as therapists actually do. (Trainee, London 2005)

When tragedies occur, whether in the form of suicide or in less severe instances of 'backsliding' or patient termination, an enormous amount of guilt may follow. Another therapist continues:

When a professional is entrusted with responsibility for stemming a patient's bad fate and fails, there are actually several objective levels of guilt that are triggered... They are part of the job. One is—how can I enjoy my life and work when this human being—the patient—no longer can? Sometimes there is also guilt over hostile impulses that were (quite naturally) within the therapist's soul and *might* have contributed to the patient's sad outcome. Another is guilt for not really trying hard enough... (Charny 1996, p. 24)

The various stresses therapists endure are more testing for those lacking the armoury of experience. For trainees these encounters might be raw, formative, and powerful—striking deep into areas unprotected by the confidence won from years of practice. These stresses again can generate fantasies in abundance. Patient assertions that leave seasoned practitioners unruffled can easily unsettle novices. Perversions, dark fantasies, and confessions of self-hate resonate more forbiddingly in unaccustomed ears, filling the interstice of inexperience with trepidation. So while tested practitioners might 'just know' when a suicide threat is critical, novices rarely trust whether they do. They are more wary, cautious, and fretful than their seniors, usually more to their own than to their patient's detriment.

When facing these pressures, it is understandable that trainees look to elders for a steady arm—supervision provides opportunity for this. And so the regression that 'patients in need' undergo in relation to the 'needed therapist', is strangely replicated between supervisor and trainee—similar dynamics emerge; parallel gratitudes, allegiances, and dependencies crystallise. We thus envisage a chain of reliance from patient to trainee to supervisor to institute. For the first time trainees merge into a communal task—the united experience of healing. With this union they are now distinguished from outsiders. The trainee's progress into the domain of practice is therefore also a movement into community, into an *insider* status won by experience alone. In Houseman's and Severi's (1998) terms, we might say that by embarking on practice trainees have taken a decisive step on their incremental movement towards 'inclusion' in the dominant pole, the qualified, as their identity with the lesser pole, the non-ratified, is simultaneously being shed.

All these features (fear of failure, of readiness, of patient decline) I would argue constitute the second suite of subjective conditions, themselves generated by social conditions, rendering trainees more susceptible to the leadership and suggestions of the learned. In the next section I describe a third susceptibility—one not emerging from the many apprehensions and fantasies accompanying training, but one generated by the trainee's desire to accrue clinical mastery and confidence as training proceeds.

THE PULL AND THRILL OF MASTERY

The final susceptibility does not emerge from the many apprehensions and fantasies that accompany certain rites of training, but rather from the delight of accruing practical mastery as training proceeds. Authors such as Liberman (1978b), Bandura (1977) and Calestro (1972: 97-9) have shown that patients respond well to practitioners who are assured and confident in practice: as patients learn to understand and cope with their distress from an authoritative other they gain a sense of control over their problems, which is vital for healing. Other anthropologists, if only in passing, have referred to how 'developing expertise' facilitates processes of professional transformation. Following authors such as Torrey (1986) and Ehernwald (1966), for instance, the anthropologist Kleinman (1988: 188) points out that therapists must believe in their power to heal if they are to embody the comfort essential to successful practice. As Samuels has said:

> It is well-known that patients benefit when the analyst
> has conviction (or faith) in his theoretical ideas and
> clinical practices, no matter how deviant these may
> seem to be. (Samuels 1989: 7)

However, such comfort with, and conviction in, one's theoretical beliefs and growing expertise, as Luhrmann has shown in the
case of psychiatry (Luhrmann 2000: 203-30), on the flipside might
encourage undue confidence in one's ideas and abilities which in
turn may support a kind of rigid or dogmatic form of practice. Cassell's (1987) work also explores some negative consequences of belief in mastery: she shows that as a surgeon's expertise grows, his
or her propensity to deny or project doubt and paranoia onto unsuspecting 'others' (nurses, junior doctors) develops proportionately.[145]

While these explorations of the merits and demerits of mastery
differ in their points of emphasis, none of them overtly contradict
the observation that to *feel* masterful in any given endeavour neces-
sitates certain noticeable preconditions—and as these preconditions may be operative for the psychoanalytic practitioner let me
elaborate on them further.

To start, a sense of mastery is rarely experienced by those
doubtful of the worth of their craft. To use techniques that are sold
as efficacious but that are felt to be coloured with falsehood engenders more disquietude than confidence. Distrust in one's practice, as the psychiatrist in Peter Shaffer's *Equus* laments, often endows practitioners with feelings of fraudulency. If my craft is questionable, and I sense its questionability, then I dispense it with
great unease. And while it is true that this equation by no means
universally applies—indeed, we can recall Lévi-Strauss' discussion
of the young sorcerer, Quesalid, who, despite his disbelief in the
project of sorcery, managed to practice his craft with the veneer of
conviction (Lévi-Strauss 1963: 175-178)[146]—it is also clear that in
most cases it is essential for practitioners to largely concur with the
claims of their craft if they are to acquire the clear conscience
needed to delight in its employment; for indeed, even Quesalid became a believer in the end.[147]

In all my formal and informal encounters I very rarely met therapists who denied to therapeutic claims any objective validity.

Therapists, philosophically speaking, were more 'realist' than this, seeing their theoretical utterances as largely mapping psychic actualities. While in their public roles it is true that they often conceded that psycho-dynamics, as one therapist phrased it, 'could not be seen through microscopes' and that therefore they were largely 'hypothetical', it was also true that therapists privately attributed them with far more factuality than the term 'hypothetical' denotes. Emotionally speaking, these linkages resonate for therapists to the extent that belief in them constitutes a kind of meta-belief, making the use of 'hypothesis' a lip-serving device to appease those unconvinced by the reality of unconscious dynamics.

If believing in the merit of one's system is a precondition for acquiring a 'sense of mastery' then a further precondition is the belief that seniors perceive you as proficient in your craft. The fruits of being seen as possessing technical flair (e.g. peer respect; and, for the trainee, the privileges of the committee's regard), is not only the inspiration prompting the novice onwards, but the incentive to submit to the instruction of the learned. The approval of seniors is crucial since perceiving oneself as competent is largely dependent on the agreement of those 'in the know'. It is in this sense that the *subjective feeling* of competency can be said to be *socially ascribed*, as it stems from the approval of those qualified to judge. Thus trainees are dependent upon such approval since without it they are in danger of experiencing their self-belief as illegitimate. Dependency is likely to make trainees more partial to the instruction of seniors, since, as we have seen, seniors are regarded as embodying the standards of good practice, and so trainees are more prone to emulate their ways as these are the ways proven to be effective. Thus a route to acquiring the elders' approval is to follow their example and instruction.

To illustrate this fact let me now provide a concrete example of one technique trainees hope to master with the guidance of seniors.

THE TECHNIQUE OR DEVICE OF 'CONFRONTATION'

One supervisor stated:

Knowing theory is just cerebration unless it can influence how you are with the patient... It's about paying attention to significant moments which others would ignore, and then using these moments to give force to your interventions in ways that will shift patients towards insight and health... you have to expose to patients the aspects of themselves they are unable to see. (Psychodynamic Supervisor 2004)

Before illustrating the technique of using 'significant moments' to draw the patient's attention to hidden aspects of themselves as an example of a skill the trainee must master, here is a third-year trainee elaborating metaphorically on the means by which therapists encourage patients to apprehend hitherto concealed aspects of themselves; a technique formally known as 'confrontation':[148]

It is as if you have a mirror which you must hold up to the patient at just the right time, to say—look, do you see! This is more difficult than it sounds as the reflection you show isn't always pleasant—it can be grossly disturbing, actually demonic [for the patient] —and so you are never sure how the patient will react (defensively, psychotically, they might crumble, resist, or be illuminated). Things that have been repressed always return with an emotional charge. (Third Year Trainee 2005)

Shane, a fourth-year trainee, in the following extract provided an example of 'confrontation' at work. This patient in question was a thirty year-old man who still lived with his mother. This patient to his own regret had never experienced a lasting intimate relationship. In what follows Shane recounts the moment when he leads his patient to apprehend the bearing living with his mother has had on his relationships with women:

Well it was during this one session when he was going on in a kind of monologue, but this time about a woman he'd met during the week, so I was alert—he was saying, she was this she was that, a 'bit fussy', a 'bit dull', she was on the whole 'not right'. So I questioned him:

'Not right?'

'Well you know,' he replied flippantly.

I was silent momentarily, and then said very carefully,

'I know what?'

He responded again in an offhand kind of way, 'Well, you know.'

'Actually,' (I pushed a little harder now) 'I don't know—why don't you tell me?'

Now he looked visibly irritated and responded: 'If you don't know I shouldn't have to tell you.'

I was silent again and then said.

'Again, tell me what?'

This was the final straw and he finally snapped: 'Look, isn't it clear? I could never live with my mother and a woman like that!'

At this his hands went up to his mouth and his eyes looked about distractedly as it slowly dawned on him what he had actually said. (Fourth Year Trainee 2005)

Learning to seize opportunities to 'confront' the patient is a subtle affair as such opportunities can easily be squandered. Another fourth-year student illustrated with palpable regret how she let one such moment pass:

I am struggling to get this one patient to *feel* things—he is so in his head. During a recent session he said that I judged him. Now this comment was significant because my patient had always felt severely judged and this feeling has inhibited him in many areas of his life. So now I had something important here, this confession, but instead of getting the patient to stay with this feeling, I said: 'Isn't it interesting that you should feel this way about me!' Now that was completely the wrong thing to say—the word 'interesting' took him back into his head (he thought 'does she think I am wrong then?'—'is this something I should be con-

cerned about?' and so on) and so I'd lost my opportunity to remain with the feeling... [and] encourage
the projection... [and thus] make him confront through
me the internal judge that has been plaguing him for
so long. (Forth Year Trainee 2005)

This trainee conveyed this story to me with a self-recrimination
that was illustrative of how crucial 'getting it right' is for the therapist. The therapist feels the art of making successful interventions
is so essential to master since opportunities to 'shift' patients come
by rarely—therapists can work for weeks or months struggling to
gain the patient's trust and to obtain the facts required to make effective interventions. Thus, instruction is sought-for not solely because it offers a means for winning approval (which is a precondition for feeling competent), but since it is also thought to offer
genuine insight into how to succeed in the art of psychotherapy.

The institutional conditions so far identified provoke powerful
subjective states disposing trainees towards conformity and dependence. This is consistent with Frank and Frank's (1993 [1961]:
195) comments regarding dependency: that it inclines trainees to
'imitate' supervisors and leaders. While such imitation or 'model-
ling' has been shown to be one of the most powerful mechanisms
of learning, especially in children (Bandura 1977), in psychotherapy this mechanism is activated by conditions unique to the training context: while supervisors' guidance alleviates the anxieties of
inexperience, supervisors also stand as the 'embodied answer' to
the question 'what do trainers want?'—Imitation, then, not only
provides a source of learning, and a source for feelings of self-com-
petence, but also a palliative for 'evaluation apprehension' and its
associated fears (i.e. fear of failing, of negative judgement [and
what this means], etc.).

In sum, although I found no evidence that the conditions of
training were *consciously* designed to arouse susceptibilities to conform to seniors' expectations, deeper inspection of such conditions
reveals how instrumental they might be in securing trainee conformity and re-organising the trainee's subjectivity. That transformation occurs under stressful conditions is a fact long known by
anthropologists (La Fontaine 1985; Richards 1956; Herdt 1987;
Turner 1967), but what is particular to this context is not only the

configuration of stresses aroused, and the tacit conditions which help to produce them, but the unique modes of practice and belief to which these institutional conditions give rise.

CONCLUDING CHAPTERS SIX AND SEVEN

I commenced this chapter by cataloguing psychoanalytic aetiology within a wider system of classification. I did this to apprehend clearly, through contrast and comparison, the exact species of aetiology embraced. I then discussed how this understanding of causality guides psychoanalytic interpretation and intervention, endowing practitioners with conviction that they have something vital to offer the emotionally troubled.

Furthermore, I described some key stressors fostered by the conditions of the institute, noting how they render trainees susceptible to the convictions and leadership of senior members. By recognising 'institutional stressors' as creating 'private susceptibilities' I have indicated that clinical supervision cannot be read as a disembodied event, shorn from the subjective mood that the social conditions of the institute generate. Supervision, as with all other aspects of training, transpires in an atmosphere in which subjectivies are largely poised in postures of receptiveness. This receptiveness strengthens the therapeutic imagination and facilitates the embodiment of the *internalising mono-directive* practice characteristic of psychodynamic intervention.

To account for the existence of these susceptibilities by recourse to 'institutional stressors' and the 'thrill of mastery' in no measure exhausts the matter. As I recalled mid-way through this chapter, trainees enter the institute with a disposition of partiality towards the theories and techniques they hope to master. Owing to this we might say that trainees already possess a susceptibility to be susceptible to the conditions which facilitate the embodiment of psychoanalytic practice and belief. In the next and final chapter I wish to plunge headlong into an investigation of this primary susceptibility, one which makes psychotherapy so alluring to those who decide to undergo the trials of professional socialisation. What is it about the profession of psychotherapy that so appeals? How does the transformation it brings affect the new therapist's life? And what do we mean precisely when we say that training transforms the individual?—to what effect, and in what direction? I shall now invest my energies in exploring these questions, for I believe that by doing so not only will we take one step further towards understanding the deeper meaning of psychoanalytic socialisation, but through this we will approach nearer to discerning the aims of the psychoanalytic movement itself.

CHAPTER EIGHT
THE TRANSFORMED PRACTITIONER

In the preceding chapters I have followed as a process the core stages of psychodynamic training. After describing in chapter one the socio-historical scene in which the psychodynamic institute is situated, in chapters two and three I proceeded to consider the therapeutic encounter through which all trainees must pass. I argued that pre-training therapy is the first domain in which the psychodynamic imagination is cultivated. In chapters four and five I turned to the second stage of training: the seminar encounter. Here I focused on the transmission of therapeutic knowledge and the methods of doubt management the institute can call upon to safeguard the psychodynamic vision from the provocations of dissent. I illustrated that psychodynamic socialisation is predominantly circumscribed and 'affirmative', preferring the fostering of dispositions that are consonant with institutional aims. Finally, in chapters six and seven, through assessing the final stage of clinical supervision, I described not only the kind of aetiological vision therapists learn to adopt, but also some of the institutional stressors evoked to hasten transformation in institutionally desired directions.

With my discussion of the core stages of therapeutic socialisation complete, in this my final chapter I wish to now pass beyond the stages of professional socialisation in order to gain a clearer impression as to the bearing assimilated psychodynamic dispositions have upon the transformed practitioner's life. By this method I aim to uncover the background against which the deeper significance of psychotherapeutic socialisation can be revealed. There are two means by which to achieve this end. In the first place I shall expose some of the tacit commitments that the therapeutic project subtly demands. By considering data gathered from informal surveys and from my participatory observations, and by relating these data to certain hidden ethical, political, and communal commitments that the psychoanalytic ethos obliges, I will highlight how the 'professional' ethos permeates the 'private' sphere of therapists' lives. I shall argue that it is the trainee's desire to be subject to this very permeation that largely constitutes their primary susceptibility to the world of therapy, as I discussed in the previous chapter. Secondly, by studying the personal biography of one seasoned practitioner, I shall show how these commitments play themselves out in the practitioner's total life. By considering these commitments through the prism of his person, we will gain insight into why the genealogical structure is ordered as it is, and further reveal that therapy, aside from its position as a clinical practice, takes up a central place in the practitioner's search for private meaning and personal orientation.

The Mythic World

Earlier in chapter two I mentioned that anthropologists such as Dow (1986), Kleinman (1988), and Calestro (1972) have emphasised the centrality of the therapist's myth in facilitating healing. They understand by 'myth' a system of interlinking symbols and ideas which, on composite, provides a frame of orientation through which the origin and nature of the patient's problem can be framed and understood. Healing transpires when patients become attached to this system and learn to articulate their private world in its terms. That this composite is itself linked to wider systems of meaning ensures that its adherents enjoy a wider integration— private experience is given public orientation and through this reconciliation the straying individual is once again incorporated within the whole. Dow (1986) labelled this system a mythic world —'mythic' because for him and others the question whether this explanatory system corresponds to empirical reality was not the essential fact. What mattered was whether it held experiential truth for its users, since it was from such 'belief' that its efficacy was

gained. In this they diverged little from Lévi-Strauss' attitude towards shamanic myth:

> That the mythology of the shaman [or psychoanalyst]
> does not correspond to objective reality does not mat-
> ter. The patient believes in it and belongs to a society
> that believes in it. The protecting spirits, the evil spir-
> its... are elements of a coherent system which are the
> basis of the native's concept of the universe. The pa-
> tient accepts them, or rather she has never doubted
> them. (Lévi-Strauss 1967: 217)

At this point it is interesting to note that the symbolists, by referring to the therapeutic system as 'mythic', have not strayed far
from the attitude Freud sometimes took regarding his own theoretical construct. When defining his theory of the instincts he wrote:

> the theory of the instincts *is so to say our mythology*. In-
> stincts are mythical entities, magnificent in their indef-
> initeness. In our work we cannot for a moment disreg-
> ard them, yet we are never sure that we are seeing
> them clearly. (Freud 1977 [1932]: 127)

The difference between the symbolists and Freud is that while
Freud himself located the efficacy of the myth in the close correspondence it bore to reality, the symbolists, like Lévi-Strauss, located its efficacy in the adherent's 'belief' that it corresponds—a belief endowing the mythic with active power to both affect the individual and to influence the social world (Calestro 1972: 97).[149]

By locating the effective power of the myth in belief, these
scholars studied the psychotherapeutic 'mythic world' from a very
specific standpoint. As pointed out in chapter three, they were not
concerned with how the myth worked alongside other forms of
healing (e.g. sensory healing) to effect individual change, and
neither did they show, as I shall soon illustrate, that the inspira-
tional authority the myth wields acts as a scaffold supporting and
endowing meaning to the lives of those administering it. That they
overlooked this latter point is understandable, firstly because they
were more interested in how the myth heals the patient than how it

sustains the practitioner; and secondly because their investigations endeavoured to illustrate psychotherapeutic healing as but a subset of symbolic healing—an emphasis explaining their indifference to the role the myth played in the therapist's professional or private life. Therefore, as the aim of their investigations was to understand how the mythic / symbolic furthered psychotherapeutic healing, they pursued a question quite different from the one that we must try to answer here: for those who administer the myth, for those supposedly already healed and integrated, what function does the myth perform?

To address this question we must concentrate our interest on the function of myth, not for the patients it transforms and heals but for the therapists it serves and supports. It is fitting at this point to quote Malinowski on myth, the first anthropologist, it must be remembered, to truly engage Freud in a battle of ideas:

> Studied alive [i.e. by the anthropologist] myth... is not an explanation in satisfaction of a scientific interest, but a narrative resurrection of a primeval reality, told in satisfaction of deep religious wants, moral cravings, social submissions, assertions, even practical requirements. Myth fulfils an... indispensable function: it expresses, enhances, and codifies belief; it safeguards and enforces morality; it vouches for the efficiency of ritual and contains practical rules for the guidance of man. Myth is thus a vital ingredient of human civilization; it is not an idle tale... but a pragmatic charter of primitive faith and moral wisdom. (Malinowski 1971 [1926]: 79)

It is with these words in mind that I shall embark upon an exploration of three such functions of the therapeutic myth—the ethical, the political, and, in the end, the communal.[150]

THE ETHICAL

A moral scheme which came to dominate Europe from the twelfth century until the early modern period can be traced to the Nicomachean Ethics where Aristotle draws a fundamental contrast between two states of man: between 'man-as-he-happens-to-be' and 'man-as-he-could-be-if-he-realised-his-own-essential-nature' (MacIntyre 2004 [1981]: 52). Ethics thus conceived is a rational enquiry into how we might successfully move from our 'given' state to our 'transformed' state. The following investigation seeks to reach clear proscriptions that will guide individuals towards their telos, their end, towards a kind of existence where their 'essential nature' becomes actualised. This idea of human transformation presupposes a potentiality in individuals to convert their raw, instinctual nature into more polished examples of humanity. If we are to move into the full-born state of human completion, our desires and impulses must be put in order by the cultivation of habits and the embodiment of precepts consistent with these highest aims.

The Aristotelian idea that reaching our full potential requires a transformative act has resurfaced in different redemptive projects that have on occasion added to, if not sometimes complicated, the foundational idea that salvation presupposes ethical transformation (MacIntyre 2004 [1981]: 53). Whether predominantly rationalistic, empirical, or symbolic foundations have been used to buttress a given ethic, the generic feature of all such ethical projects is that their legitimacy is derived from their appeals to authority, whether this authority is scriptural or rational, revelatory or empirical, symbolic, or some integration of these.

The relevance of these comments when assessing the system of psychotherapy becomes palpable if we acknowledge that psychotherapy as it exists for the majority of its practitioners constitutes a system with a transformative imperative at its heart, an imperative, as with other such systems, which comes complete with legitimating pillars of symbol and concept. It is in this sense that the psychotherapeutic system differs little from systems which legitimate the transformations they endorse by having recourse to wider systems of knowledge and meaning, whether symbolic, empirical, or rationalistic in kind.

With this said, my first step is to show how the ethic and the mythic are linked in psychoanalytic psychotherapy—i.e. how the therapeutic system can be seen as an ethical system. Therefore let me first identify the ethical aim integral to dynamic psychotherapy by looking to the various therapeutic objectives as outlined by some of its foremost contributors. This teleological perspective reveals that all psychodynamic schools possess ethical imperatives despite these imperatives and the means to reach them being variously defined. Whether these goals are subsumed under the concept of 'genitality' as in libido theory; under 'active creative will' as in Rankian theory; under 'social interest' as the Adlerians once stressed; or whether in terms of the 'integrated self' of Sullivan; the 'productive personality' of Fromm; the 'secure personality' of Bowlby; or the 'mature personality' of Stern—all such utterances, as Marmor has commented, express the differing but decidedly ethical aim of helping the individual to achieve greater emotional maturity, to love unselfishly, to sustain and create healthy relationships, to work effectively, and to be a socially responsible and productive human being within the limits of his or her capacity (Marmor 1962: 288). In other words, while there is disagreement about the exact ideas concerning how to conceptualise personality development, and about the nature of the human telos, there is a firm consensus that the route to health always entails a qualitative and thus ethical transformation. To provide an example of this ethical imperative it is useful to turn to Freud's mature theory where his ideas on 'civilisation' and the 'purpose of life' are revealed at their fullest.

With regard to the treatment of the individual, Freud in his mature stage was more occupied with an ethical aim than is generally believed. This interest is reflected in his ideas on the principle human instincts. These are understood in terms of a dualistic scheme which traces all psychological phenomena to two basic but contrary drives—Eros and Thanatos, the life and death instincts. In respect of Thanatos, for example, the compulsion to repeat, technically known as 'repetition compulsion', a compulsion which is central to his ideas of regression, repression, and human aggression, has its ultimate ground, as Freud tells us, in that instinct

> inherent [in] inorganic life to restore an earlier state of things which the living entity has been obliged to abandon under the pressure of external disturbing forces. (Freud 1955 [1920]: 36)

When we inquire as to what exactly this instinct aims to achieve, we are told:

> If we are to take it as a truth that knows no exception that everything living dies for internal reasons—becomes inorganic once again—then we shall be compelled to say that 'the aim of all life is death' and, looking backwards, that 'inanimate things existed before living ones'. (Freud 1955 [1920]: 38)

This primordial pull towards dissolution in the inorganic is the drag of the death instinct—a force permeating all phenomena and acting contrarily to the force of Eros, the drive towards life. If the death instinct tends to inertia, the life instinct alternatively finds its fullest expression in what Freud regarded as the highest of human activities—the perpetuation and development of civilisation. He characterised civilisation as:

> a process in the service of Eros, whose purpose is to combine single human individuals, and after that families, then races, peoples and nations, into one great unity of mankind. But man's natural aggressive instinct, the hostility of each against all and all against each, oppose this programme of civilisation. This aggressive instinct is the derivative and the main representative of the death instinct which we have found alongside Eros and which shares world-dominion with it. And now, I think, the meaning of the evolution of civilisation is no longer obscure to us. It must present the struggle between Eros and Death, between the instinct of life and the instinct of destruction as it works itself out in the human species. This struggle is what all life essentially consists of, and the evolution of civilisation may therefore be simply described as the struggle for life of the human species. And it is the battle of the giants that our nurse-maids try to appease with their lullaby about Heaven. (Cited in Storr 1989: 53)

What long ago began as a medical cure in a small Austrian consulting room, at its end wins for itself a decisive place in this cosmic struggle between the forces of dark and light.[151] As Freud tells us, the essential role psychoanalysis is to play in this unfolding epic consists in effecting 'the liberation of the human being from his neurotic symptoms, inhibitions, and abnormalities of character'—an essential liberation required to strip individuals of the illusions keeping them trapped in primitive stages of human development (Freud 1955: 316). When consciousness expands to uproot repressions and to place fortifications against future regressions, greater freedom, liberation and consciousness will be attained. Freud likened the task of augmenting consciousness to certain mystical objectives which seek to move the individual towards more evolved stages of humanity. As he says:

> we have to admit that the therapeutic efforts of psychoanalysis have chosen a similar point of approach. Its intention is to strengthen the Ego, to make it more independent from the Super-Ego, to enlarge its field of observation, so it can appropriate for itself new parts of the id. Where there was Id there shall be Ego. (Freud 1977 [1932]: 112)

Indeed, where there was darkness there shall be light. And therefore once the ego owns more of the internal expanse it can now participate more fully in the correct business of life:

> The neurotic who is cured really becomes another man, he has become what he might have become at best under the most favourable conditions. (Freud 1975 [1916-17]: 486-7)

From these observations it is clear that psychoanalysis has a transformative agenda at its heart, an agenda, as I will show, that has not only remained a quiet and steady pulse throughout the history of psychotherapy, but, as we can see, and as is the case with many other redemptive projects, has gained its momentum from a symbolic or conceptual base which inspires the personal aspirations needed to attain the ethical end.

From my discussion here and in other sections (see chapter three) I have shown that since the psychotherapeutic myth holds that greater release from unconscious determinants equips individuals with greater personhood (a quality indispensable to furthering civilisation), it is embedded within a larger cosmology linking individual transformation with a grander project of the progress of human existence. Furthermore, as the mythic contains claims that if it is followed it will safeguard against the ruinous eventuality of poor mental health, the mythic can evoke in adherents concern to act in ways consistent with its suggestions and imperatives. So far as the mythic, then, generates aspirations to act in ways that, from the standpoint of the psychodynamic tradition, are deemed beneficial to the individual, we are obliged to speak of the mythical as supporting ethical and, consequently, instrumental life. In this sense we might say that the mythic is socially embodied, since the social actions stemming from it more or less bear the imprint of these mythic beliefs.

The fact that the redemptive aim of psychotherapy is fundamental to its design has rendered therapy for the majority of its practitioners into more than simply a medical cure. With its driving ethical aim it promises its own kind of salvation which might be won in ever greater degrees—not only for the patients it heals but for the practitioners it supports. In other words, if Freud has argued for the importance of therapy in curing the neurotic, let me provide some evidence for its importance in sustaining the practitioner in both the consulting room and in his or her wider life. To achieve this end I shall invoke the results of an informal survey sent out to experienced psychoanalytic practitioners based in London and the South East.[152]

In this survey, which I intend only as an informal investigation, I asked a series of open questions about what it means to be psychotherapist. The relevant question for our immediate discussion concerned whether or not therapists had submitted to more personal therapeutic analyses since graduation. Out of the 42 surveys returned, 38 respondents admitted to re-entering therapy after they had completed their training and training analysis. Of these respondents, 11 had embarked on one further long-term analysis; 12 had submitted to two further analyses; 4 had been in analysis a further 3 times; 1 a further 4 times; and 2 more than 6 times. In all, only 4 therapists out of the 42 respondents claimed to have never re-entered personal therapy after completing training.[153]

When asking therapists why they had returned to analysis, we find some interesting responses:

> Analysis is never complete: with new life stages there are new life problems to be dealt with... therapy has helped me at these times.

> I have used therapy to overcome resistances to patients and to work out problems in my own life.

> It has helped me with my ongoing personal development.

> My analyses have helped deepen my understanding of myself and the therapeutic process.

> My training analysis was with a woman, so I thought I would learn something new from therapy with a man—new transferences, etc.

> Continuing personal growth.

> Help me progress professionally and personally.

In short, not only do the majority of therapists submit to additional therapy over the course of their careers, but the reasons they gave for this attendance were just as much to do with their personal as with their professional growth and development. For most therapists, then, personal exploration does not cease with training, but continues via the medium of personal therapy. And because therapy is itself supported by the mythic, the therapeutic myth supports practitioners' ongoing personal development through their submission to further personal analyses.

This supportive function of the myth is further suggested when considering figures gathered on whether qualified practitioners continue to engage in self-analysis throughout their careers. ('Self-analysis' is here defined as 'the monitoring of their unconscious processes'.) Of the 42 asked, 41 unequivocally asserted that self-analysis played a very regular and prominent part in their lives. As different practitioners tell us:

> My work with every patient includes self-analysis in thinking and processing—this is central to my work and my life.

> [*How often do you engage in self analysis?*] All the time.

> Continuously.

> Self-reflection many times a day—not sure I call it self-analysis.

> Most of the time—it is a way of life not something to do in organised 'sessions'.

> YES, especially if difficulties occur in the treatment of patient—I discuss with my supervisor.

> Who doesn't?—Every day and all the time.

> Constantly—unconsciously to a greater extent, but consciously due to my long hours of work and my personal needs.

> Every day.

> Informally all the time, probably.

> I continue to monitor and examine and explore myself every day.

> Yes, of course, who doesn't?

> Psychoanalysis becomes a 'way of living' and one goes on using it to understand oneself and others all

one's life. I always try to be honest about my feelings
and behaviour.

Later in this chapter I shall look at the methods by which such
self-analysis is assisted, but for now let it suffice to say that these
comments should not surprise us given what we have already
learned about the redemptive and thus transformative project of
psychotherapy; a project that is obvious enough in respect of patients, but which is less so when considering the lives of practitioners. In short, psychotherapists believe that therapeutic ideas pronounce just as much on the state of their own souls as on those of
their patients. For trainees learn early to believe that the reach of
the psychoanalytic imagination extends to the whole variegated
domain of human peculiarity—hence the conclusion that it may be
profitably applied to their own peculiarity. For those living under
the influence of these imperatives continuing self-analysis and personal therapy follow as natural responses. This justification for the
self-administration of therapeutic ideas explains why the mythic is
not something merely believed but something personally embodied and, ultimately, enacted.

THE POLITICAL

During the period of the London Blitz the psychoanalytic community was in crisis. Anna Freud and Melanie Klein, at that time
the dominant figures of the psychoanalytic movement, were irreconcilable on a principle point of developmental theory—the rift
was such that the Institute of Psychoanalysis was on the brink of
irrevocable fracture. To avoid this, a series of discussions (now
known as the 'controversial discussions') were arranged by the
president of the British Society, Donald Winnicott. On the same
evening when one of these talks were in process, the German air-
force was raiding London. The first indication of the attack came
with the sirens, a warning which the members seemed determined
to disregard. It was not until the explosions approached in ever
nearing degrees of proximity, that Winnicott finally rose from his
President's chair to suggest that 'as the debate was very crucial we
must not let its outcome be decided by a bomb'. Perhaps more
troubled by this thought than by the threat to themselves, the

members gathered up their belongings and made for the door in search of a safer place to continue their discussion.[154]

This anecdote is a wonderful allegory on what many have believed to be the psychoanalytic attitude to the world 'out there'. The bombs are the mess and dirt of society's folly, while the discussion is representative of civilisation's advance amidst the barbarism of governments and their wars. This nonchalant and lofty attitude towards the business of life, if arousing some approval on this occasion, has at other times provoked reactions of a less friendly sort. To provide an example of this apolitical and asocial spirit of interiority, a spirit which has agitated so many commentators critical of psychoanalysis, here is a letter by Ernest Jones, the longest-serving president of the IPA, sent to discourage certain IPA members from making psychodynamic theory a foundation for social or political activity.

> We see once more that Politics and Science do not mix any better than oil and water. We know, as psychologists, that the motives impelling men to change a given social order are of the most varied kind, a medley of laudable and ignoble impulses in which the desire to ascertain truth seldom plays any but the most subordinate part. So that anyone engaging in such activities must necessarily be impelled by motives other than scientific ones. The master of our school, though well-known to be strongly imbued with humanitarian for the betterment of human life, has always known how to keep these strictly apart from his scientific work, which has therefore never suffered in its purity. In this, as in so many other respects, he has set us an example we should do well to follow. There are not wanting among us signs of impatience with social conditions and eagerness to engage in changing them. From what I said it follows that whoever yields to such impulses becomes by so much the less a psychoanalyst. And to attempt to propagate his particular social ideas in the name of psychoanalysis is to pervert its true nature, a misuse of psychoanalysis which I

wish to firmly denounce and repudiate. (Cited in
Young 1993: 134)

Two things here are important. Firstly, that these warnings were
not simply scaremongering. Those who tried to make an overt
political message of psychoanalysis were indeed punished. For instance, Wilhelm's Reich's expulsion from the IPA, as Steiner recalls,
was due to Reich's offensive act of 'forcing psychoanalysis to become political, psychoanalysis has no part in politics' (Steiner 1989:
59). On other occasions, as we have seen in chapter five, there have
been members, such as Karen Horney and Erich Fromm, who were
estranged for their more socio-political psychotherapy.

The second important point concerns Jones' claim that Freud
kept politics and psychoanalysis wholly separate. While this suggestion seems correct at first glance, if we probe deeper it is only
true in the most limited sense, since, as I now shall argue, it is not
so clear that psychoanalysis was entirely free of political intent. As
this query about the link between politics and psychoanalysis is essential to my immediate discussion, let me enter this controversy
further.

Many commentators have criticised the 'interiority' of the psychoanalytic community, its apolitical stance and its complicity with
the status quo. Herbert Marcuse (1966 [1955]), for instance, while
lauding psychoanalytic theory as in some sense radical, commented that what it produced in the consulting room did little to affect
social change:

> psychoanalytic therapy aims at curing the individual
> so that he can continue to function as part of a sick
> civilisation without surrendering to it altogether.
> (Marcuse 1966 [1955]: 245)

Ernest Gellner (1985) in his *The Psychoanalytic Movement* also criticised the apolitical propensity of psychotherapeutic culture:

> Freudianism was different [from Marxism] from the
> beginning it had within itself a certain tendency to-
> wards political quietism. Salvation lay in adjustment,
> a term which, in effect, depth psychology introduced

into the moral vocabulary of modern man. By implication or overtly, it preached acceptance of the external
order, which turned out to cause a measure of embar-
rassment during the Hitler period. (Gellner 1985:
xxxv)

Andrew Samuels (1993), one of the few psychotherapists who
are fearlessly critical of the tendency of psychoanalysis (and in particular the 'object-relations' school) to support the social consensus
also concurs:

Object relations theories unwittingly perpetuate the
political *status quo*... [they] focus on intrapsychic and
interpersonal explanations for personality development and dysfunction. They tend to rule out sociopol-
itical or other collective aspects of psychological suffering... For us in the West, this implies that the per-
sonality-idea (to coin a phrase) will reward personality theories that are congruent with our humanistic-
romantic-individualistic traditions... Object relations
theories may have attained their popularity, not because they mount a challenge to the existing order, but
because of this secret alignment with the existing order. (Samuels 1993: 276)

Among these commentators we might count American critics
such as Masson (1989), Lasch (1979), Sennet (1976) and Halmos
(1973), all of whom carried the same critique. The existence of this
widespread commentary raises some curious questions when set
against the fact that the founder of this apolitical movement, was,
until his eighteenth year, gripped by the ambition to become a
great political leader and social reformer.

Erich Fromm (1959), in a book dedicated to exploring Freud's
leadership aspirations, showed with impressive clarity how this
desire was a hallmark of Freud's youth. Starting from Freud's early
attachment to his closest school friend, Heinrich Braun, who was
later to become one of Germany's most prominent socialists,
Fromm shows how Freud's political aspirations directed many of
his academic choices. Fromm quotes much evidence supporting

this claim including a letter Freud wrote many years later to Braun's widow explaining their friendship:

> In the Gymnasium we were inseparable friends... All the hours of the day which were left after school I spent with him... Neither the goals nor the means for our ambitions were very clear to us. Since then I have come to the assumption that his aims were essentially negative ones. *But one thing was certain: that I would work with him and that I could never desert his party.* Under his influence I was also determined at that time to study law at university. (Fromm 1959: 74-5)

His second strong identification was with the leader of the Austrian Democratic Party, Victor Adler, whose apartment at 19 Berggasse Freud once visited as a young man. Such was Freud's regard for this place (which was known to everyone else as stuffy and impractical) that when it came up for sale some years later Freud eagerly purchased it and made it his home for the next forty-seven years. Fromm explains Freud's immediate attraction to this unattractive and untidy little home in terms of Freud's identification with the political leader for whom Freud's admiration, at the time of the sale, must have been exerting an unconscious affect.[155]

If we are to accept Fromm's claims concerning Freud's early political ambitions, how do we reconcile this young man full of heady aspiration to study law and enter government with the founder of a movement later decried for its political quietism? One possible answer is that Freud's aspirations underwent a radical transformation, turning from the brightest light to something comparatively dim. And this indeed is Jones' theory:

> what is significant is the extraordinary change that must have set in about the age of sixteen or seventeen. Gone is the pugnacious child who fought vigorously with his playfellows, the boy full of military ardour, the youth who dreamed of becoming a Cabinet Minister and ruling a nation. Was, after all, the two days' encounter with a country girl so very fateful? (Cited in Fromm 1959: 85)

Jones hints that Freud's first romantic encounter might have prompted this change. This suggestion Fromm flatly rejects. As he explains:

> Jones is simply mistaken in the assumption that all these youthful fantasies were gone. They had simply taken new forms, and partly they were less conscious. The boy who wanted to become a Cabinet Minister had become one who aspired to a new knowledge... a knowledge which was the last word in man's understanding of himself and the world. Not nationalism, not socialism, not religion could be trusted as guides to a better life; the full understanding of man's mind could show the irrationality of all these answers and could lead man as far as he was destined to go: to a sober, sceptical, rational appraisal of his past and present... Freud saw himself as the leader of an intellectual revolution, which made the last step rationalism could make. Only if one understands this aspiration of Freud to bring a new message to mankind, not a happy but a realistic one, can one understand his creation: *the psychoanalytic movement*. (Fromm 1959: 87-8)

For Fromm, then, at the age of seventeen Freud's aspiration for political leadership was repressed rather than extinguished. Thus it continued to exert a covert influence on his life playing a decisive part in Freud's eventual founding of the psychoanalytic movement, an institution providing an outlet for his leadership aspirations and for his hope to bring a new means of redemption to society.

And yet, even if we accept the plausibility of these explanations a crucial question still remains: in what sense could Freud be said to satiate his social reform tendencies if the psychoanalytic message was as anti-political as Jones, Gellner, Marcuse and others have claimed? One interesting way to approach this question is to analyse the quote from Virgil's *Aeneid* with which Freud opened *The Interpretation of Dreams*—the book which for him was to launch psychoanalysis. It runs: *flectere si nequeo superos acheronta movebo* (*Aeneid* 7: 312). 'If I cannot bend the higher powers, I will move the infernal regions'.

The only explanation Freud offers as to why after long deliberation he chose Virgil's line, is contained in a letter to Wilhelm Fliess where he briefly states that the quotation provides 'a reference to repression' (Freud 1985: 361). But what did Freud mean by this curt explanation? One reading is that given the book's principal message (i.e. the repressed will return through dreams and thus by deciphering dreams we will understand what has been repressed) the quotation communicates the secret intent of the repressed desire: 'if I cannot move your conscious intent then I shall trouble the unconscious'. This reading is satisfactory only if we ignore the wider theoretical context in which this book was situated; namely, the broader vision of the personality that Freud by this time had begun to construct.[156] If interpreted in the light of his wider vision (where Virgil's 'higher powers' alternatively refers to society and the 'infernal regions' the unconscious) then the line takes on a new meaning: 'If I, Freud, cannot bend society directly then I shall do so by moving the depths of man'.[157]

Interpreting Freud's use of Virgil in this manner is not only consistent with Freud's later ethical aim (i.e. I shall move the depths of man to create 'civilisation' on earth—helping *Eros* triumph over *Thanatos*), but it is also consistent, as we have seen, with the psychoanalytic understanding of aetiology which locates the cause of much discontent in psyche not society—an understanding of aetiology legitimating the project of tackling discontent (and its wider social consequences) through psychoanalytic intervention. In this respect we must agree with Fromm that the political agenda lives on, only now it finds its dominant outlet by making the personal the political—by bringing social salvation through individual means.[158]

One apostate psychoanalyst sums up what I am suggesting here to be the essentials of psychoanalytic social policy, by stating what a successful analysis will accomplish. She writes:

> the achievement [of healing] will have not only personal consequences for the individual and her family, *but also far-reaching significance for society as a whole.*

People who discover their past with the help of their feelings, who learn through therapy to clarify these feelings, to look for their *real causes,* and to resolve the transference, will no longer be compelled to displace their hatred onto innocents... Once they dare to see who brought them to their plight and how it was done, they will be better orientated in the present reality and able to avoid acting blindly, unconsciously. (Miller 1994:126, italics added)

In Freud's *The Future Prospects of Psycho-Analysis,* one of his first essays on the future social relevance of psychoanalysis, Freud himself writes:

The gain from illness provided by the neurosis is nevertheless on the whole and in the end detrimental to individuals as well as to society... All the energies which are to-day consumed in the production of neurotic symptoms serving the purposes of a world of phantasy isolated from reality, will, even if they cannot at once be put to uses in life, help to strengthen the clamour for the changes in our civilisation through which alone we can look for the well-being of future generations. I should therefore like to let you go with an assurance that in treating your patients psycho-analytically... you are not only giving your patients the most efficacious remedy for their sufferings that is available to-day; *you are contributing your share to the enlightenment of the community from which we expect to achieve the most radical prophylaxis against neurotic disorders along the indirect path of social authority.* (Freud 2001 [1912]: 150-151, italics added)

These ideas follow from the principle that the struggle for human salvation is not primarily decided on the social field and the manner in which it is structured and managed, but rather on the intimate ground of the human psyche which, *ex hypothesi,* precedes and presupposes society. That this social policy of self-realisation is solipsistic and supportive of an individualism corrosive of community ties and obligations is an argument rejected by therapists who consider this policy to be not at the expense, but to the advantage of, society at large.[159] To substantiate the prevalence of this attitude in the community let me place these reflections in the context of real-world data by once again citing some comments from practitioners I knew and interviewed.

In the same survey discussed in the section on ethics, and by exploiting the dichotomy between society and the individual, I asked respondents whether they believed that social reform will be better served ultimately via individual means (through changing people) or via social means (via social policy). I found their answers to support broadly the conclusion that individuals should be the point of departure for social change. For instance, although 18 out of the 31 respondents asserted that 'both' means were necessary, all 18 indicated a deep preoccupation with social policies aimed at the individual level. Viewing this in the light of the fact that 8 respondents asserted individual means, leads us to conclude that out of the 31 respondents only 5 *prioritised 'social means' as a vehicle for social reform.*

We can glean a clearer understanding of the respondents' concerns by looking at a random selection of their answers verbatim. It thus becomes clear, for instance, that of the 18 who emphasised that 'both' social and individual means were important, 12 came down on the side of education:

Social policy influencing education and support—especially for children and families

In spreading understanding in interpersonal relationships.

Educating the young thoroughly in the natural sciences.

We need politicians to effect change, but first they need some psychological insight which they don't have.

Society's 'betterment' can only come through changing attitudes (educational) and attitudes are influenced by the social policy we apply.

[Policy works] through reaching children at school /
supporting parents and families who are vulnerable.

Social policy (but this must act by changing people).

Through educating people especially in more humanistic and interpersonal ways.

And again, of those stressing the importance of individual
means we find such comments as:

I have been able to effect change through my therapeutic work.

I prefer portraits to landscapes.

Progress is more likely if it springs from individual
choice rather than being imposed by authority.

I am interested in individualist not social policy.

There is a quote from Margaret Little, I can't remember it exactly—'never believe that small groups of
people will not succeed in changing the world. It is
the only thing that has ever done so'.

I believe that improving early development and childhood experience is the key.

I am a staunch believer that in changing people we exercise the deepest kind of social policy.

I believe in individual means, I wouldn't be a therapist otherwise.

These findings of course do not allow definitive conclusions, but rather only permit the suggestion that the majority of therapists, if preferring social means, or 'both' social and individual means, do so with the caveat that these means must concentrate on reforming individuals—especially through education and early family socialisation. The conclusion they allow is thus tentative and provisional—namely, that the political preferences of those psychoanalytic practitioners who responded to the question broadly supported policies aimed at shifting the micro-processes of individuals. This reflected the wider belief that the personal is a point of departure for political change. To illustrate further evidence for this preference let me cite some impressions gathered during my time in the community itself.

The feeling for social policy which promotes therapeutic and educational agendas I observed as being far stronger than that felt for most other kinds. For instance, the therapists I knew felt passionately about disseminating therapeutic practices in deprived areas or local communities. They also expressed interest in government policies concerning education and health services—especially policy bearing upon mental health provisions in the NHS. Moreover, any projects that would further the expansion of psychotherapy into wider institutional culture were largely embraced —e.g. therapists widely supported the instituting of therapy and counselling in universities, in the work place, and in familial settings. Again this is supported by considering informal survey figures on activities expanding the therapeutic domain: of the 33 respondents asked whether they had worked to increase the institutional base of therapy, an impressive 29 asserted that they had been involved 'in some kind of promotional activity'. This might vary from setting up peer groups to founding new trainings or therapeutic services. This kind of activity is reflected in the data offered in chapter one on therapeutic expansion, which is partly explained by a public demand for therapy and partly by the colonising tendencies of those within the profession itself.

It would be untrue to say that these informal figures speak of the partiality of all therapists. The conclusion they allow is more tentative—namely, that relative to more politically active professional communities (we might think of legal and journalistic communities) psychodynamic practitioners tend in their political preferences towards policies directed at shifting the micro-processes of individuals. This reflects an attitude that I have tried to argue is not only consonant with psychodynamic theories on human transformation (civilisation as the offshoot of evolved persons) but complements and legitimates the *internalising mono-directive* practice I discussed in the previous chapter. These forms of theory and instrumentality inculcated through training thus provide an intellectual basis to the notion that the personal is a political domain. In this sense we might affirm along with Littlewood and Lipsedge that:

> Psychotherapy or 'holistic' approaches are perhaps less innocent, less free of social and political ideologies than biomedicine. (1997 [1982]: 309)

This is because they have the potential to control individuals by leading those subject to psychoanalytic ideas to embody specified modes of social action.

THE COMMUNAL AND IDENTITY

If the ethical and political lives of therapists are more congruent than not with the dominant claims of their assimilated 'mythic world', then in some measure we can speak of these claims as being analogous to and supportive of practitioners' ethical and political proclivities. To concern ourselves now with the last of the three suggested dimensions that the mythic supports, let us supplement the conclusions so far with a discussion of the communal.

As the mythic is vouchsafed to trainees during the various stages of training, here I shall argue that the mythic forms the basis of a human community or association that provides identity and belonging to its graduate members. Furthermore, I shall argue that this association is fostered in particular via processes of 'identification' and 'differentiation': identification being the process by which graduates come to associate and identify with certain therapeutic ideas and schools, while differentiation is what leads trainees at the same time to distance or disassociate themselves from competing schools. That these identifications and differentiations ultimately uphold the fractured state of the community is a further point I shall explore.

Before proceeding to analyse these two processes, let me first make some introductory comments about the role of the mythic in supporting the communal. The psychodynamic community builds its identity substantially around a specialised body of knowledge and organised enquiry; in our case what we have called the mythic world. This is partly in keeping with Larson's suggestion that professions develop an 'exclusive cognitive identity', which not only provides the basis for the goods or skills particular to that profession, but which enables the profession to convert its specialised knowledge and skills into social and economic rewards (Sinclair 1997: 14). If Larson is interested in linking professional identity to economic action, it is clear that other linkages exist. In other words, many communities, professional or otherwise, possess identities that entail a multiplicity of commitments and incentives not reducible to the purely economic. Alliances sustained in social clubs, trade unions, or old-school syndicates, for instance, often constitute groups based on deeper ties of association and obligation than those established on pecuniary interests alone; while communities formed predominantly on the basis of shared ideals, beliefs, and aspirations will often contain members who invest themselves far more personally. We might think here of charismatic groups (Csordas 2002), contemporary witchcraft covens (Luhrmann 1989), New Age movements (Heelas 1996), Freemasonry societies (Hutton 1999), and in our case, psychotherapeutic groups. What is essential is that communities of this latter kind will invariably contain a high proportion of members who are personally and often passionately involved, since beliefs, whether religious, political or philosophical, constitute a vital part of a person's sense of identity (Storr 1989). Furthermore, as these binding commitments are considerably strong, and are, as is the case in psychotherapy, continually under threat by neighbouring movements and wider social trends (see chapter one), tendencies to bind closely together through identification as well as inclinations to distance others through differentiation are features that might be particularly pronounced. To now clarify these two processes of identification and differentiation and to show that they are embedded in wider social processes, I shall relate them to the existing concepts of 'social consensus' and 'social conflict' of which we can say they are accompaniments.[160]

LOOKING TO DURKHEIM, MARX, AND EVANS-PRITCHARD

The first social theorist to put the idea of social consensus at the heart of social enquiry was Emile Durkheim (1915). He believed that social institutions (e.g. the religious, the legal, the political, etc.) by working in interdependent and harmonious relationship, secured the smooth functioning of the particular society in which they operated. These interrelations had an analogue in the human body where the health of the organism depends upon each organ fulfilling its proper function. And just as in biology where the function of each organ can only be understood when related to the functioning of other organs, so in sociology no social institution could be studied in abstraction from other institutions with which it interrelates. Durkheim's belief that such interdependence characterised all societies provided the basis for his general methodology: the relationships existing between institutions within one society must be identified so that they could be compared with institutional relationships occurring in other societies. This comparative approach aimed to arrive at generalisations about the functioning of 'society' per se.

While Durkheim's sociology clearly offered a 'consensus' model of society (its comprising institutions worked harmoniously for the good of the whole), other theorists believed that it was the 'conflict' existing between institutions that defined society. Marx and many of his followers saw the dominant social institutions (classes) as expressions of the material foundations of production which, when working with the social relations of production, together constituted 'modes of production' that served the interests of particular groups. As the economic success of one group rested upon the economic disadvantage of another, Marx asserted that society did not function for the good of the whole (as Durkheim supposed) but at the expense of certain groups or classes. Social relations were thus in a perpetual state of either covert or overt conflict.

These two approaches, which stressed consensus and conflict respectively, found an unlikely and rarely acknowledged integration in the 'segmentary model' of society advanced by Evans-Pritchard in his study of the Nuer (1959). Evans-Pritchard realised that in lineage systems where descent was defined in terms of individuals' identifications with successively more distant apical ancestors, both consensus and conflict became indispensable mechanisms in maintaining social cohesion. The institution which thrived on consensus and conflict was the acephalous or 'headless' non-centralised political system. This system maintained tight social organization despite the absence of overt leadership. It did so by depending upon a 'relativity of identity'—this is to say, it relied upon its individual members being able to frequently shift their social allegiances for the good of the social group. For example, two groups who reside in angry relationship within the one society, must be able to form an alliance when threatened by an external superior force. Thus groups which reside in conflict at one point in time should be able to unite themselves for the good of the social whole at another point.

While it is true that these different theorists were not directly concerned with understanding how humans use their identities, each model of social functioning implies a different idea as to how identity is used to support society. From the perspective of Durkheim's 'consensus model', an individual's identity is formed from their deep association with the group to which they belong—thus keeping these group associations strong and secure (largely through ritual practice) was thought essential if the social group were to survive. Alternatively, Marx's 'conflict model' stressed the oppositional nature of identity—individuals defined themselves primarily through differentiation: 'I am what I am not'. Thus strategies like conspicuous consumption ('I am going to consume what you can't afford to show how different I am from you') and the propagation of ideology ('I shall sell you ideas of how your way of life must be protected—protected because it supports and funds my own'), were integral to constructing 'us' identities felt to be inherently different from 'them'. Finally, in Evans-Pritchard's 'segmentary model' both processes were stressed as integral: individuals strategically aligned themselves, via identification, with groups whom on other occasions they would oppose, via differentiation. Thus in segmentary societies, identities had to be both mul-

tiple and shifting, making use of both identification and differentiation.

With these comments now firmly in mind let us return to the psychodynamic community. As I have already noted in chapters one
and five, the segmentary nature of the therapeutic community is
one of its palpable features. And as any system that is 'segmentary'
needs its members to be able to shift their allegiances and identities, we would expect to find operating in psychotherapy processes
fostering both identification and differentiation.[161] Let me turn to
an assessment of these processes.

In the first place, it is clear that the psychotherapeutic identity
takes up a central position in most practitioners' lives. Of the 42
who answered our survey, for instance, all but one stressed the
central role this identity takes in how they view themselves. When
asking how important a position it took, there emerged unequivocal responses:

> Yes, it is central, it says something about my approach
> to myself and others—to do with being concerned
> with personal growth and understanding. Also
> provides me with a professional/social status which
> reflects my intelligence, personality and achieve-
> ments.

> It is very important to me because it is through my
> work as a therapist that I feel I have found part of my-
> self I haven't encountered in a safe and bounded en-
> vironment before.

> It reflects a great deal of who I am, how I think, how I
> create meaning in my life.

> Yes—it gives me a professional identity separate from
> family and domestic—and I use it for thinking about
> myself, others, and the world.

My identity as a therapist is very important to me.

Important, as it influences that way I feel and see the world.

Yes—it is my most important identity along with being a mother.

Of course it is! I value my work for myself and my patients. I am a professional—I can earn money and hope I am contributing in a small way to improving mental health in the community.

Yes—as a vehicle for future personal development and living.

My identity as a therapist is important in that it integrates areas of work, family and gender successfully—a psychoanalytic perspective addresses the self within all these roles.

Yes—I am a psychologist and psychotherapist, and have been both for many years. I feel that both contain and largely convey my values and choices in the world.

Yes, I like to see myself as a healer of some kind.

Given what I have said about the selection, training, and assessment of psychotherapists in previous chapters, that the psychotherapeutic identity becomes a core identity for practitioners might not surprise us. What is more interesting, however, is that this so-called 'core identity' is not some kind of uniform garment worn by all. Rather the profession is a kind of syndicate league comprising many different uniforms. For it is clear that encouraging strong school allegiances has a dominant place in the formation of therapists' identities. We have seen how trainees are taught to internalise and identify with the doctrines of key figures, while being led to disassociate or distance themselves from others residing outside the theoretical body (chapter four). In fact, from the following comments it becomes clear that those trained in the teachings of a particular school ultimately end up supporting and identifying with that school's main proponents: 10 out of the 15 respondents trained at a traditionally Kleinian institute quoted Klein as a therapist of identification, while of the 15 therapists trained at a non-Kleinian institute only 2 respondents expressed allegiance to her beliefs and teachings. Similar trends can be found elsewhere—e.g. not one therapist trained in the classical Freudian tradition mentioned Jung in their list of identifications; while nearly all who trained at the major Jungian institute emphasised Jung. In fact, of all 42 psychoanalytic therapists who responded *not one of these emphasised a non-psychodynamic practitioner as a mentor*—thus the whole field of nondynamic therapists, humanists, existentialists or anthropological psychiatrists were excluded from their minds. This trend continues when observing more diverse trainings in the genealogical structure—humanists tend to prefer humanists; existentialists, existentialists; transpersonal therapists, transpersonal theorists and so on.

The nature of the 'psychotherapeutic identity' is thus quite patchwork and segmentary—while it might seem broadly unified from the standpoint of an outsider, it is fragmented when seen from within. The 'affirmative' nature of therapeutic training (which places boundaries around the theoretical body), the strong allegiances encouraged between senior and junior members, the confidence won by associating one's style of practice with the 'true' tradition, and the subjection of self to the ideas learnt to understand the complexities of others—are all devices fostering identification with fellow members of a given school. For psychotherapists, as do many others, gain assurance when associating with people who think and feel in ways similar to themselves. And this assurance is ever more deepened when these associations are legitimated by authoritative symbols, bodies, myths and institutions. As one therapist put it:

> Yes I suppose I would feel more comradeship with a Kleinian if we were sitting among a group of accountants than with a group of therapists. I think it was Johnson who said that if an English worker and an aristocrat met in the heart of Paris they would experi-

ence camaraderie, but if the same two encountered
each other at home, convention would say they have
nothing in common. (Psychotherapist 2005)[162]

As the therapeutic community is internally fragmented by processes of 'identification' this is helped by concomitant processes of
'differentiation' that are also operative in training schools. We have
already witnessed such seeds of differentiation not only in the institutional nurturing of school allegiances, but also in the institutes'
management of doubt and dissent where attempts to integrate dissociated objects (theories, theorists) are discouraged. We have also
seen how these dismissed elements can themselves pull rank and
form anti-groups, which in the history of psychotherapy have often become mirror-images of the bounded systems they originally
opposed—the evidence for this being most clearly revealed in the
manifold splits to which the community has been subject. These
splits and disassociations are further highlighted if we accept that
the identifications which training establishes promote not only
high levels of conformity, but also some measure of *dependence*
upon the objects identified with, a dependence encouraged by the
benefits of identification: security, status, a sense of belonging,
membership to an association promising referrals; all advantages
rendering expulsion or dis-identification a costly enterprise.

That identification brings personal gains might explain why an
attack which challenges the objects identified with, could be felt as
a personal attack. This threat of attack is repelled by denigrating
the attacking object through many possible devices—through expulsion, denigration, reverse attack, disregarding or dissociating
from it. These processes of identification (embracing one's group)
and dissociation (defining oneself against others) perform a definite social function: they ensure a community structure in which all
'schools' and 'individual members' have their identities and positions affirmed.

In view of these comments it is not surprising, then, that the
mythic, its inculcation, its adoption, and its ultimate fracture, is reflected as we have seen in the community's genealogical structure,
which is broadly divided along doctrinal lines. This diversification
of the mythic therefore can be seen as a scaffold supporting a complex web of disparate schools and traditions—a web which in turn

serves to solidify and protect the identities of the members comprising its constituent parts.

THE CASE STUDY

I have argued thus far that the psychotherapeutic myth sustains much more than simply clinical practice since it supports certain ethical, political, and communal proclivities in the practitioner's life. As the evidence for this claim has been derived from general observations and surveys, rather than from the inspection of a single practitioner's biography, we might still feel strangely remote from the living pulse of the individual. To rectify this I shall now consider data relating to a single practitioner's professional story, so that we might not only more roundly apprehend the intimate intricacies of personal transformation, but also what I mean when I speak of 'transformation'.

I have selected the following practitioner because of the positions he has taken in the psychodynamic community—at one time orthodox, training at an orthodox institute, at another more independent from the psychodynamic mainstream. By inspecting some of the personal transformations this practitioner underwent, we can elaborate through the prism of his person the refraction of the mythic on the community. This method I believe consistent with one of Dan Sperber's more popular assertions, that:

> the transmission, the maintenance, and the transformation of culture, takes place not uniquely but in part in these individual psychological processes... culture goes through them, and through their minds and their bodies and that is, in good part, where culture is being made. (Sperber 2005: 1)

The transmission of therapeutic culture I shall now study via the 'mind and body' of Michael Jacobs—a senior member of the psychotherapeutic community, well-known and widely-published. This biographical account draws from his autobiographical writing and from my personal interviews and correspondence with him.

Michael has not always been a psychotherapist. He was first a Curate in The Church of England after graduating in theology in his early twenties. Confronting a church reality for which his youthful fantasies of ecclesiastical life had not quite prepared him precipitated 'a period of great turmoil' in which he undertook a serious reappraisal of his chosen vocation. Unhappy with his new position, and increasingly at odds with the social milieu into which he was expected to integrate, he was forced to consider alternatives. The decisive moment came, as he said to me in conversation,

> when I received a letter from my old university tutor saying that he had a sabbatical and whether or not I would like to teach for him whilst he was away. And so I said that I would of course be delighted, as I was desperate to do some reading. So he put me in touch with a chaplain whom he felt could guide my reading. I went to the chaplain and mentioned that I was interested in studying psychoanalysis, perhaps Jung. He quickly replied 'Oh, don't read Jung he is unscientific, you must read Freud!' And so, guided by his suggestion, I started with Freud.

Encountering Freud during this period of doubt eventually resulted in his leaving the Church for the alluring world of psychotherapy; a new world offering fresh possibilities of vocation, expertise, and belonging. As to why psychoanalysis so gripped him, he reflects in his autobiographical essay:

> [In retrospect psychoanalysis] appealed for a variety of reasons... Psychoanalysis had a substantial body of knowledge that had hitherto sustained my intellectual interest and my emotional fervour... It asked similar questions, if phrased rather differently, to those that had clearly appealed to me in religion. Freud too had wanted to resolve 'something of the riddles of the world' ...just as I had been previously engaged in trying to solve the riddles of existence and the universe,

and in a rather more microcosmic way pursued the same quest.

What I did not see at the time, *but has become so much more obvious to me since, is that psychoanalysis also appealed because it was cultic like a church... Therapist and counsellors often feel passionate about their therapeutic schools and positions, and I was no exception.* Psychoanalysis beckoned with a type of certainty... It had its dogmas; indeed, as I begun to discover, it had its creeds, and in some societies woe betide the person who tried to step outside them. It had a whole set of moral views—although they are called 'psychopathology' rather than 'sin'. I could 'analyse' people rather than hear their confessions. I could help relieve their guilt, rather than pronounce forgiveness. I could achieve a new kind of status, because as the status of clergy declined, the admiration of counsellors and therapists came in.

I exaggerate slightly, but in order to make the point. Psychoanalysis suited me: it fitted, if not quite like a glove, at least enough to support my personal characteristics. Indeed, what is ironical is that I was leaving the Church because it was dogmatic, intolerant and narrow in much of its public thinking, and I felt that it had no place for my more radical, questioning and independent mind. That I should have allied myself to psychoanalysis is now not at all surprising, given the power of the 'return of the repressed': this is one of Freud's greatest discoveries which I still hold true, and which sometimes makes me think that very little changes—even as a result of years of therapy. In some ways I went from the frying pan into the fire. (Jacobs 2001: 16-17, italics added)

Michael's characterisation of his switch to psychoanalysis as 'moving from the frying pan into the fire', implies that at some point he became aware of the constraining factors in psychoanalysis. For although psychoanalysis replaced the role of the church in his life, it did not completely.

[B]ecause I did change, at least in my conscious mind, and I like to think those changes seeped a little lower into a layer or two of my unconscious... [For while the 'return of the repressed' referred to his need to replace one authoritative structure (i.e. the church) with another] it also applied to [the return of] my free-thinking spirit. If I was on the one hand rather conformist —public school, Oxford and the church—on the other I had always been uncomfortable with the conformity of others and of institutions: a careful rebel at school, somewhat radical in the church, and now [today] independent within psychotherapy, and hence able to reach a point where I could see how psychoanalysis might entrap me. (Jacobs 2001: 17-18)

When asking Michael what alerted him his replacing the church with the unifying system of psychoanalysis, he reflected to me:

Well, [my awareness of the possibility] came gradually, that is my transformation from a less questioning to a more reflexive practitioner. In the chapter you read [and from which I quote here] I was looking back from a place where I could see what might have happened to me. I hope it is an accurate reflection. But at the time when my attitude was changing, I am not sure whether I was wholly aware that it was happening. It is only now in retrospect that I am aware of three factors that seemed to have helped it.

The first factor he stated was his growing maturity as a person. Accounting for the second factor he says:

I had a supervisor who was rather rigid in psychodynamic thinking, although she did soften somewhat as the years went on. But on the whole there was a very strong very Freudian line; and that was attractive when you are trying to find yourself as a practitioner, and when you want some answers and so on. So to begin with I must have found that very valuable. But then my supervision with her virtually dropped down to once a week and then to nothing at all because she retired. And at that time I was just attending peer supervision. So I think that this is the second factor that shifted things, since I gradually weaned myself of her supervision.

The third factor Michael sees as due to his not undergoing a formal training. In his biographical account he elaborates:

[Because of this] I was fortunate... Fortunate because training with a psychoanalytic society or association—especially in London—tends to produce a mindset which finds it difficult to question accepted wisdom, both of theory and practice; or it makes it very difficult to voice this within what remains a largely conservative profession... [such institutes create practitioners] and I come across many of these, who wait for permission to express their doubts and uncertainties, not having learned that it is safe to do so in their training. (Jacobs 2001: 17-19)

By now we might have sympathy for Michael's comments given what we have so far discovered about training ourselves—that it is 'affirmative' and uneasy with opposition or dissent, that it is bounded and encourages dispositions of conformity.

We must not read Michael's comments as suggesting he had no formal training in psychotherapy; indeed, he had trained in adult psychodynamic psychotherapy at the prestigious Tavistock Clinic for two years, although this did not lead to a professional qualification or membership in the Tavistock association.

When looking more closely at Michael's professional story it is fair to say that he underwent two transformations: one from priest to therapist, and the other from therapist to a more 'reflective' practitioner. As I have already said, his first transformation, when leaving the Church for psychotherapy, was marked by a season of considerable 'turmoil' and tension. About this period he says:

In those days [the days of his leaving the church and beginning training] I became much more withdrawn socially, as if the observing, careful, non-disclosing therapist had leaked into my life outside the consulting room. *I think now this was because I was needing to find a new identity as a therapist in place of being a priest, and therefore needed to hide in my shell until that identity was firm enough to risk its fuller exposure.* (Jacobs 2001: 20, italics added)

He continued during his interview with me:

This was a tough time, indeed; and I think it took me a good three years before I began to feel at the beginning of each day that I was looking forward to seeing patients... So it was a long time before both my sense of who I was and my humour returned.

[After this tense initial period was at its end] my natural personality began to feel safe to emerge again with patients. I think what I found very difficult when I began as a therapist was this notion that I couldn't be myself. You had to be this blank screen, that sort of thing. I found that very frustrating to the extent that when the odd occasion arose when I could go off and give a lecture or a talk or something, I would feel fantastic relief—here I at least could be exhibitionist again... I enjoy the public arena and therapists do not tend to have a public arena, it is a very private arena; so performing publicly allowed my old self to come through—the one that was more regularly used during my time in the church.

Michael did not lecture in the formal institutes, for he did not hold the requisite qualification.[163] Rather his lectures took place in more independent settings privately run for clergy and lay people, contexts that we might confidently suppose were free from the teaching restrictions discussed in chapter four.

With the first transformation now complete, and with his confidence and good-humour retuned, Michael was ripe for his

second and more gradual transformation—from orthodox to reflexive therapist. To gain an impression of what this second transformation would ultimately yield, let me cite some of his current
attitudes towards the psychodynamic community. The first feature
he gradually became aware of was its 'displaced sadism', which, as
he explained,

> appears to make some psychoanalytic therapists,
> teachers and supervisors hypercritical. Whether or not
> they show this to their patients I do not know, but I
> see considerable evidence of it *in the way some students
> and supervisees experience those who teach them*. That hy-
> percritical, hyperanalytic attitude is one I knew my-
> self, in relation to myself perhaps more than to my cli-
> ents, *and in relation to other forms of therapy which did
> not appear to fit the model that I had chosen for myself*.
> Whether it is a return of my questioning spirit, or the
> influence of the *rapprochement* I perceive taking place
> across many of the therapies; whether it is the soften-
> ing that comes with maturing years, *or whether it is in
> relation to so much persecutory teaching and supervision
> that I hear about from those who come to study with me*:
> what has changed is that I make my analytic com-
> ments about myself and others with a lighter touch,
> without the persecutory edge, trying to empathise
> and understand, rather than to label and put down.
> (Jacobs 2001: 22, italics added)

Furthermore, commenting on his growing awareness of the
political dimension of the psychodynamic, he writes:

> his [Freud's] emphasis on phantasy as playing as an
> important a role as actual events in the aetiology of
> hysteria set in train an exaggerated concern for the in-
> ner world in psychoanalysis generally, and a neglect
> both of the political dimension and actual history, col-
> lective or personal... [Because of this] psychoanalysis
> has been very narrow in its actual impact, *concerned*

more with its own politics than with the wider world. (Jacobs 2001: 13, 23, italics added)

However, he places himself as an object of his own criticism:

I am not generally political as a therapist, or even as a private individual, even though I take interest in politics—both of the profession and in what sometimes seems more like the 'real world'. Perhaps it is therefore unfair to chide psychodynamic therapists for being indifferent. (Jacobs 2001: 24)

Finally his 'second transformation' bringing his growing 'reflectivity', highlighted to him the need for more tolerance in the profession:

Tolerance is not something I perceive to be obvious in the psychoanalytic world, and the splits within psychoanalysis, including the perpetuation of divisions in psychoanalytic therapy in Britain, are witness to the fact that may others prefer to put their emphasis on standards rather than on tolerance. If I am intolerant, it is of this in-fighting, which may not only be true of psychoanalysis: the Jungians have their own splits (Casement 1995), and I imagine that there must be tensions between the different humanistic therapies too. But the therapeutic 'family' which I have chosen seems preoccupied with internal quarrels, and this would distress me were I not still sufficiently individualistic to say 'a plague on all your houses', and go my own way. (Jacobs 2001: 22-23)

Commenting on how he managed to 'go his own way', and survive as an independent in a largely orthodox profession he tells us:

I... [was] fortunate to have initiated a psychodynamic psychotherapy training, and to belong to a psychodynamic association which I helped found, which can, in many ways, described as tailor made. (Jacobs 2001: 22-23)

Michael's new vision, institutionalised in a new psychodynamic training, provided him the freedom to define the style of teaching and the curriculum in accordance with his own preferences. In this sense, and recalling Weber, Michael has cast off his 'priestly' role to become his own more 'prophetic' spirit.

ANALYSING MICHAEL'S PROFESSIONAL TRAJECTORY

Michael's story is intriguing for a number of reasons. Not only does it reiterate some of the problems that I have shown to belea- guer the profession, but it also provides through the prism of his person an insight into how the genealogical structure is expanded and maintained. Expanded, since his solution made yet another addition to the stock of trainings; and maintained, as this addition expresses a social dynamic in which individuals can institutional- ise their departures from the mainstream.[164]

Despite Michael's movement into reflexivity, he has neverthe- less remained an active member and passionate promulgator of psychotherapy. For both himself and his patients, the mythic as an ordering principle still retains its magnetism. He thus remains in the league of psychotherapeutic identity even if wearing a specific 'independent' brand. What is rejected is the brand formed by, and associated with, the dominant forms of psychodynamic socialisa- tion, which, as we have seen, are largely 'affirmative' and conser- vative.

WHAT IS THIS TRANSFORMATION?

With these facts set down before us, might we now better under- stand what is meant by saying the practitioner through training is somehow transformed? In the first place, to speak of the trainees' transformation I refer to that general human phenomenon which accompanies the acquisition of new knowledge, experiences, and expertise. What is unique in this case is that such transformation is facilitated by a specific set of institutional devices which instil not only idiosyncratic beliefs and dispositions affecting both professional and personal spheres, but particular identities and differentiations that follow the preferences of the assimilated tradition.

I have identified this unique collection of absorbed dispositions not by studying the psychological mechanisms of transformation (cognitive, dynamic, behavioural), but by firstly recognising the social and institutional devices aiding transformation; by secondly, identifying the consequences of these devices in terms of the specific culture they inculcate (e.g. dispositions, identities, practices and preferences); and by finally showing what this inculcated culture socially entails (further institutional and personal practices).

That the institute can so function and thus assist personal transformations, requires two indispensable preconditions: the institution's capacity to entice new adherents to act in ways consistent with its aims; and a tendency in the prospective adherent to 'drift' or 'transform' in the institutionally specified direction. As I have spoken of the institution's capacity to entice adherents in previous chapters (its promises of competence, referrals, and expertise), let me here focus on the second precondition—that there must exist in prospective adherents a propensity to transform.[165]

THE PROPITIOUS CONDITIONS FOR TRANSFORMATION

The question whether there are factors disposing individuals to 'transform', and if so what might these be, will constitute the final concern of this chapter and thus of this book. The first step to approaching an answer comes from recalling a fact I discussed in chapter two—namely, that it is mostly the case that psychotherapeutic trainees are individuals who originally entered psychotherapy to help themselves and then from this experience elected to train to help others.[166] Thus in the majority of cases the need to resolve some kind of private conflict precipitated their involvement. At this point there are at least two ways of interpreting the causes of these precipitating conflicts. From a psychological standpoint, and to invoke C. W. Mill's distinction (2000 [1959]: 9), we can trace these conflicts to 'personal troubles'—that is, to factors whose origins rest in the psychology of individuals. Or we could trace them sociologically to 'public issues'—that is, to factors whose origins lie beyond the range of the person's inner life, and thus in the social world. Since many in the psychoanalytic community, as we have

seen in chapter seven, might interpret psychologically the problems which lead them to seek out and train in psychotherapy, I
here intend to address what many overlook—the possibility that
many such conflicts may be partially rooted in social factors and
'public issues'.[167]

Before discussing certain sociological theories which try to account for why individuals seek out psychotherapeutic intervention, let me first identify the social group from which the psychoanalytic community largely recruits. I shall do this by inspecting
the ethnic, educational, and class categories in which practitioners
place themselves. Firstly, and in respect of class, of the 42 respondents who answered the open question not one classified themselves as 'working class'; rather 37 stated that they were 'middle
class', 2 referred to themselves as 'professional class', and 3 as 'up-
per-middle class'. When asking in what class their parents placed
themselves at the time of the respondent's secondary schooling, 8
said 'working class', 4 'upper-middle-class', and the remaining 30
'middle class'. On the matter of ethnicity, 2 stated they were 'African', one 'white-Greek', one stated 'complex', while a full 39 stated
'white' (one prefacing this with 'European', another with 'Scottish',
and another with 'Jewish'). Finally, the responses to questions on
education were thus: only 2 out of the 40 who answered the question held no first degree. Thus 38 held undergraduate degrees, and
20 held post-graduate degrees.

These figures are consistent with existing claims as to what
kinds of people dominate the psychoanalytic profession (Littlewood 1999: 403), and like them reveal that the psychodynamic
community contains predominantly university-educated, white,
middle-class, British professionals.[168] This delineation of the social
group with which we are dealing, places us in a better position to
identify the characteristic 'public issues' bearing upon it; issues
that may well prompt certain members to turn to psychotherapy
for solutions.

SOCIOLOGICAL THEORIES AS TO THE APPEAL OF THE PSYCHOTHERAPEUTIC

The first anthropologist who sought to account for middle-class reliance on psychotherapy was Ernest Gellner. Gellner's explanation
for psychotherapy's appeal suggests psychoanalysis offered along

with Marxism a way out of the *anomie, alienation,* and the *disenchantment* wrought by the shifting social realities of twentieth century European life. Psychoanalysis, he argued, successfully articulated through its 'pseudo-scientific' doctrine a *pays legal* (explanatory system) that accorded with the *pays reel* (what everyone 'knows' to be instinctively true—namely, the belief that until we become aware of all the hidden forces shaping our lives our fate is out of our hands). It entailed a kind of Old-Testament wager, a heroic gamble asking all those who would risk adherence to it to follow what a rejected religiosity once asked of the believer: to act in spite of fear, to have faith in spite of doubt, to believe its promise but also its threat. The decline of moral and communal solidarity which accompanied the growth of industrialism and modern capitalism, Gellner believed, left people starved of the personal webs of meaning and relationship that the dissolution of local communities brought. Modern individuals thus became partial to any system where relationship, intimate and revealing, was offered as a means by which personal salvation could be won.

In locating the appeal of the therapeutic in how it purported to offer palliation to specifically modern issues, Gellner belongs to a tradition of commentators who look to socio-historical factors to make sense of psychotherapy's allure and ascendancy. For instance, Heelas (1996), although focusing upon the rise of New Age movements, argued that the 'various uncertainties of modernity' made attractive new visions of personal redemption that could palliate the 'various identity problem[s]' engendered by the demands modern life (Heelas 1996: 137).

To take one example, Heelas quotes what Berger calls the 'problem of work' as one major factor at the root of this confusion; a factor accompanying the rise of capitalism. Berger says of this problem:

> The two spheres [public and private] are geographically and socially separate. And since it is in the latter that people typically and normally locate their essential identities, one can say... that they do not live where they work. 'Real life' and one's 'authentic self' are supposed to be centred in the private sphere. Life at work thus tends to take on the character of pseudo-

> reality and pseudo-identity... The private sphere, espe-
> cially the family, becomes the expression of 'who one
> really is'. The sphere of work is conversely apprehen-
> ded as the region in which one is 'not really oneself',
> or... one on which one 'plays only one role'. (Berger,
> cited in Heelas 1996: 146)

Heelas argues that this state of affairs, rending and confusing
individuals, is partly resolved by the 'New Age Movement' which
re-infuses meaning back into 'public' activity by asking its members to assume professional activities consonant with its 'world-
healing' aims. By bringing public endeavour in line with private
belief, it largely resolves the public / private divide to which modern individuals have been made painfully subject.

While the differences between New Age and psychodynamic
systems are at once deep and manifold, one obvious similarity is
found in the fact that psychotherapy also offers a response to the
'problem of work' identified by Berger. For it is clear that the psychoanalytic ethos is not confined to the 'public' sphere alone: not
only are patients largely seen in therapists' homes (which is a symbolic gesture *par excellence* of the collapse of this dichotomy) but
the mythic, while publicly enacted is, as we have seen, privately
believed and embodied. Its ethical, political, and communal dimensions are thus not confined to the walls of the consulting room.
In home, in treatment, in 'self', and in 'other', the therapeutic ethos
wields palpable influence. Expanding Richard Sennett's (1976:
6-13) insight that psychotherapy has helped erode the distinction
between public and private life in modern society, therapy also offers the clearest example of a discourse that successfully merges
within its own precincts the two apparently distinct domains.[169]

That psychotherapy intimately penetrates private life, and that
it is this very infiltration that partly explains its attraction, is a
point further developed by Furedi (2004). Like Gellner, Furedi argues that psychotherapy is a response to what Weber called the
'disenchantment of everyday life'—a kind of rise of the bureaucratic society which has dislodged traditional systems of morality and
meaning.[170] It is this dissolution of the moral and meaningful that
Furedi argues has contributed to the rise of the psychodynamic. As
he says:

the fragmentation of a moral consensus had forced individuals to look for their own system of meaning.
Without a socially accepted moral compass to help
people negotiate the problems they face, ambiguity
and confusion surrounds the question of how to make
sense of existence. The weakening of shared values
fragments this quest for meaning... Therapeutics
promises to provide answers to the individual's quest
for the meaning of life. (Furedi 2004: 89)

Furedi does not suggest here that psychotherapy is a kind of
surrogate religion, since, as he perceives it, therapy promotes an individualism and anti-communalism antithetical to the support of
communal cohesion, shared webs of meaning, and the collective
forms of ritual worship that mainstream religions promulgate and
uphold (Furedi 2004: 91). However, since Furedi's comments were
largely advanced with the lives of patients in mind, patients, who,
through their solitary excursions to the therapist's couch, learn to
'unearth' and to some degree weaken their early parental and familial ties, we must ask how far his comments are relevant to the
experience of practitioners. For it must be said patients' and practitioners' experiences are quite different: for one, patients' participation in the community largely ceases after their therapy concludes,
while for practitioners their professional transformation, as we
have seen, offers at its end institutional affiliation and networks of
sociality into which any willing therapist will be welcomed. Indeed, just as in traditional religion, from which Furedi distinguishes psychotherapy, for the practitioner, psychotherapy not
only provides a non-material, non-corporeal other with which one
must continually interact (the unconscious), and a hierarchical
structure in which one can be located (via institutional membership), but a shared idiom by which experience can be interpreted
and articulated, a ritual and social network by which it can be supported, and finally an elaborate symbolic or 'mythic' system by
which it is legitimated.

While not wanting to strain this analogy too far, it is not difficult to see the fragmentation of psychoanalysis as reminiscent in a
structural sense to that affecting the protestant institutions of the

nineteenth century (and in a wider sense with that affecting Christianity from the Reformation to the modern age). Within the broad framework of primary Protestant tenets (faith, reliance on scripture, and personal relations with God, etc.) there were innumerable divergent interpretations as to how these different aspects were to be practised, related to, conceptualised, and enacted. These divergent visions laid a broken ground of diverse and contending institutions not unlike that upon which we have seen psychotherapy rest.

If we can pull back from this analogy for a moment in order to check the plausibility of what this 'surrogate' hypothesis presupposes (i.e. that for therapists psychotherapy is a dominant system of meaning), we might benefit from considering some statistics concerning psychotherapists' religious affiliations. Of the therapists I surveyed, when asking whether they had any religious faith, and, if so, whether it had strengthened since they become therapists, 7 stated that they had never held any religious faith and 9 that they no longer held any religious faith (of these 9, a total of 4 lost their faith around the time of training, 3 lost it before training, and 2 after[171]); 9 continued to have some kind of 'spiritual' or agnostic faith, while only 3 of these had experienced a constant attachment to an organised religion. Therefore, of the 23 practising therapists who answered the question only 3 were involved in organised religion.

Naturally, these figures alone do not validate the surrogate hypothesis. However, when interpreted against the background of this chapter we see that psychotherapy in some of its formal structures contains elements associated with religious institutions and beliefs. If these comments might tempt us to reduce the rise of psychotherapy to the demise of traditional religion, the arguments of others commenting on the rise of therapy might give us pause for thought—mainly because they collectively imply that the sources for therapy's attraction are numerous.

Anthony Giddens (1991), for instance, saw therapy as responding to the 'risk' and 'uncertainty' that modern conditions have generated. By creating a subjective sphere over which a certain degree of control can be exerted, adherents win a sense that certain aspects of life are controllable—a soothing proposition for those living in the reality of an uncertain world. In a similar vein, Peter Berger

(1965: 39) stated that the complex fabric of roles and institutions in which individual lives are woven, means that people are increasingly subject to manifold social forces, the motors of which remain largely incomprehensible to them. Rather than making these motors comprehensible, the psychodynamic imagination attaches this 'incomprehension' to an idiom promising eventual self-understanding and mastery; it therefore not only captures a general experience generated by modern society, but endows individuals with the belief that through studying the 'self' alone full understanding will follow. Incomprehension of social life is recast as incomprehension of self—thus plumbing the unconscious replaces the investigation of society as the primary means by which to acquire comprehension of and control over reality.

That psychotherapeutic understanding has replaced social and traditional understandings of personal conflicts has also been emphasised by Michael Smail (2001). He locates the attraction of psychotherapy in its congruence with the rise of medicalisation and its adjunct, 'psychologisation'—namely, the process of reconfiguring the problems of everyday life in psychological terms such as trauma and neurosis. Such processes, which accompany the rise of medical hermeneutics, inevitably engender the belief that the successful management of subjectivity can only be facilitated by clinical experts. Self-trust is thus eroded by the belief that only 'trained professionals' hold the keys to subjective understanding. This belief is that which compels patients to seek out, and (we might say) trainees to attain, psychotherapeutic expertise. This equation creates a market for therapeutic services, which apportions these services with ever more power.

Other commentators have stressed the link between the rise of psychotherapy and the demise of politics. They argue that psychotherapy appeals to the modern mind as it provides a focus for energies once spent in political action and concern. For instance, Christopher Lasch (1979: 43) believed that as 'collective grievances' are being increasingly transformed 'into personal problems amenable to therapeutic intervention' (or as Mill would say, as 'public issues' are being recast as 'personal troubles'), individuals channel the pleas for change once levelled at the political domain into the narcissistic arena of 'self-reform'. He sees this as serving Reaganite, Thatcherite social policy consistent with Conservative ideologies of self-determination and 'choice'—if the individual is the locus of responsibility then reduced state involvement is justified. This idea is finally supported by Halmos (1973: 24) who also interprets the decline in political action as both the cause and accompaniment of the rise of psychotherapeutic belief and intervention, which holds that the 'self', rather than the environment, is the best site for radical reform.

THE SOCIOLOGICAL THEORIES UNIFIED

What unites these diverse anthropological / sociological analyses is not where they locate the sources of psychotherapy's allure, for they variously emphasise different social causes, but rather their broad attempt to clarify the *social roots* of why therapy seems a viable option to Western, educated individuals. By resisting the invocation of psychological ideas to explain the rise of psychotherapy, and by preferring instead to identify the social conditions of personal despondency, these authors evade a psychologistic circularity (i.e. explaining the rise of therapy in terms of therapeutic theory). They are also unanimous in insisting that psychotherapy dulls a socio-political action by psychologising the roots of personal despondency.

The objective of this short review has not been to identify the precise social factors that have given rise to therapy's ascendancy (e.g. economic, political, professional, religious etc.). For even if I were able to unravel such complexity, such an investigation would take me far beyond my immediate concerns. Rather my aim has been more modest: to illustrate that therapists are largely called to the therapeutic profession by the disconsolations of their own predicaments; predicaments whose origins, in contrast to what trainees are taught, might very well have some of their causes in the conditions of the society in which they live.

CONCLUDING CHAPTER EIGHT

In this chapter I have argued that for practitioners therapeutic practice is more that just a species of clinical expertise. It obliges ethical, political, and communal commitments whose embodiment can provide solutions to aspects of the practitioner's total life. That most therapists enter therapy to grapple with their own private troubles I have seen as a fact of considerable significance. Psychotherapy wins its appeal by interpreting personal crises through a unifying system which can provide answers to certain ultimate questions. It achieves this by recourse to an overriding hypothesis about the inner 'dynamics' and the *telos* of persons. By assuming this hypothesis participants gain security and learn to know in what direction they are to strive; and in 'uncertain times', by initiating themselves into this powerful system of meaning, there is not only won a community of peers and upholders, but a quasi-ritualised organization (expressed through forms of continuing 'self-analysis', 'supervision' and personal therapy), whose ideal foundations are formally consecrated in institutional practices and protected texts. It is in this sense that we may argue that the therapeutic myth bears marks reminiscent of what previous traditional interpretive and ritual schemes once offered individuals.

I have advanced the various facts and arguments of this final chapter in order to uncover the background against which the deeper significance of psychotherapeutic socialisation can be revealed. In so far as I have managed to achieve this general aim, I shall at last pull together my final conclusions.

CHAPTER NINE
THE CONCLUSION

That psychotherapy brings to the facts the philosophy it claims to derive from them is a charge that can be levelled against many interpretive enterprises, including the one I have undertaken here. And yet, the anthropologist could insist that far from approaching phenomena with a fixed set of questions in hand, as might the experimental or quantitative researcher, he or she must remain an open book, hesitant to affirm anything until the relevant range of details are in. If we accept this view then anthropologists are in a far less enviable position than most, since they rarely know beforehand the kinds of questions their observations will force upon them. Through sustained submersion in a distinct community they will encounter many facts not of their choosing. At once all manner of seeming peculiarities, perplexities, and unforeseen happenings will crowd their field of vision. And yet through the fog of these countless impressions they must still find their way to certain connections that the misty opaqueness conceals. Facts are considered in their total surroundings; regularities are sought for beneath veils of the arbitrary; subjectivities and structures, their conflicts and concordances, are traced for relations and interdependencies, while theoretical reductionism is simultaneously eschewed in the name of a more holistic and analogical enterprise.

In my ethnography of the psychotherapeutic community I have not escaped any of the obligations that this particular vision of anthropology demands. Confronted with a plethora of socio-cultural curiosities, I could not generate questions until what had first perplexed me yielded its meaning; meaning only revealed by 'living the community'. From the many questions raised during my participant observation I then had to select a workable few. And this meant rejecting many. Consequently what has been written is in no measure a complete representation of the community. My selection has unveiled but a portion of the picture (indeed other stories could be told). To reveal what I did, however, and as partial as it may be, only after the facts were in and the questions selected did I turn to established anthropological knowledge to guide interpretation.

Before I summarise the conclusions this approach has generated, let me make explicit the two fundamental questions of anthropological importance that this book has addressed: What are the distinctive aims of the psychodynamic institute? How do these influence the professional socialisation of trainee practitioners?

The psychodynamic community, as we have seen in chapter one, is under siege by manifold external threats. Challenged from media and from academe, from psychiatry and from new therapeutic schools in the genealogical structure, the psychodynamic closes its ranks and affirms its value and vision. While the sociology of the professions teaches that such affirmation is a feature of most established professions (e.g. via various strategies they protect universal aims of wealth, status, and power acquisition), I have illustrated anthropologically that 'maximising' and economic interests alone cannot account for why psychodynamic training proceeds as it does. Other factors are at play.

What is distinctive about psychodynamic institutes is that they inculcate a body of specialist knowledge that has an intimate bearing on 'self'. The mythic recommends to novice practitioners new possibilities of self-knowledge, identity, and belonging, along with the privilege of discerning both professionally and personally in what direction as persons they are to strive. Institutes are thus organs of transition in a particular sense, for not only do they pass on clinical expertise, but also membership to an established and self-healing tradition. Psychodynamic socialisation, while avowedly aiming to heal the patient, thus also promises personal sustenance and meaning to practitioners. It achieves this largely through imparting a circumscribed, totalising body of knowledge, and thus a frame of orientation by which self, society, and the other may be understood.

Throughout my chapters I described psychoanalytic socialisation as 'affirmative' since it inculcates largely conservative dispositions. By the circumscription of the theoretical body (chapter four), by appeal to shared concepts of personhood that legitimate role asymmetries (chapter four), by devices of secondary elaboration, displacement, and doubt management (chapter five), by the circumscription of aetiology which renders candidates convinced that they have something vital to offer clinically (chapters six and seven), and by the creation of susceptibilities which dispose trainees to submit to the instruction of seniors (chapter seven), trainees are institutionally coaxed into embodying a professional habitus which builds upon the foundational dispositions of 'partiality' and 'imagining psychodynamically' instilled ritualistically in pre-training therapy and assured avowedly by candidate-selection procedures (chapters two and three).

If these affirmative devices promote a tacit 'social contract' of conformity, peer-fellowship, and a union of aims between novices and the initiated, I have also shown that they may generate low tolerance for individual transgressions of institutionally defined norms and boundaries. Whenever transgressions occur, and when more rarely such mutinous visions are institutionalised, competitors and thus conflicts are born. And yet, as we have seen in previous chapters, such 'conflicts' do not engender total community fragmentation. While conflict may dissolve friendly ties between psychotherapeutic fractions (as I have emphasised in chapters one, three and eight), it can bind individual members of each fraction together against a greater external foe. In an anthropological sense, shared sentiments of conformity and solidarity thus unite the single school as effectively as do shared antagonisms towards rivals. Far from being indifferent to the dissociated and antagonistic 'other', then, from this other the 'disassociator' gains its identity, affirms its principles, and solidifies its aims.

If the therapeutic myth when fragmented extends *outward* into what I have called the genealogical structure, I have also argued that the myth extends *downward* into the institute itself. Trainees are judged as persons as well as practitioners (chapter seven); and as the criterion of judgement is culled from the psychodynamic

myth trainees are treated like patients. This treatment is legitimated by 'role asymmetry' (between seniors and trainees) which is
in turn legitimated by recourse to concepts of personhood (chapter
three). Dissent is managed via the 'psychologisation' of complaints
(chapter four), and appreciated trainees, just like good and willing
patients, are those who submit to the guidance of the learned. The
therapeutic ethos is therefore not confined to the therapeutic
frame, but spills out in every direction: it is applied to the patient
(in healing), to the patient/trainee (in training), it is applied by the
practitioner (in practice), and by the leader (in teaching). It thus re-
fracts in manifold contrary directions—*outwardly into community
structure, and downwardly into training device.*

If the myth as I have observed permeates these different domains of the psychodynamic enterprise (the person, the institute,
the practitioner, the trainee), where exactly does the significance of
this fact lie? In the first place, exposing such permeation I believe
reveals why the reform many therapists keenly desire is slow in
coming. This is to say, as the myth is a pillar propping both 'system' and 'self', *to undermine the myth is to undermine much that legitimates the affirmative project along with the personal advantages such a
project secures.* This conclusion might explain why objectives such
as the following are rarely taken up in traditional institutes:

> Our aim then must be, not just 'therapy', but a self-re-
> flexive practice which examines its own prejudices,
> ideology and will to power, which is aware of the
> ironies and contradictions in its own formation, and
> which is prepared to challenge them. (Littlewood and
> Lipsedge 1997 [1982]: 309-10)

The fact that weakening the myth, via reflexivity, would
destabilize all that the mythic supports, raises two important concerns. The first must be the psychotherapist's: does affirmative socialisation (which protects the practitioner's community) undermine what by any account must be the ultimate goal of training—
namely, the creation of the most effective healers? As this question
can only be answered by first defining what is meant by the 'effective healer', rather than enter the normative ground that making
such assertions would oblige, I shall instead clarify the central

problem for those practitioners who desire reform and who therefore believe that affirmative socialisation compromises standards.
Since conservative trainings establish the conditions for the maintenance of their conservatism (i.e. by instilling affirmative dispositions in trainees) how are they to be transformed? Might Sinclair's
suggestion (Sinclair 1997: 321) that medical training must be reformed by impositions from without also apply in this context?

In confronting this issue we might first recall that affirmative
socialisation, despite its conservatism, also creates opposition.
Secondly, we must remember that affirmation creates opponents
who, once being expelled for their diverging visions, can later be
reintegrated back into the fold (as in the BAP, chapter one). These
two insights lead us to the paradoxical conclusion that affirmation
itself can be reformative, albeit indirectly. In this sense the question
shifts from Sinclair's concern about who reforms training institutions (e.g. the outsider or insider) to that of how reform transpires
and at what pace. When considering how it transpires we would
look to the external pressures which force segmentary alliances
and thus bring new proximities and integrations. When considering the pace of reform, we would ask whether indirect reform is as
radical and swift as reformers desire, and thus whether from their
standpoint it adversely affects patients by denying them the fruits
of prompt reform. The moral dilemma for the dissatisfied, then, is
whether relying on indirect reform alone is the fairest option for
patients. *This* must be the therapist's concern: shall the community
be reformed by default, or shall it be reformed actively, purpos-
ively with greater rapidity, reflexivity and awareness? And if the
latter choice is made, in which direction must reform strive? Towards ever deeper conservatism and protectivism, or to greater
openness, reflexivity and integration? If we choose reflexivity and
integration then we might do well to further accept that the certain
training devices identified in this book may well be factors block-
ing reform; a reform which many believe is needed if psychoanalysis is to exist as a viable and vital profession in the twenty-first
century. This is the choice for the psychotherapist.

The next concern is the anthropologist's: what does the reproduction of the myth via the institute teach us about this form of socialisation? As we have seen, in this book I have identified a species of professional socialisation which surreptitiously requests a

robust ideological commitment. That it makes this request distinguishes it from other forms of vocational socialisation in which the ideological is less covertly or overtly insinuated. We might think here of trainings in industry, in the manual professions, in certain artistic, bureaucratic or scientific pursuits. Psychodynamic socialisation also distinguishes itself from medical training, for in the latter 'concepts of the person' are less explicitly declared than mutely implied, and the content transmitted neither shores up socialisation devices nor an energetic self-redemptive project (Sinclair 1997; Luhrmann 2000; Becker et al 1976).

Furthermore, unlike trainings in more skill- than idea-based professions, where practical attainments can reach high levels of perfectibility, the kind of abilities garnered from psychodynamic socialisation are characterised by non-completion. Like in Kabyle rituals where material exchange binds people in unending cycles of reciprocity (Bourdieu 1979), the project of the institutes, as with the project of therapy, never reaches completion. The gift given in training obliges a return—a lasting commitment. The trainee has thus entered a story whose narrative extends infinitely—personhood is never fully obtained, and the final aims of analysis are never achieved (chapter three). There is no denouement at graduations' end, for the myth will pronounce on the person interminably. Thus as with religious adherence so with psychodynamic: the only way out of the unbroken commentary comes via the renunciation of belief, since that believed-in obliges perpetual self-analysis as a condition of belief. As the institutionalisation of this non-completion finds its source in the specifics of the myth, here again we observe the myth's permeation of the institutional ground—and through the works of the institute, the ground of the person.

In view of these comments we might envisage a scale of professional socialisation from those most explicitly ideological (e.g. political, religious, psychotherapeutic) to those more practically driven (manual, technical, industrial, bureaucratic). Future research might work to identify the structural and often tacit devices used by each species of socialisation. For example, in what features and forms do, say, seminary trainings resemble military or psychotherapeutic? What are the training conditions under which inflexibility or else flexibility in professionals is furthered? And do comparable forms of socialisation create similar community structures and fragmentations? Furthermore, for the ethicist, could a normative scale of socialising forms be contrived for the better regulation of professional affairs? And again, how do wider socio-historical conditions relate to how differing forms of socialisation evolve and operate? Indeed, as much power in the West over the long-term has moved from centralised civic and governmental institutions to professional communities, investigating the sites where the professions are maintained offers a critical way of unearthing the hidden and powerful machinations and aims of the professions themselves.

Through this work, in sum, I have laboured to show that psychodynamic training inculcates commitments which are not explicitly recognised by the institutes as such—and yet the power of these commitments is so palpable as to pattern institutional directives and aspects of practitioners' lives. In this sense, the institute seeks to reproduce in individuals in the form of dispositions its norms, its underlying presuppositions, and its modes of organising experience. This is assisted as members of the institute, 'partial', 'susceptible' and dwelling in states of forced self-inspection (forced by the conditions and devices of the institute) are so engaged as to rarely think of challenging the structured roles and rules. These structured 'others' thus become firm and constant standards against which 'the self' can be orientated.

The reality of the institute is then a fixed entity into which people must fit and make their way. And as the objectives of training fashion dispositions that become such integral markers of 'self' as to feel indispensable, the public (institutional) infiltration of the private (self) creates persons who can be relied upon to reproduce the community project. And as affirmation is a precondition for fragmentation, that community fragmentation has been constant throughout the history of the profession is testament to the affirmative project's ability to reproduce itself over time—a reproduction that shows the power the psychodynamic myth holds for all those who use the training institutes as an initiatory route down which they may enter a new professional and moral home.

APPENDIX ONE
THE DISTINCTION BETWEEN ANALYTIC AND INTERPERSONAL
OR 'OBJECT RELATIONS' THERAPY

Psychodynamic psychotherapists who err towards the analytic pole, follow closely in the tradition of Freud. For Freud and the early analysts (e.g. Ernest Jones and Georg Groddeck, Karl Abraham, etc.) the patient's problems were 'intra-psychic'—that is, the tensions emerging from the opposing demands of ego and instinct cause neurosis. The analyst's job was to reduce these tensions through bringing to awareness the unconscious conflict. This theoretical emphasis on the intra-psychic origins of discontent entailed the *clinical* stance that was mainly analytical—that is, the therapist investigated objectively and disinterestedly the patient's intra-psychic life and offered interpretations that were thought to heal by bringing insight. The relationship between *certain internal dynamics within the patient* was therefore more significant than the relationship between the *therapist and patient*.

In distinction to the analytical therapists the interpersonal or 'object relations' therapists stressed the primacy of the inter-personal rather than intra-psychic relationship. As Fairbairn says, this relational stance 'may be formulated in the general principle that the libido is not primarily pleasure seeking [as the analytical psychotherapists urge], but object seeking' (Fairbairn 1952: 137). That is to say, the libido finds its primary goal though forging healthy relationships with others, not in seeking the pleasure through gratifying tensions. The primary drive at the outset of life

257

thus becomes the establishing and maintaining of good object relations, not of satisfying instinctual needs. This shift in emphasis also has its resultant clinical stance: therapists in large part heal the patient through relationship—that is, they 're-parent' the patient, providing that which was lacking in the child's early years. Thus for the interpersonal therapists, exploring the relationship between therapist and patient with all its reparative possibilities is the crux of analysis. In sum, analysts heal largely through analysing and interpreting patient material, while interpersonalists heal through providing a reparative relationship.

It must be emphasised that the new 'interpersonal' or 'object relations' approach does not subvert the analytic stance but rather builds upon it. For example, it still takes basic classical psychoanalytic theory and technique as axiomatic: the structure of the psyche and the characteristics of the unconscious, childhood sexuality and development, as well as psychic mechanisms such as defence and displacement, symbolisation, symptom formation, repetition, resistance, transference neurosis and working-through (King and Steiner, 1990). All these are expanded upon and developed, but never dismissed. This means that despite there having been considerable changes in psychodynamic therapy since the time of Freud, a general psychodynamic orientation has nevertheless remained constant throughout its history. It is this constancy that has enabled the UKCP to classify all these therapies under the rubric of the 'psychodynamic', and the BPC under the 'psychoanalytic'.

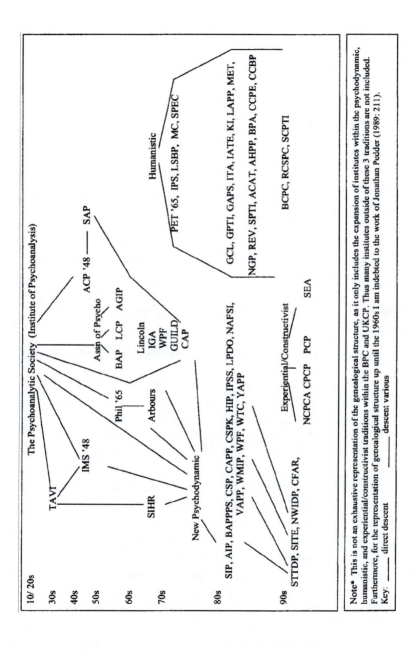

Note* This is not an exhaustive representation of the genealogical structure, as it only includes the expansion of institutes within the psychodynamic, humanistic, and experiential/constructivist traditions within the BPC and UKCP. Thus many institutes outside of these 3 traditions are not included. Furthermore, for the representation of genealogical structure up until the 1960s I am indebted to the work of Jonathan Pedder (1989: 211).

Key: ——— direct descent   ——— descent various

The following list of abbreviations and organisations refers to the diagram on the previous page.

SIP	Severnside Institute for Psychotherapy 1980s
ARBA	Arbours Association founded 1970s
AGIP	The Association for Group and Individual Psychotherapy 1974
AIP	The Association of Independent Psychotherapists 1988
BAPPPS	British Association of Psychoanalytic and Psychodynamic Psychotherapy Supervisors 1980
CSP	Cambridge Society for Psychotherapy 1980
CAPP	Centre for Attachment-Based Psychoanalytic Psychotherapy 1992
CFAR	Centre for Freudian Analysis and Research 1985
CSPK	Centre for the Study of Psychotherapy 1981
GUILD	Guild of Psychotherapists 1974
HIP	Hallam Institute of Psychotherapy 1985
IGA	Institute of Group Analysis 1971
IPSS	Institute of Psychotherapy and Social Studies 1978
LPDO	Liverpool Psychotherapy and Diploma Organisation 1980
NAFSI	NAFSIYAT 1985
NAAP	Northern Association for Analytical Psychology 1981
NWIDP	North West Institute for Dynamic Psychotherapy 1991

PA	Philadelphia Association 1965
SITE	The Site for Contemporary Psychoanalysis 1997
SPMP	Society for Psychoanalytic Marital Psychotherapy 1990
STTDP	South Trent Training in Dynamic Psychotherapy 1998
TMSI	Tavistock Marital Studies Institute 1948
VAPP	Vaughn Association of Psychodynamic Psychotherapists 1982
WMIP	West Midlands Institute of Psychotherapy 1980
WPF	Westminster Pastoral Foundation 1980s
WTC	Women's Therapy Centre 1980s
TAPP	Yorkshire Association for Psychodynamic Psychotherapy 1970s

PSYCHODYNAMIC TRAININGS WITHIN THE BCP

BPS (IPA)	British Psychoanalytic Society (Institute of Psychoanalysis) 1913
BAP	British Association of Pyschotherapists 1951
CPP	Centre for Psychoanalytic Psychotherapy 1979
LINCOLN	The Lincoln Centre for Psychotherapy 1967
LCP	The London Centre for Psychotherapy 1974
NEATPP	Northern England Association for Training in Psychoanalytic Psychotherapy 1992
SAP	The Society of Analytical Psychology 1936
SAPP	The Scottish Association of Psychoanalytic Psychotherapists 1972
TAVI	The Tavistock Clinic 1920

HUMANISTIC AND INTEGRATIVE TRAININGS IN THE UKCP

ACAT	Association for Cognitive Analytical Therapy 1980s
AHPP	Association for Humanistic Psychology Practitioners 1980s
BCPC	Bath Centre for Psychotherapy and Counselling 1990s
BPA	British Psychodrama Association 1984
CCPE	Centre for Counselling and Psychotherapy Education 1984
CTP	Centre for Transpersonal Psychology 1973
CCBP	Chiron Centre for Body Psychotherapy 1983

GLC	Gestalt Centre London 1980s
GPTI	Gestalt Psychotherapy Training Institute 1980s
GAPS	Guild of Analytical Psychology and Spirituality 1987
IPS	Institute of Psychosynthesis 1975
ITA	Institute of Transactional Analysis 1980s
IATE	Institute for Arts and Therapy in Education 1985
KI	Karuna Institute 1982
LAPP	London Association of Primal Psychotherapists 1986
LSBP	London School of Biodynamic Psychotherapy 1970s
MET	Metanoia Institute 1980s
MC	Minster Centre 1978
NGP	Northern Guild for Psychotherapy 1983
PET	Psychosynthesis and Education Trust 1965
RCSPC	Regents College School of Psychotherapy and Counselling 1990s
REV	Revision 1988
SCPTI	Scarborough Psychotherapy Training Institute 1990s
SPTI	Sherwood Psychotherapy Training 1988
SPEC	Spectrum 1976

EXPERIENTIAL AND CONSTRUCTIVIST TRAININGS IN THE UKCP

NLPCA	Neuro-Linguistic Psychotherapy and Counselling Associaton 1992
CPCP	Centre for Personal Construct Psychology 1990s
PCP	PCP Education and Training 1990s
SEA	Society for Existential Analysis 1988

In order to gain ratification from the BCP traditional psychody-namic trainings must organise their curricula in accordance with its training standards. This will explain why the following institutes engage in a uniform rejection of works residing outside of the psychodynamic canon. This includes not teaching a historical / sociological perspective on psychodynamic psychotherapy, or surveying any relevant literature from related disciplines. Below I review the curricula of five traditional psychodynamic institutes—all members of the BCP (British Confederation of Psychotherapists).

The Lincoln Centre for Psychotherapy

It defines its curriculum thus:

> The Lincoln Centre aims to provide a course to further the skills, understanding and technique of psycho-therapists who already have a qualification equivalent to our basic training and experience in psychoanalytic psychotherapy [which provides a basic introduction to Freudian concepts]. Seminars are conducted by psychoanalysts and Lincoln training psychotherapists. The orientation is that of the British Psycho-Analytical Society, representing the work of the Contemporary Freudian, Independent and Kleinian schools.[172]

Upon speaking to a member of the institute I was told that the theorists taught were Freud, Abraham, Ferenczi, Klein, and the object relations theorists Winnicott and Fairbain. The topics that I was told were covered are borderline states, depression, psychosis, perversion, thinking and symbol formation, dreams, psychopathology, sexuality, advanced study of clinical concepts, techniques of interpretation, diagnosis, assessment, and analysability. There was no inclusion of any works outside the psychodynamic tradition—that is, from authors who are not themselves psychodynamic practitioners. Also there was no social perspective taught in training.

The London Centre for Psychotherapy

It defines its curriculum thus:

> The qualifying course is committed to providing a sound understanding of unconscious processes through the teaching and critical evaluation of the work of the Freudian, Kleinian, Object Relations and Jungian schools, with a firm grounding in related clinical technique. The curriculum has been devised to familiarise the trainee with the theory and practice of each school of thought, presented coherently throughout the length of the training. The theoretical seminars begin with an in-depth study of Freud, moving on to the work of Jung, Klein and her contemporaries, Bion, and British Object Relations including Winnicott. This is followed in the second year by more contemporary theoretical developments, including American psychoanalysis.[173]

When asking whether these contemporary theoretical developments included the work of those commenting on the profession from outside the tradition (e.g. anthropologists, sociologists, philosophers, etc.) I was told that 'we are more concerned with teaching good psychoanalysis—and so these concerns are tangential'. It was also made clear to me that no socio-historical perspective was taken on the psychodynamic tradition.

THE SEVERNSIDE INSTITUTE FOR PSYCHOTHERAPY

It defines its curriculum thus:

> The course covers the theories, clinical concepts and techniques of Freud, Jung, Klein, and the British Independents in their classical and contemporary forms.[174]

Like the Lincoln, London, BAP, and other trainings, here too in the curriculum there is no inclusion of work that reflects either socially or historically on the psychodynamic tradition.

THE CENTRE FOR PSYCHOANALYTIC PSYCHOTHERAPY

The Director of the institute informed me that the key works studied are those by Freud, Klein, Winnicott, Kaper, Balint and Bion. These authors are studied in order of their history of contribution. Thus trainees start with Freud and the early Freudians, proceeding through Klein, to the object relations theorists, and then to post-Kleinian work. Again, no work is taught that dwells outside of the psychodynamic bounds.

NORTHERN IRELAND ASSOCIATION FOR THE STUDY OF PSYCHOANALYSIS

The British Guide to psychoanalytic psychotherapy trainings defines the curriculum thus:

> The theoretical orientation of NIASP is psychoanalytic and the educational curriculum includes the leading theoretical schools within psychoanalysis.

Like the aforementioned curricula, this curriculum is bounded —never transcending the bounds of the psychodynamic. The head of training told me that the main theorists studied were Freud, Klein, Winnicott, Bion, Balint, and the post-Kleinians.

Notes

[1] Such anthropologists are thus more interested in research contexts closer to 'home' than with those so-called 'exotic' and 'far-flung' contexts with which anthropological research is most commonly associated. To reverse a tested adage for a moment, they opt to expose strangeness in the familiar rather than what is familiar in the strange. And by focusing on the minutiae of local training, they furthermore have tried to produce insights of wider social importance, mainly because by investigating the transmission of power, knowledge, and belief at the local level we can reveal why influential professions come to function in the world as they do.

[2] For Becker 'student autonomy' refers to the collection of ideas and actions that comprise the 'student culture'. This culture includes all that students collectively perceive as the right thing to do and to think during their training; ideas which might conflict with the official ideas of the faculty. This culture is therefore to be distinguished from the total culture of the medical school which consists of all the values, directives, and expectations either explicitly communicated by the faculty or lived out in the structures of the institution (Becker *et al* 2002 [1977]: 437).

[3] Apart from the authors so far mentioned we could add studies by Katz (1984), Cassell (1987) and Fox (1980). Their theories of 'practitioner certainty' shall be discussed in chapter seven.

[4] This point is aptly made by Lave and Wenger (1991). In following them I am implicitly critiquing here the cognitive theory of knowledge acquisition which generates for itself a number of problems. Mainly because it assumes a division between learning and other kinds of activity; secondly, because such theories cannot account for moments of creation which produce the knowledge upon which cognition works; and thirdly, because cognitive theory assumes a universal homogenous cognitive apparatus free of social influence. For an alternative critical emphasis see Chaiklin and Lave (1993: 12), authors whom I am paraphrasing.

[5] As we shall soon see, the activities of the psychotherapeutic field, as with other fields of politics or medicine, are circumscribed by collec-

tions of rules, symbols, etc., whose ownership is contested by various sub-groups comprising the field itself (Webb et al. 2002: 22).

6   A useful compendium of such studies has been gathered in *Understanding Practice* edited by Chaiklin and Lave (1993). It gathers together anthropological and educational theorists who study learning in terms of how practices affect 'being', rather than how didacticism affects cognition.

7   As Bourdieu writes: there is a distinction 'between apprenticeship through simple familiarization, in which the apprentice insensibly and unconsciously acquires the principles of the 'art' and the art of living—including those which are not known to the producer of the practices or works imitated... at the other extreme [there is] explicit and express transmission by precept and prescription, every society provides for structural exercises tending to transmit this or that form of practical mastery' (Bourdieu 1977a: 88).

8   For Bourdieu subjectivity and society are inextricably woven entities that could reside in either dialectical or mechanistic relation. More reflexive individuals through acquiring 'cultural literacy' would exist more dialectically in relation to the social fields; a dialectic allowing such individuals in turn to react upon the structures that shaped them. Thus agency could be won, but only by those reflexive enough to grab the reins of the deterministic field so as to shrewdly guide them. And as such extremes of reflexivity were evidently scarce, these individuals were invariably few. I say 'leaning' rather than 'stance', for a stance is always taken against a contrary and thus implies a dichotomy, and as Bourdieu claims: 'Of all the oppositions that artificially divide social science, the most fundamental, and the most ruinous, is the one that is set up between subjectivism and objectivism' (Bourdieu 1999b: 25).

9   For instance, so far as the scientific standing of the profession in the eyes of wider society affects the profession's internal dynamics, then the scientific standing is of anthropological importance since it bears upon the internal dynamics of the profession.

10   'Ideas do not succeed in history by virtue of their truth,' said Peter Berger, 'but by virtue of their relationship to specific social processes' (Berger 1965: 32). Thus as the truth of these beliefs is subsidiary to the social implications of what either belief or un-belief in them generate, it is with what is generated that I shall be concerned.

11   Some more examples would include Hinshelwood's (1985) application of a Kleinian social defence theory to account for the schismatic forces keeping psychotherapy organisations in a stance of mutual suspicion (i.e. persecutory and depressive anxieties based on fear of retaliation are projected onto bad objects—namely, competitors in the field, etc.) Another would be Bruzzone et al (1985: 411), who stress that the regression students experience in their training therapy (making them use words such as 'mummy' and 'daddy' to refer to their therapists, and referring to a good training experience as a 'good feed') is sometimes inadequately *contained* and thus spills out into the learning situation and the training. It is then a short step to feelings of persecution and paranoia about the student's personal pathology. Finally, Figlio (1993: 326) argues that as trainees internalise key figures such as the

therapist and the institute, when they encounter others holding to other (often opposing) internalised figures a mutual hostility ensues.

[12] I thank Dr Louise Braddock for these comments which she presented
at the psychoanalytic seminar series (St Johns College, Oxford) in sum-
mer 2005.

[13] The information about psychiatric training is derived from my discussions with senior psychiatrists in the Day Centre at the Warneford Hospital, Oxford where I underwent a short-term psychiatric placement.

[14] A final caveat: it is important to note that in this book I shall not consider the training of either Lacanian or Jungian practitioners.

[15] Quoted by J. Brunner (2003: XXI); forward to E. Gellner (2003 [1985]).

[16] Personal communication (2004).

[17] My rejections were numerous (there are more institutes today, and thus
more from which one can be rejected). Furthermore the reasons for
these rejections often remained unclear: admittedly some rejections
were as unequivocal as 'we do not engage in fieldwork experiences',
while others were far more abstruse: 'it would be unethical for us to allow this study', without it being explained why it would be unethical.
Other institutes ignored my requests (at one institute I had to press for
six months before they sent out a rejection letter). On another occasion
I was asked to submit a proposal which was turned down some twelve
months later.

[18] In short, the principle I adhered to when approaching informants for
data was that of *right to informed consent*: all informants were made
aware of the nature of the research to the extent that they could make
an informed decision about participation or non-participation. To get
around the problem that disclosing the nature of research might compromise the data, I had the obligation to tell as much as would not
compromise the research (letting the interviewee know what is happening). In cases where interesting things were said in informal conversation I would make a point of requesting that I make use of the information offered. In cases where conversations were recalled from
memory at a later time, either I would return and check with the informant for their consent or if unable to do so quote the data anonym-
ously. In all case material I checked with the contributors for their approval, and where requested I have sent them finished versions of the
work for their perusal.

[19] Feelings towards psychoanalysis in British medicine can be gleaned
from assessing the British Medical Journal from 1910 through to the
Second World War. Here most of the articles that treat dynamic psychotherapy err on the side of hostility. Many of the principle psychiatrists of this time wrote hard critiques. Crichton-Brown (1920), for instance, then a leading figure in British psychiatry, firmly argued for
links between reflex cerebral activity and associated mental development implying that brains could be literally modified by the appropriate medical reactions whether by correct feeding, re-education, or 'psychological massaging'. There was no suggestion of the worth of the
talking cure. Other professional objections were voiced. W. McDougall
(1908), who urged a multiplicity of instincts, rejected reducing all
symptomatology to the sexual urge. Other psychologists and psychiat-

rists such as A. G. Tansley, W. Brown, H. Crichton Miller, as well as W. H. R. Rivers, urged a psychological level-headedness to counter the scientific immoderation of the Freudians (Porter, 1996: 389). The eminent psychiatrist Charles Mercier was also a staunch critic who portended the downfall of the psychodynamic: 'psychoanalysis is past its perihelion, and is rapidly retreating in to the dark silent depths from which it emerged. It is well that it should be systematically described before it goes to join pounded toads and sour milk in the limbo of discarded remedies' (quoted in Porter 1996: 389).

20 Unlike the British reaction, American psychiatry embraced psychoanalysis from the start. As Forrester writes: 'in the United States, the history of psychoanalysis was intimately part of the history of medicine, in particular of the history of psychiatry. For a period, from the late 1930s (at the latest) to the 1960s, psychoanalysis was an indispensable part of the American psychiatrist's training and authoritative knowledge, and certainly a crucial component of his or her social status' (Forrester, 1994: 183). This was to change from the 1960s onward where the rise of the psychotropic was by the early 80s to almost eliminate psychoanalysis from medical psychiatry.

21 The Royal College of Psychiatrists now recommends that psychiatrists in training gain some experience in psychotherapy during their professional training. This training is not as thorough as the training psychotherapists receive in psychotherapy training institutes. It also may not focus specifically on dynamic therapy, often preferring to school young psychiatrists in cognitive / behavioural approaches (personal correspondence 2004).

22 The emphasis in these centres was on the training of mid-term and short-term psychotherapy for individuals and groups—long-term psychotherapy was not practised see, Holmes (2000)

23 See Donna Lafromboise 'One of their own blasts therapists for their shoddy work', *The Montreal Gazette* 11 January 1997. Cited in Frank Furedi (2004: 9).

24 This is the number for 'registered' counsellors, that is, counsellors who can practice. However, at the time of writing the BACP has a further 20,000 members many of whom are in the process of working towards full accreditation.

25 This table is based on that appearing in Michael Jacobs (2000: 457). However as his table only gave figures up until 2003 I have modified it according to my own research at the UKCP, BPS, and the BACP.

26 After the Second World War, in little time psychological expertise began to be deployed in many new administrative situations. As Porter comments, 'Psychological personnel and techniques became involved in the testing of individual conduct and the handling of personal problems in the armed forces, in job applications and selection for employment, and in hospitals, schools, and prisons. Aptitude and intelligence testing became routine, and new psychological specialisms gained ground—clinical psychology, criminal psychology, educational psychology, industrial and military psychology.... This gradual but significant planting of people with psychiatric or psychological training in posts of social influence—in education and employment, in the law courts

and the probation services, in the armed forces and in industry—represented at least a partial fulfilment of the aims of the mental hygiene lobby, articulated through the National Council for Mental Hygiene... From the first Report of the Board of Control after the First World War and the Report of the Royal Commission on Lunacy and Mental Disorder (1926), down to the Report of the Feversham Committee... the philosophy of mental hygiene became incorporated into official thinking' (Porter 1996: 396-7).

[27] Figures on the changing rate of depression have been gathered by the Cross-National Collaborative Group (1992: 3098-3104). On long-term trends in the presentation of depression, see Edward Shorter (1994: 118-148).

[28] This claim is based upon the observation that the British Association of Counselling and Psychotherapy, the United Kingdom of Psychotherapy have more non-psychodynamic members than psychodynamic. It was also informally communicated to me by one of the sub-directors of the BACP that there were more private non-psychodynamic consultancies registered and practising than psychodynamic.

[29] This diagram is not exhaustive. It neither includes all traditions nor all schools—it is therefore only offered to illustrate how the system is ordered.

[30] I arrived at these generalisations from an informal survey I conducted among a randomly selected group of psychotherapists and counsellors of different theoretical positions. I asked 25 interviewees to rank in order of status the various psychotherapy trainings within the UKCP. The Institute of psychoanalysis was placed at the top of the list by all but two interviewees, 22 placed the BPC second, 21 the UKCP third, and a full 24 placed counselling in the BACP last.

[31] Having asked a spokesperson for BACP as to why the change in name, I was told that the members themselves requested that it be altered as a number of psychotherapists were members. Asking whether someone who had passed through a counselling training could then legitimately call themselves a psychotherapist now that the BACP had changed its name I was told that 'we have no legal liberty to stop people calling themselves whatever they like.' Although the amount of years needed to become a counsellor is fewer (two years of training) than the amount needed to become a psychotherapist (minimum four years), there is nothing legally binding members of the BACP who have only passed through a counselling training from labelling themselves 'psychotherapists'.

[32] These figures were gathered from the British Association of Cognitive and Behavioural Therapies, the United Kingdom Council for Psychotherapy and the British Confederation of Psychotherapists. These figures only treat the *traditions* of CBT, psychodynamic and humanistic / integrative psychotherapy. I have also excluded data on the proliferation of trainings in the BACP—thus this is not so much a total representation of the expansion of the genealogical structure than an illustration of the expansion of three traditions within it.

[33] I refer here to the Lincoln Centre and the British Association of Psychotherapists.

34 In 1989 what I have called the UKCP (United Kingdom of Psychotherapy) was then called the UKSCP (United Kingdom Standing Conference for Psychotherapy), only changing its name to the UKCP in 1992.

35 Today it is still the case that anyone can set themselves up as a private psychotherapist in Britain, as the profession is still in the process of acquiring statutory registration from parliament. Until such registration is attained this state of affairs will remain. However, as bodies such as the UKCP and the BPC gain more credence and popularity, employment in the public sector is only given to those therapists belonging to one of these bodies. Also, only registered therapists are allowed on the therapeutic registers, which, however does not stop unqualified practitioners from advertising privately.

36 The UKCP, then, is an umbrella organisation of psychotherapy institutes and traditions. The current traditions it oversees are the sections of Analytical Psychology; Behavioural and Cognitive Psychotherapy; Psych-hypnotherapy; Experiential Constructivist; Humanistic and Integrative Psychotherapy; and finally, Psychodynamic Psychotherapy (including Marital, Sexual therapy, and Psychoanalytically Based Therapy with children). Each of these traditions contain more or less training units.

37 Traditional institutes proudly display their histories at application meetings. For more immediate evidence of this, see the website of The Institute of Psychoanalysis: http://www.psychoanalysis.org.uk [Accessed June 2004].

38 Institutes such as Metanoia, the Westminster Pastoral Foundation, and Regent's College in London are a few of the growing number of institutes looking beyond the genealogical structure for ratification. These trainings enjoy patronage from Middlesex University, University of Surrey, and City University respectively.

39 This iconoclastic spirit is firmly embodied in the ethos of new integrative training schools which oppose the idea that trainees should be inculcated with the teachings of only one tradition. The real spirit of psychotherapy, they argue, is found in those practitioners who can draw form an array of different traditional approaches to meet the varying needs of their diverse patient-base.

40 The Principal of one such training said in interview with me: 'The whole point of Freud's original vision was that it was scientific, that it grew, changed, and evolved along with our increasing understanding of psychology... at many institutes they teach a gospel, not a fluid body of knowledge which is to be only accepted provisionally' (Interview 2004).

41 Under the BCP now sit twelve institutes, many of which give preference to the teaching of a particular school. For example, the Lincoln Centre privileges Kleinian analysis, whereas the London Centre promotes integration between various psychodynamic schools; an integration which trainings such at that in Freudian analysis at the Institute of Psychoanalysis flatly reject.

42 The equivalence paradox has elsewhere gone under the name of the 'Dodo Hypothesis', this stresses that there is no evidence that one mode of psychotherapy is superior to any other assuming the same

amount of contact time between patient and therapist—see Luborsky & Luborsky (1975).

43 More recent meta-analyses seem to endorse the equivalence theory, albeit with certain qualifications. For example, a meta-study conducted by a psychotherapy research team at University College London, identified key factors that may account for therapeutic success. This study started from the widely-accepted view within the profession that psychotherapy works, and then moved to answer why it works and what works for whom. It involved a meta-analysis of hundreds of efficacy studies conducted over recent decades in the United States and Europe. The conclusions drawn concerning therapeutic efficacy were that theoretical orientation is less a determining factor for success than the level of therapist training, the ability of the analyst to develop a healthy alliance with the patient, and the skilfulness and personal qualities of the therapists. Although in some problems such as PTSD certain therapies such as CBT seemed to generate better results—see (Roth and Fonagy 1996).

44 For an extended discussion of the rise of cosmetic pharmacology see Shorter (1997: 314-25).

45 These methods evolved out of the early requirements for training established in 1920 at the Berlin Institute for Psychoanalysis (Falzedaer 2000), and are now seen as fundamental to any psychodynamic training.

46 The correlation between a training institute's status and the number of weekly hours of pre-training therapy it requires, tempts the conclusion that the amount of hours expected of candidates is one means by which institutions achieve distinction. As I will show later in this chapter, one community myth holds that deeper analysis makes for better practitioners—those institutes asking for more therapy hours might thus believe they produce better practitioners.

47 These figures are based on many informal interviews I conducted with trainee practitioners. The quoted was calculated from 20 interviewee's claims (randomly selected) about the amount of time spent in pre-training therapy.

48 These two motivations were stated with almost clockwork regularity. Others emerging with less frequency included the desire to enter a profession where the hours are more flexible and where there is both a strong intellectual and practical component; also many trainees stated that they wanted to 'give back' something to a profession that has helped them.

49 As the psychoanalyst Johannes Cremerius comments: 'Only three associations within the IPA [International Psychoanalytic Association] have introduced the "open system" in which instead of training analysis a personal analysis is required which is not the responsibility of the institute. These are the French, the Canadian and the Swiss psychoanalytic associations' (1990: 124). Here, as a prerequisite for acceptance to training, the applicant must have finished the personal analysis or be quite advanced in it before being admitted to the program.

50 For a suggestion that we should distinguish between 'therapeutic efficacy', which is essentially articulated from a biomedical point of view,

and 'therapeutic success' which is a social scientist's assessment, see E. Hsu (1996b). The idea of 'therapeutic success' honours the notion that treatment might make us 'feel' better despite there being no noticeable biomedical change. (1999: 65-6).

51   We might think here of researchers such as Georges Devereux (1970) and Ari Kiev (1964)—see Roland Littlewood (1992: 51).

52   Dow seconds this: 'Many elements of psychoanalysis [its methods of practice] are also found in other forms of symbolic healing, but psychoanalysis does not offer the universal model of therapy' (Dow 1986: 57).

53   Theorists such as Frank (1961) and Torrey (1986) have abstracted from a wide variety of therapeutic systems certain fundamental features that characterise many therapeutic systems. Marmor's (1971) list of these factors includes: the release of tension though catharsis; cognitive learning through cognitive stimulation; learning though rewards and punishment; identification with the therapist; reality-testing through 'practising' in the learning process (paraphrased in Zatzick and Johnson 1997: 219). A more comprehensive list can be found in Kleinman (1991 [1988]: 115-6).

54   Patients learn to re-evaluate and re-frame their past and present experiences in terms of the new system of categories. And once patients have assimilated a new interpretative system, they can proceed to construct a narrative of their past, present, and likely future. This narrative may include insights on how to proceed out of illness (Hoshmand 2001).

55   From this brief summary we can identify the symbolist tradition out of which these anthropological ideas emerge. For while the symbolist approach, broadly stated, maintains that beliefs and ritual action should be understood as statements about the social order (Leach 1954: 14), it also emphasises that the meaning adherence to such beliefs and action generates consequently performs necessary social functions. And it is this latter function of symbolist thinking, as Desjarlais (1996: 150) has mentioned, that these theories of therapeutic healing emphasise. We can trace the genesis of this tradition to the work of Ferdinand de Saussure's (1959 [1916]) and his understanding of the sign: de Saussure defined the concept of the 'sign' as a union of two elements: the *signifier*, which is the word or emblem that represents a *signified*—the mental image we have of an object, idea, or experience. A sign is thus the resultant of a signifier being combined through association with a signified (i.e. when a word is associated with a mental object). Because any signifier can be associated with any number of signifieds, signs are complex and multi-levelled. Turner (1967) when developing this idea postulated a distinction between sign and symbol. A sign captures the 'indexical' (a simple) relationship between the signified and the signifier—that is, the signifier is associated with objects *in the world*; while the 'symbol' denotes an 'iconic' (a complex) relationship between signifier and *inner experience*—hence his saying, 'we master the world through signs... we master... ourselves though symbols' (Turner 1967, italics added). The symbol denotes an association between inner experience (signified) and the representing emblem, whether word or form (signi-

fier). A key characteristic of symbols for Turner, then, *is that they are always attached to deep subjective or emotional meanings.*

56   In many respects symbolist theories when applied to the understanding of psychotherapeutic healing presuppose a conventional view of dynamic therapy that it is primarily a semantic and analytic encounter in which the patient reconfigures self-understanding in terms of a new conceptual / symbolic system. This conventional view falls obsequious to connotations inherent in the term 'psychotherapy', a term which, as Hinton and Kleinman (1994) has expressed, constitutes a Western ethnocentric bias so far as it privileges changes in mind or psyche over changes in behaviour, feeling, or bodily symptoms.

57   Finally, in diverging from dominant symbolist understandings as to what constitutes the primary force in psychotherapeutic healing, I follow a tradition of anthropologists who have highlighted aspects of healing other than those revealed by the symbolists. For instance, Katz's (1982) study of the Kung's ritual dance which enhances *kun*, or the spiritual energy of healers, to the extent that *Kia*, or their state of mind, begins to alter. The experiencing of Kia heals not only those directly experiencing it but those who are in the proximity of those experiencing Kia. Thus the ritual heals by removing individual symptoms, by arousing universal protecting powers to help the patient, by re-establishing balance in the individual, and through healing the communal tensions which threaten group cohesion (1982: 34). It re-energises the whole society by re-connecting it with the divine energy of the Gods. Elisabeth Hsu (1999), on the other hand, has studied 'interpersonal interaction'. Studying ritual healing in contemporary Chinese medicine Hsu (1999) highlights many ritual features characteristic of Chinese medicine, two of which are the power of secrecy and words. The adornment of secrecy as a healing device confers on the healer an element of mystery that increases the value of his personality—the status of the healer may facilitate healing (p.56). In ritual the correct use of spoken words convert them into emanations with the power to induce change (p.51). The link between words and secrecy comes where secret transmission of knowledge, apart from legitimating the power of healers and allowing control of the distribution of knowledge, excludes the possibility of critically evaluating the healing power of words (p.51). Secrecy and words are welded together in service of therapeutic success. Desjarlais writes: 'while both intellectualist and symbolist positions have helped to explain the structural logic of religious rites throughout the world, I find neither to be particularly useful in explaining how or why Yolmo shamans heal' (Desjarlais, 1996: 49). This is to say that the successes of Yolmo healing cannot be accounted for in symbolist or intellectualist terms alone. For example, the Yolmo shaman relies more on arousing the patron's sensory experience than on particularising symbols or on effecting cognitive transformations. In this sense the shaman changes the way persons feel by altering the sensory stimuli around them. Through the use of imagistic poetry, touch, tactile images, music, and taste, that is, through the rich sensory impact of varied dramatic media, the shaman works to 'wake up' the patient by revitalising the senses and imagination. This activation takes place to 'reform the cognitive and perceptual faculties that in large part

make up a person' (p. 160). These theories, which stress the ritual / performative aspects of healing, are just some of those which offer a different understanding of how healing works. The theories I shall draw upon to assist my investigation of psychotherapeutic healing are those articulated by Antze and Lambek (2004), Laderman (1986), and Sharma (1996).

58 This description is derived from my various observations, participatory experiences, and extensive interviews in the field of psychotherapy and offers an 'ideal outline' of the therapeutic session as it is taught in the training schools. Gilbert Lewis urged that to trace an ideal over an individual interpretation of a healing ritual required checking the individual case against the general rule lest we take what might be an anomalous case as representative of standard practice (1980: 22). As Lewis put it: 'An obsessional neurotic man may express his fears through private ritual and we may come to understand his ritual as symptomatic of these fears. With this understanding we may learn about the personality and experience of the performer but learn little about the society in which he lives' (Lewis 1980: 22). In other words, as we examine the rules guiding 'healing' action in a community, rules widely taught and practised in the therapeutic profession, we learn about the preferences and objectives of that particular community— namely, about the type of practice communally desired, rather than about one idiosyncratic practice which may be unrepresentative. With this said, however, although I describe here more the ideal than the particular session, the examples used to illustrate points of practice are pulled from real practice. Therefore I speak of 'ideal' practice not in the Weberian sense, but in the sense that it defines the ideally preferred practice, the one held aloft in training schools as the prototypical version new practitioners should emulate. As I have checked the accuracy of my representation with a number of psychodynamic practitioners, the interpretation I shall now present is one mutually agreed upon rather than my own.

59 For a comprehensive introduction to a psychodynamic understanding of the therapeutic frame see Gray, A. (1994).

60 For a succinct summary of 'acting out' see Rycroft (1995 [1968]: 1).

61 I have also heard analysts say that a transgression which could be accounted for on practical grounds (the bus was late, etc.), should not also be taken at face value. This is not to say that the patient is deceiving the therapist, but that their unconscious might have had a role in sabotaging the conscious intent.

62 At one particular training institute where I conducted my fieldwork, the psychotherapist Anthony Storr was considered an authority on the importance of the setting in facilitating healing. On his advice concerning sealing the consulting room from extraneous sounds see Storr (1979: 4).

63 As discussed in chapter one, as British Psychiatry wards increasingly opt for non-dynamic therapies such as CBT, working privately is becoming ever more the province of the dynamic therapist.

64 Again, Storr emphasises the following: 'If the bookshelf is full of devotional works and there is a crucifix upon the wall, he is likely to alien-

ate the patient who is agnostic or a convinced Protestant.' (Storr 1979: 3). This will make the more sensitive patient more reticent in broaching religious matters lest he or she offend the therapist.

[65] Because what the patient might be attached to is less the therapist's person (rarely do they know his person) than the sense of belonging and attention that the therapist provides, it is crucial that nothing sabotages the patient's 'getting what he needs'—namely, the care and attention that he was denied in early childhood. For a comprehensive discussion of psychodynamic attachment, see Bowlby (1969).

[66] Such separation Jose Bleger (1967: 245) calls 'de-symbiotization'—the process by which the patient evolves out of a parent / child transference into a less symbiotic and more independent adult posture.

[67] In Gestalt therapy, for instance, the use of objects is considered integral to the healing process. Patients are asked to use objects to express emotional states, these arrangements are analysed for meaning just as a therapist would analyse images in dreams.

[68] See Charles Rycroft (1995 [1968]: 185-6).

[69] Please refer to appendix one for the distinction between 'analytical' and 'interpersonal' therapists.

[70] Freud (1915a) quoted in (Rycroft, 1995 [1968]: 1).

[71] D. Yalom (2001), a humanist and existential psychotherapist, draws a distinction between 'healthy' and 'counter-productive' self-disclosure. For fuller discussion see chapter 26.

[72] Melanie Klein (1952), perhaps the most celebrated analyst in Britain in this intermediary period, worked these ideas into a controversial distinction between 'counter-transference' and 'projective identification' —to understand this distinction we must take a momentary detour into her work. Starting from her understanding of the paranoid-schizoid position, Klein argued that the new-born baby employs mechanisms of defence against feelings of excessive loneliness and anxiety. Rather than experience these feeling in the full, the baby separates them from conscious awareness creating an inner 'split' in her psyche. This splitting of 'the good from the bad' was a defence which had the result of colouring the child's perception of reality: the child comes to see the 'external world' as she experiences her 'inner world' and so separates the external world into good and bad part-objects. The bad objects then, as opposed to being owned, are denigrated and projected. For Klein projective identification is symptomatic of this paranoid-schizoid position in which aggressive expulsions of disowned feelings are split from awareness. These disowned feeling are then projected outward towards an unsuspecting other, eliciting in them the very emotions that have been split off and denied (Klein, 1952). Klein's concept of projective identification, a phenomenon which she saw occurring in only schizoid patients, was later believed to occur in all patients to some extent whether schizoid or not. Thus her concept came to greatly influence all modern psychodynamic practice encouraging it to move out of the 'analytical' (assessing only patient's transference) towards the 'interpersonal' pole (assessing counter transference). Therapists were soon to take account of their own reactions as statements about the patient's subjectivity (Casement 1985).

73   Analogies have been drawn between family therapy and the ritual encounter, while the dyadic encounter which I describe here has not been so commonly compared (see, Roberts 2003 [1988]; Whiting 2003 [1988]).

74   A clear although popular example of how a therapist practically speaking contains strong emotion is found in the in the film *Truly, Madly, Deeply*. Here a deeply distressed woman expresses her intense grief at the recent death of her husband—although her despair is extreme the therapist remains calm, providing a counter-weight to the despair her patient is experiencing.

75   Aristotle's *Metaphysics*, translated by R. Hope (1952), quoted in Fromm (1960: 101).

76   For an extended discussion of this distinction in relation to 'embodiment' and 'representation', see R. Littlewood (2001: 30-149).

77   The term 'psychical analysis' was first coined in Freud and Breuer's (1895) *Studies on Hysteria*. The following year, in March 1896, the term 'psychoanalysis' was first used. See, Ferris (1997: 26).

78   For a discussion of Freud's views on determinism, causality and freewill and their relationship to the scientific thinking of his time see Jones (1953) Vol. 1. ch. 17.

79   As I shall explore more thoroughly in chapter six, while Freud's mechanism remained constant through his career, the type of causes he saw as all-determining would change. During his early work with Breuer, for example, he postulated the primary causes of neurosis as due to childhood seduction and early trauma (1895), while in his mature theory he relocates the primary causes to either over- or under-gratified childhood sexuality (1905). Psychodynamic thinkers contemporaneous with and subsequent to Freud, such as Donald Winnicott, Melanie Klein, Harry Guntrip, John Bowlby, etc., continued to relocate the primary causes of neurosis to different parts of childhood experience, yet despite this casual-shifting, like Freud they remained faithful to the overriding idea that 'the ego is not the master in its own house' (Freud 1973 [1915-1917]: 326).

80   Quoted in Campbell, J. ed. (1971: 511-12).

81   See, for example, Bass (1985) and Rudnytsky (1985).

82   Tanya Luhrmann, in her ethnography of psychiatric practice, writes of this caveat: '[Therapists] believe that the "why" is inherently unknowable, because aspects of one's own psyche are always hidden and an observer can never see clearly because his own unconscious intentions distort his vision. But analysts also believe that you can come to know more than you did, even if you can never know everything. The psychodynamic ethos, then, focuses on the honesty with which you try to know and the caring in the way you try to help another person know. If what really counts for the psychiatric scientist is knowledge, what really counts for the psychoanalyst is coming to know' (Luhrmann 2001: 182).

83   Because the correlation between the degree of pain and the severity of disease or injury is coloured by the patient's subjectivity, doctors naturally do not solely rely on this device for diagnosis—more 'objective' standards of measurement are preferred. Thus, all I assert is that the

medical doctor who might use this barometer as one tool among others for discerning the nature of the complaint.

84   See R. Porter's history of medical concepts of pain (1999)

85   R. Porter, comparing 'classical' and 'modern' medical attitudes to pain, notes how much more important is 'pain relief' in the modern doctor's outlook: 'What is undeniable is that the medical profession has become more responsive to the widespread clamour for pain relief. Sedatives and narcotics had long been used to quell pain... but painkilling was not central to the agenda of the Classical physician' (Porter 1999: 375).

86   Laderman's study of Malayan birth incantation seeks to answer the driving question: 'If the patient lacks a thorough comprehension of mythic details, how can the incantation change her physiological processes' (Laderman 2003: 293).

87   For example, while a therapist might act in a manner conducive to eliciting the transference (e.g. never disclosing personal information), it is rare that he or she would ever explain to the patient upon demand why this action is necessary, let alone explain or even name the concept that obliges this clinical action. Asking a psychodynamic supervisor as to why it is important to honour this distinction whenever a patient asks the therapist to explain his behaviour, he replied: 'I do not offer an explanation. I might acknowledge the patient's anxiety and that it must be difficult for him not knowing why I do what I do [not self-disclosing for instance], but then I would ask them to trust me, trust that there is a rationale behind what I do. On top of this I might say "your question suggests there is some anxiety about this process, I am wondering whether you might be finding it difficult to trust our work together..." Ultimately, avoiding meta-analysis means deciding to be a therapist over a teacher... Once you take up the didactic stance it is easy to get locked into it... answering one question only invites the patients to ask more' (Supervisor 2005).

88   Naturally, these need not be mutually exclusive especially when we deny Cartesian duality.

89   This is an abridged version of the theoretical program at the BAP (British Association of Psychotherapists). See Morgan-Jones and Abram (2001: 89).

90   Evans-Pritchard also made use of this distinction between priest and prophet in his analysis of the Nuer (1956: 304). For Evans-Pritchard the priest derives authority from his office, the prophet from personal qualities and charisma.

91   B. Morris, paraphrasing Beidelman (1971), pointed out that Evans-Pritchard neither acknowledges this point nor the converse point that prophets often sought to routinise their charisma by establishing a more stable authority (see, Morris 1996 [1987]: 201).

92   In fact he goes further to say that not only do our roles gain identity through contrast and opposition, but that the self is nothing but a composite of the various roles we play.

93   In Needham's polemical work *Structure and Sentiment* he rejected causal questions preferring to stress analogical relationships. Neither sphere of interest being either the cause or model of the organisation of the other (1962: xxvi).

94 But therapy is never complete. For most it is open-ended. Thus contact with a therapist is maintained after the end of therapy. As with indigenous treatments by a Taiwanese practitioner, reported by Kleinman and Sung (1979), clients may continue to keep in contact with the healer in an informal 'non-clinical' manner. Similarly, the therapist will often leave open the possibility of 'follow up' sessions—these can go on sporadically for years after the personal therapy is complete. I shall provide exact figures in chapter eight.

95 Arlow, commenting to Kirsner on how some trainers in the psychodynamic academy used 'secrecy' as a device of distinction, says: 'The feeling was that there was a way of knowing the true essence of existence, which was granted only to very special people, usually by virtue of extreme piety and scholarship. There emerged alongside of it feelings of special endowment which came from possession of secret knowledge, the kind that was not to be imparted to the general populace. The authority for that secret knowledge was transmission from one generation to another tracing the authenticity of this material to Moses' (Kirsner 2000: 32).

96 Kernberg (1996) noticed that many teachers conveyed that any critical analysis of Freud's conclusions had to be postponed until students had read Freud completely (and until they had much more experience and knowledge of the psychoanalytic field). The assumption being that any clear appraisal of psychotherapeutic concepts could only be won after more time spent in personal therapy. Until therapy was more or less complete the trainee's perspective lay unfinished.

97 Unlike in TCM, then, such knowledge is not directly denied to the novice, but only indirectly: it is denied as a consequence of the belief in how personhood is attained.

98 Another psychoanalyst speaking of his lineage says that his analyst: 'had been [analysed by] Sandor Ferenczi, and he idealised him. There was a bust of Ferenczi in his consulting room, together with one of Freud. You smile, and you should... it's the most primitive kind of family romance—my parents are aristocrats, I am descended from royalty, all that sort of stuff... you would be surprised by the number of people in and out of establishment psychoanalysis who hold these childish fancies about their royal descent' (Malcolm 2004 [1983]: 50).

99 Although Hsu is not explicit about this, she has implied it when she likened the personal to traditional authority in Weber's sense (Hsu 2000).

100 Furthermore, this assumed correlation between deeper experience and deeper knowledge also reflects the status imbalances obtaining between different schools in the genealogical structure (outlined in chapter one). This prompts the conclusion that the hierarchical relationship between trainee and leader extends into the social structure of the psychotherapeutic community: just as trainers have greater status by virtue of their deeper experience, so do those institutes that demand the 'deeper experience' from their trainees (i.e. five therapeutic sessions per week), and that can further claim an 'illustrious lineage', believe that they are entitled to reside higher up in what I called the genealogical system. Their graduates are held by the elite institutions

at least, to have had the more thorough education and thus in principle are worthy of their higher standing. Such is the taken-for-granted nature of these rationales for community stratification that in much of the psychodynamic world therapists pay little heed to how these consulting room beliefs inform relationships both within and between therapeutic institutions.

101 There are however two newer psychodynamic trainings in the UKCP which stress a strong social perspective. This is especially the case with Nafsiyat, The Intercultural Therapy Centre, founded by Professor Roland Littlewood and others; and also with the Institute of Psychotherapy and Social Studies founded in 1976 by Dr. G. Doron. Two further schools in the UKCP also emphasise a social perspective to a lesser degree: The Site for Contemporary Psychoanalysis, established in 1997; and the Philadelphia Association, founded in 1965 by R. D. Laing and Aaron Esterson. None of these, however, are members of the BPC.

102 Gorer does not make clear the anthropologists to whom he refers. But anthropologists known to have submitted to their own psychotherapy at the time Gorer was writing include George Devereux, Edmund Leach, and Max Gluckman. Also, Leach and Gluckman at different times urged their students to enter analysis before fieldwork so as to curb the influence of the 'personal equation' (Heald and Deluz, 1994).

103 This standardised knowledge is further bounded in the final sense that the 'relativity' of therapeutic ideas is not considered. Relativism consists in the view that any system is as good as any other; that the truths of that system do not correspond to an ontological reality, but are only as true as they are perceived to be by the community in question. Some commentators and a growing number of creative therapists slowly insist that therapy more resembles a hermeneutic than scientific endeavour (Holmes 1999; Hillman 1993; Spence 1987), thus implying that therapists do not unearth the real causes of patients' distress or the real choices available for the future, but simply construct narratives which order the mind and provide the healing illusion that a firm ground of certainty has been discerned (Frosh 1999 [1987]: 54-57). These therapists might insist that human subjectivity is formed in discourse, passed through meshes of 'language games' and shaped in order of their terms (p.257). The relativistic stance which minimises therapeutic aims is not an understanding of psychodynamic therapy taught in seminars, not only because relativism is largely seen by therapists to be uncommitted to the analytic project, counting it as it does as one system among numerous others that hold no privileged access to truth, but more importantly because relativism is seen to invite trainees to doubt the very heart of the system—an invitation, as I will later show, that institutes prefer not to accept.

104 This is captured in the words of a 43 year-old female trainee: 'A lot of what was taught in seminars was startling to me. Before coming here I was in long term analysis [five-times-weekly Kleinian psychoanalysis for four years], which taught me a great deal about myself... but still I was often confused by some of the actions and interventions my analyst made in the sessions... I only became knowledgeable about the theory as my training went on. I slowly found myself with a code I could

use to unpick the actions of my analyst... for me surprisingly my seminar learning became about unravelling why my therapist did what she did. This was very exciting as I would learn a bit of theory and then suddenly think "Ah yes, now I see what she was getting at, I understand why she did that"—I am still making sense of her actions now and through re-evaluating what went on during those years going through a kind of second analysis' (Interview 2004).

[105]   It is at this point that the symbolist understandings of therapeutic success discussed in chapter two have their applicability, since it is at this stage of the trainee's education that the therapeutic imagination is dressed in symbolic / conceptual form.

[106]   Practically this is continued throughout the trainee's education, since the trainee remains in personal therapy till graduation.

[107]   The psychoanalyst Sandor Ferenczi epitomises the analytic attitude to therapeutic failure in the following: 'I have had a kind of fantastical belief in efficacy of depth-psychology, and this has led me to attribute occasional failures not so much to the patient's "incurability" as to our own lack of skill—a supposition which necessarily led me to try altering the usual technique in severe cases with which it had proved unable to cope successfully' (cited in Malcolm 2004 [1983]: 132).

[108]   Other trainings attempting to enter either the IPA (International Psychoanalytic Association) or the BCP (e.g. the Lincoln Centre and the BAP) on their training days stressed these affiliations, and by implication their growing dissociation from the less illustrious UKCP.

[109]   As an aside, John's 'dissent' provides an instance of how effective pre-training therapy can be in vetting candidates who are doubtful as to the veracity of psychodynamic ideas—a fact I pointed out in chapter two.

[110]   See M. Valentine (1996: 174 -81).

[111]   I quote Valentine's description of 'wild analysis': 'In Laplanche and Pontalis' *The Language of Psychoanalysis*, they make the following points about "wild analysis": it is not restricted to the ignorant or inexperienced practitioner, it is based on a certain attitude adopted by analysts who justify their power by appealing to a "superior knowledge", it is a kind of compulsive analysing, and is a search for omnipotence' (Valentine 1996: 182).

[112]   This was gathered from my personal communication with Dr. Young (2004).

[113]   For the published account see, Young (1996b: 5)

[114]   This was disclosed to me by Dr. Young during our personal communication (2004).

[115]   As Marguerite said in interview, 'I waited till I had graduated before I made my concerns heard; it would have been dangerous to do it before'. While Robert said to me, 'Well actually my protest is still being punished, as my training institute has not sent me one referral since I graduated'.

[116]   Freud represents the birth of psychoanalysis as one great act of dissent against conventional thinking: 'In classical antiquity great importance was attached to dreams as foretelling the future; but modern science would have nothing to do with them, it handed them over to supersti-

tion, declaring them to be purely "somatic" processes—a kind of twitching of a mind that is otherwise asleep... But by disregarding the excommunication that had been pronounced upon dreams... psychoanalysis arrived at a different conclusion' (1925: 43). He speaks of the ostracism that followed: 'This time I was applauded, but no further interest was taken in me. The impression that the high authorities had rejected my innovations remained unshaken... I found myself forced into the Opposition... I was soon afterwards [1886] excluded from the laboratory of cerebral anatomy' (1925: 15-16). He continues: 'For more than ten years after my separation from Breuer I had no followers. I was completely isolated. In Vienna I was shunned; abroad no notice was taken of me' (1925: 48). And finally, '[Breuer] was the first to show the reaction of distaste and repudiation which was later to become so familiar to me, but which at that time I had not yet learnt to recognise as my inevitable fate' (1914: 12).

[117] This institute had close ties with leading members of the American 'culture and personality school' of anthropology. During the winter of 1941-2, for instance, an impressive list of speakers appeared by invitation at monthly meetings, including Margaret Mead, Franz Alexander, Ruth Benedict, Abram Kardiner, and David Levy (Quinn 1987: 354).

[118] Lacan's 'heretical' seminars were attended by and influenced many of the most respected French intellectuals: Sartre, de Beauvoir, Derrida, Levi-Strauss, Merleau-Ponty, Barthes, Althusser, Kristeva, and Irigaray. See Grosz (1990).

[119] Further in the chapter his *ad hominem* arguments against detractors such as Wilhelm Stekel and Alfred Adler further confirm his pathologisation of dissent. Of Adler he says: 'My own impression of Adler was that of a morose and cantankerous person, whose behaviour oscillated between contentiousness and sulkiness. He was evidently very ambitious and constantly quarrelling with the others over points of priority in his ideas' (p.147). And again: 'To accuse Freud of despotism and intolerance for what had happened [i.e. Adler's reluctance to accept his ideas and his consequent expulsion] *has too obvious a motive behind it to be taken seriously*' (p.150, italics added). Of Stekel he says: 'Stekel had no critical powers at all, and when he once cut himself loose from the amount of discipline that common work with colleagues imposed his intuition degenerated into wild guesswork' (p.152). And again: 'Stekel had, however, a serious flaw of character that rendered him unsuitable for work in an academic field: he had no scientific conscience at all. So no one placed much credence in the experiences he reported. It was his custom, for instance, to open the discussion on whatever the topic of the day might happen to be with the remark: "Only this Wednesday I saw a case of this kind", so that Stekel's "Wednesday patient" became proverbial' (p.153). 'Enough has been said to indicate that Stekel was an unsatisfactory editor of a serious periodical, and that to a man of Freud's literary taste and scientific integrity working with such a collaborator could only be extremely irksome' (p.154).

[120] The BAP introduced the Jungian training into their syllabus in 1963. This training was recognised by the International Association of Analytical Psychologists (i.e. the international Jungian association), in 1982

(Abram and Morgan-Jones 2001: 87). Another BCP training that reintegrated Jung into the curriculum is the London Centre for Psychotherapy, founded in 1973.

121 See the biographies on Freud by Webster (1995) and Ferris (1997).

122 Erich Fromm (1959) has eloquently explored all these factors in his book *Sigmund Freud's Mission* which constitutes a psychosocial investigation of Freud's character.

123 See *Standard Edition of the Complete Works of Sigmund Freud* (1977) Vol. 20: 34.

124 For instance, Diana Russell's influential study conducted in 1986 showed that sexual abuse occurring under the age of 18 affected almost 38 per cent of the female population. Her definition of sexual abuse was 'any kind of exploitative sexual contact that occurred between relatives' (p.145). These are figures for the United States.

125 Freud's views on patriarchy are well documented. I refer the reader to works by Webster (1996) and Gallop (1985).

126 This series of clinical supervision took place in early 2005.

127 See S. Johnson's (1994: 21-54) discussion of 'character styles' where 'avoidant' and 'schizoid' personalities are discussed in depth.

128 Although this supposition is only hinted at in this transcribed session (the supervision speaks of masochism more generally rather than of Arya's masochism) it was clear from my discussion with him after the session that he felt exploring Arya's submissive and masochistic tendencies would constitute a large part of the work. This belief was made more explicit and accepted by the trainees in the following supervision session.

129 'Inspecting' the relationship is a key diagnostic device in psychodynamic psychotherapy—in this case study we find two diagnostic devices at work: via inference on the one hand from the patient's material, and on the other from her relational style.

130 W.H.R. Rivers (1924) was perhaps the first to argue that there was an invariant relation between belief and action (causation beliefs explained clinical actions). Rivers' emphasis has entailed, firstly, a tradition of privileging belief over action (to understand the performative we must look first to the cognitive), and a further reluctance to acknowledge the inconsistency between the two domains.

131 As Blaxter has said: 'Medical theory and medical practice are not necessarily the same, however. Though theory may encompass the social and the psychological, practice is more usually based on treating pathologies by physical intervention' (Blaxter 1979: 160). Hsu (2005), contrasting T/CAM (Traditional Chinese Medicine) and biomedicine also writes: 'Whereas causative agents in biomedicine are often microorganisms or degenerative biological processes, T/CAM may find causative agents in variables like hot and cold, spirit loss or indulgent behaviour, which are often directly linked to social, religious, moral, political and ecological environment' (Hsu 2005: 8)—paper forthcoming.

132 The ethnographic record shows such multi-directional practice to be widespread. Turner's study of the Nedembu doctor illustrates this: the doctor conducts an elaborate social drama to ascertain the source of

communal tensions, coupling this on occasion with ritual exorcism (to expunge the soul of malevolent forces), as well as using certain herbs and potions to effect healing and calm in the body (Turner 1967).

[133] It is important to note how the various 'domains' at which action is directed are defined. We cannot expect a category such as 'body' (or the classificatory system to which it belongs) to have universal application. Thus any such system is always used for facilitating smooth translation, or in Evans-Pritchard's terms, for writing a text rendering the unfamiliar familiar to us. I define the various phenomenological domains in accordance with Lock's and Scheper-Hughes' (1996) classification of domains—body / psycho / social. I only make one alteration by adding the domain of the metaphysical.

[134] See Elisabeth Hsu's (2005) paper 'Other Medicines—Which Wisdom do they Challenge' (forthcoming). In the Chinese text of the second century BCE ideas of 'synchronous signs' implied diagnosis did not depend on establishing the given cause. Thus to assume biomedical preoccupations with causality are universal might be to impose and perpetuate a Western Biomedical ideology that is less *a priori* than constructed.

[135] Or we could say, following Hsu's work on aetiology, where there is no external / internal conceptual system to be found we must take instrumentality rather than concept as the criteria by which to classify aetiology.

[136] An example of a mono-directive (internalising) system is biomedicine: it directs alleviative action at one internal domain, the body. Mono-directive (externalising) systems direct alleviative action at one external domain (at witchcraft or the relational field). Multi-directive (externalising) systems direct action at numerous external domains (sorcery, social drama, spirits etc.). Multi-directive (internalising) systems direct action at numerous internal domains (the body, the psyche). Finally, Multi-directive externalising / internalising systems direct alleviative action at multiple domains: the body (thorough drugs, herbs, potions) and the external environment (social drama, prayer), thus defying any strict external / internal dichotomy.

[137] For example, Comaroff's (1985) study sees Zionist body-healing as a shrouded attempt to heal the oppressive social order; Kleinman's (1980) study exposes the social origins of so-called widespread 'psychological' suffering which emerged in the aftermath of the Chinese Cultural Revolution. And finally Sharp (1993) relates possession by *tromba* spirits in Madagascar to the growth of social anomie.

[138] For example, where tissue damage or excessive trauma is unequivocally implicated.

[139] Mainstream psychodynamic therapists increasingly following the diagnostic criteria laid down in DSM IV where traditional sociological concepts of suffering do not feature.

[140] For instance, during the course of my fieldwork I rarely heard the question asked 'is therapy right for this patient'. On the whole other questions were preferred: 'will this patient also need to see a social worker', 'a psychiatrist', or 'a pastoral healer'? Such alternative practitioners were often seen more as auxiliaries than replacements. In many

cases the applicability of therapy is assumed.

[141] Quoted in Joan Cassell (1984: 242-3).

[142] Such narrowing is 'legitimated' by the discourse of rationality in which it transpires (Hsu 2004: 9), a legitimacy endowing practitioners with a sense of safety and competence needed for effective practice (Kleinman 1988: 160).

[143] Such correlations, if found, would force other questions regarding the social systems in which their accompanying practice belong. Following Bourdieu (1998) in linking theory and practice to the struggles of the wider social field, we could ask how far certainty and other species of the dogmatic practice are socially induced responses to socio-historical factors of economic unknowing—that is, to the insecurity of competing with a plethora of contending traditions for resources that are scarce. If therapeutic professionals can sow the widespread belief that they have something unique to offer the emotionally distressed, then the concept of aetiology engendering this belief has economic and political correlates so far as it supports the market for therapeutic services.

[144] The fear of negative evaluation expresses itself in sinuous ways. A further sign is the free-floating stress which often manifests itself somatically. Many female trainees complained of 'feeling sick in the stomach' or of experiencing 'butterflies' before coming to the institute. Others spoke of 'not being able to sleep' the night before a training weekend or workshop—there were other complaints of nervousness. The male students appeared to complain less about these reactions, but when questioned also admitted to experiencing feelings of 'nervousness' or 'trepidation'.

[145] Finally, as noted in the introduction, Hugh Gusterton (1996: 157-164) has shown that young professionals' growing sense of mastery gradually overrides some of the moral concerns they had about their profession. He believes that this partially explains how once politically liberal young physicists who were hesitant about the nuclear arms race, can over the course of their training be turned into keen weapons scientists —the thrill of growing mastery thus becomes the force prompting individuals to rationalise their old objections away.

[146] However, it is also true that Quesalid suspends his disbelief in the end. As Lévi-Strauss says, after a period of carrying on with his craft conscientiously, '[Quesalid] seems to have completely lost sight of the fallaciousness of the technique which he so disparaged at the beginning' (Lévi-Strauss 1963: 178).

[147] Indeed, in the same essay, Lévi-Strauss tells us that the senior sorcerer whose position Quesalid usurps, after admitting to Quesalid that his practice was fraudulent and that he was 'covetous for the property of the sick men', became racked with guilt and grief, leaving the community out of shame only to return one year later as a madman. Three years later death takes him (Lévi-Struass 1963: 177).

[148] The psychoanalyst, S. Pulver, defines the technique of confrontation as 'the act of drawing the patient's attention to some aspect of his behaviour or of reality that he has either been genuinely unaware of or has denied' (Pulver 1995: 23).

[149] Calestro correctly writes that the therapist's belief is largely established through training: 'The therapist's beliefs regarding his efficacy as a curing agent generally derive from his training in and adoption of a particular school of psychotherapy. He is taught to believe that emotional distress or behaviour anomalies develop as a function of certain systematic and scientific principles. He is also taught that similar principles can be used in correcting psychological abnormalities. These beliefs, which are consistent with his assumptive world, make up the substance of his personal myth' (Calestro 1972: 97).

[150] The reader will notice that the essential method here is that used by Evans-Pritchard's (1977 [1937]) in his work on Azande witchcraft, where he looks to the 'ideal' as supporting not only legal and kinship systems, but as providing a general explanatory system by which 'unknown' causes of misfortune can be explained.

[151] The irony of this fact is pointed out in Storr (1989:53).

[152] This was survey was conducted in 2005. Although this was an informal survey, I nevertheless followed tested conventions. This was a 'mail survey' which sampled psychodynamic therapists (including psychoanalysts) in the BCP (British Confederation of Psychotherapists). Interviewees were selected alphabetically (starting with 'A') from the BCP register; interviewees were based either in London or in South East England. The survey questions were of two kinds: those which sought to elicit 'opinions and attitudes' (e.g. concerning issues of identity and beliefs), and those focusing on factual 'characteristics and behaviours' (e.g. class, religious, and political affiliations etc.) All questions were 'open' rather than 'closed'.

[153] Furthermore, although there was not a consistent correlation between the amount of years spent as a practitioner and the number of personal analyses undergone, there was a broad trend indicating that those with the longest practical experience, because they can, had more personal analyses.

[154] I heard this anecdote on a few occasions during my time in the community—on each occasion the specifics were slightly different, although I am confident that this version broadly captures the event as it occurred. The particular version is adapted from an interview conducted with a senior member of the Institute of Psychoanalysis (2004).

[155] Fromm (1959: 86) goes on to provide further evidence of Freud's various identifications with great men such as Hannibal, Columbus and Moses—a figure whom in later life Freud would write about in *Moses and Monotheism*.

[156] This wider vision is of the 'topographical' understanding of the psyche which the concept of repression presupposes—namely, an unconscious substratum into which dissociated contents are relegated from the conscious mind. For Freud at this time the mind comprises three components: the ego (conscious life), the unconscious (the domain of repressed instinct) and the super-ego (society's rules and taboos internalised).

[157] This reading is further substantiated by noticing that *acheronta* and *superos* might be better translated as heaven and hell. 'If I cannot bend the heavens I will move hell.' And as we have seen that for Freud heaven represents the ideal on earth, thus civilisation and the realm of

the social, while hell represented the inorganic state, the absence of civilisation and dominion of the realm of id, this interpretation better captures what these terms symbolised for him. A very recent translation by Robert Fitzgerald comes close to this meaning: 'If I can sway no heavenly hearts I'll rouse the world below'. The nominative singular, Acheron, refers to a river in Hades, which, by the poetic device of synecdoche (substitution of a part for the whole) refers to the whole underworld. (The plural 'Acheronta' in Virgil's poem is presumably there to fit the metre.) Given these considerations, it is reasonable to translate *acheronta* as 'hell,' with the caveat, of course, that Virgil wasn't a Catholic and that Hades, in his understanding, was a more mundane place than, say, Dante's hell. As for *superus*, it is safe to translate it as heaven or heavens or 'the ones above'. It is plural, suggesting heavenly places or heavenly powers. However, the decisive point is that the context makes it obvious that Virgil is contrasting good powers and means with evil, dark, and prohibited ways, since Juno, having failed to destroy Aeneas via godly means, is now resorting to manipulating the dark underworld. Since 'heaven' and 'hell' convey, roughly, these ideas in English, it seems fair to translate it in the way proposed. (I thank Joseph Yarborough of Cornell University for the suggestions made above.)

158 In the last chapter I emphasised Freud's complicity with his social world, while in this chapter I emphasise his desire for social reform— how can these two things be reconciled? One way would be to locate the contradiction in Freud himself, for indeed Freud was surely not free of the inner contradictions which (he postulated) assail us all. Another method, perhaps more satisfactory, would be to note that for Freud the status quo expressed society at its best, so that anything challenging the status quo must be considered threatening. Social reform on this understanding was the reform of those subversive social elements which he saw as the expressions of individual neuroses. Thus to heal the individual was to disable the neurosis whose expression when concretised would threaten civilisation.

159 In fact this view that the personal is political, and that the unconscious is a disruptive, political force, has found its theoretical justification in the work of the French thinkers G. Deleuze and F. Guarrati (1987). They postulate that human 'desire' comes directly from the unconscious which is inherently revolutionary in character—desire prompts the social action that would alter the status quo.

160 My attention was drawn to this opposition by Professor Roger Goodman, the Department of Social and Cultural Anthropology, University of Oxford.

161 This not to say that these processes eventually swamp the member's total identity (which is always multiple and defined through an interlocking set of varying social roles, obligations, and relationships), but that they annex a fresh and influential identity onto the matrix of identities so established.

162 Although two Kleinians might pull together at a party of accountants could the same be said for a counsellor and a Kleinian? Or would the anxiety of forming an unsuitable acquaintance override their acknow-

ledging the similarities this context bids them share? Alexis de Tocqueville in his *Democracy in America* offers some thoughts: 'In a foreign
country two Americans are at once friends simply because they are
Americans. They are repulsed by no prejudice; they are attracted by
their common country. For two Englishmen the same blood is not
enough; they must be brought together by the same rank... It may
therefore be inferred that the reserve of the English proceeds from the
constitution of their country much more than from that of its inhabit-
ants' (de Tocqueville 1998 [1840]: 261). We wonder if the analogy of the
English holds for the highly stratified therapeutic community.

[163] As I mentioned in chapter four, only those educated in the formal institutes would be invited to teach there.

[164] To say that these observations locate the origin, and sustenance, of this
social dynamic in the psychology of individuals (e.g. a kind of 'free
spirit' in Michael in which social structure finds it origin) is not a necessary consequence. For, as David Parkin (1995) has told us, such 're-
emergences' do not transpire in abstraction from social and cultural
contexts: the return of disavowed inclinations also have their social
causes.

[165] Another way of defining the kind of transformation produced by institutes would be to take our departure from Tanya Luhrmann's study of
contemporary witchcraft. In her monograph she argues that ordinary
middle class Londoners come to embrace witchcraft as a meaningful
system through a process of what she calls 'interpretive drift'—i.e.
when persons become passionately involved in a particular activity,
they come to gradually see the world in terms consistent with its supporting and legitimating ideas. As she puts it, interpretive drift is: 'The
slow shift in someone's manner of interpreting events as they become
involved in a particular activity' (Luhrmann 1989: 312). To the idea that
action ultimately entails belief I would add that belief, through the en-
ticements it purports to offer, provides incentives for the plunge into
action. Thus reciprocally, belief, through encouraging action, and action, through encouraging belief, set turning a reciprocal regime
whereby 'person' (as actor) and 'system' (as guardian of belief) mutually support and confirm each other.

[166] The reasons for this search I feel can be summarised under the following broad headings: 'relational problems' (i.e. problems in marriage, or
wider social life), problems with 'depression', 'anxiety' and 'fatigue' (a
general feeling that life it not progressing as it should); and finally,
problems with living or finding general life-meaning (this includes
searches for new vocations, new friendships).

[167] Of course from an anthropological standpoint this distinction appears
fluid, for the point at which 'personal troubles' become 'public issues'
will be variously defined in different societies.

[168] To the observation that training in psychotherapy or psychoanalysis remains largely restricted to the white middle classes, Littlewood adds
that it largely serves a middle class clientele. Not only is private practice frequented by only those able to afford the high fees, but, as he
says: 'The black community mental health groups which have been established such as the Afro-Caribbean Mental Health Association or the

Fanon Project's Day Centre in Brixton (MelVille, 1985; Moodley, 1987; see Ward, 1986 for details of the different projects) offers support and advice or counselling rather than the sort of formal long-term intensive therapy developed by psychotherapists in private practice' (1997 [1982]: 302). See also Littlewood (1999: 403).

169 The image of trainees being obliged on their first day of training to sit in a circle and disclose to each other their personal biographies is symbolic of this merging—here the private sphere (the intimate) infiltrates the public sphere (the interactions of strangers), something which Sennett believes constitutes the first condition for the fall of the public domain.

170 For Weber, the rise of pan-bureaucratisation and the spread of the rationalisation of the everyday unravels the spiritual, magical, and religious fabric of social existence, leaving persons estranged from traditional sources of personal enrichment, security, and meaning. Furedi argues that psychotherapy responds to this disenchantment, which at bottom 'creates an intense need to comprehend subjective experience' (Furedi 2004: 90). It does this by promising 'to re-enchant subjective experience'. What is interesting here is what Furedi overlooks: that psychodynamic psychotherapy as a social institution is largely bureaucratic, heavily circumscribed by collections of rules, obligations, hierarchies, and formal procedures. If Furedi is therefore correct to say that psychotherapy provides a response to what bureaucratisation entails, members of the community who offer this response are in an unusual position. For unlike the civil, legal, and professional bureaucracies in which Weber was mostly interested, psychoanalysis, while being institutionalised in a manner that allows it to survive in the modern bureaucratised world, still contains elements of mystification uncharacteristic of more traditional bureaucracies. This ambiguous position thus offers practitioners one solution to disenchantment: a bureaucratic system that makes the 're-enchanting of subjective experience' its particular objective.

171 Of these one was Christian in early adolescence; one left Catholicism around the time of training; one was brought up in the Church of Scotland; one between the ages of 14-16 was Christian but is now agnostic; one was a Methodist until 18; one a Unitarian until 30; one an agnostic until 60 and now a humanist; one was Greek Orthodox but became agnostic at the time of training; one stated 'once Anglican'; and finally, one was Non-Denominational before training.

172 The Lincoln Centre, 2005, official website: http://www.lincoln-psychotherapy.org.uk/background/index.htm. (Accessed December 2005.)

173 The London Centre 2006, offical website: http://www.lcp-psychotherapy.org.uk/qualify.htm. (Accessed November 2005.)

174 Severnside Institute for Psychotherapy, official website: http://www.sipsychotherapy.org.uk/id8.htm. (Accessed November 2005.)

BIBLIOGRAPHY

Abram, J and Morgan-Jones, R. (2001). *Psychoanalytic Psychotherapy Trainings—a guide*. London: Free Association Books.

Ashurst P. (1993). Supervision of the Beginning Therapist: Privileges and Problems. *British Journal of Psychotherapy*, Vol. 10 (2):139-77.

Auchincloss, E. L. and Michels, R. (2003) A Reassessment of Psychoanalytic Education: controversies and changes. *International Journal of Psychoanalysis*. 84: 387-403.

Auden, W. H. (1950). *Collected Shorter Poems*. London: Penguin.

Bandura, A. (1977). *Social Learning Theory*. Engelwood Cliffs N.J: Prentice-Hall

Barth, F. (1971). Role Dilemmas and Father-Son Dominance in Middle Eastern Kinship Systems. In Hsu, F. L. K. (ed.) *Kinship and Culture*. Oxford: Oxford University Press.

Bass, A. (1985). On the History of Mistranslation and the Psychoanalytic Movement. In: Graham, J. F. (ed.) *Differences in Translation* Ithaca: Cornell University Press.

Bateson, G. and Mead, M. (1954). *Growth and Culture*. New York: Putman.

Bayer, R. and Spitzer, R. L. (1985) Neurosis, Psychodynamics, and DSM III. *Archives of General Psychiatry*, 42: 187-196.

Beattie, J. H. M. and Middleton, J. (1964). (eds.) *Spirit Mediumship and Society in Africa*. London: Routledge.

290

Becker, H. S., Geer, B., Hughes, E. C., and Strauss, A. L. (2002 [1977]). *Boys in White: student culture in medical school*. London: Transaction Publishers.

Benedict, R. (1934). *Patterns of Culture*. London: Routledge.

Berger, P. L. (1965). Towards an Understanding of Psychoanalysis. *Social Research*, 32(1): 26–41.

Berman, E. (2004). *Impossible Training: a relational view of psychoanalytic training*. Hillsdale: The Analytic Press.

Blaxter, M. (1979). Concepts of Causality; lay and medical models. In: Osborne, D. J. (ed.). *Research in Psychology and Medicine*. London: Academic Press.

Bleger, J. (1967). Psycho-Analysis of the Psycho-Analytic Frame. *International Journal of Psychoanalysis*, 48: 551–519.

Bloch, M. (1998). *How We Think They Think: anthropological approaches to cognition, memory and literacy*. Boulder Colo: Westview Press.

Bourdieu, P. (1977a). *Outline of a Theory of Practice*, (trans. Nice, R.). Cambridge: Cambridge University Press.

Bourdieu, P. (1979). *Algeria 1960: Essays by Pierre Bourdieu* (trans. Nice R.) Cambridge: Cambridge University Press.

Bourdieu, P. (1992c). *Academic Discourse: linguistic misunderstanding and professional power* (trans R. Tesse). Cambridge: Polity Press.

Bourdieu, P. (1998). *Practical Reason*. California: Stanford University Press.

Brown, B. S. (1976). The Life of Psychiatry, *AJP*, 133: 489–495.

Bruzzone, M. et al. (1985). Regression and persecution in analytic training: reflections on experience. *Int. Rev. Psychoanalysis* 12: 411–415.

Calestro, K. (1972). Psychotherapy, Faith Healing and Suggestion. *International Journal of Psychiatry*, 10:83–113.

Campbell, J. (1971). (ed.) *The Portable Jung*. New York: Viking Press.

Casement, P. (1985). *On Learning from the Patient*. London: Routledge

Cassell, J. (1987). On Control, Certitude, and the "Paranoia" of Surgeons. *Culture, Medicine and Psychiatry*, 11: 229–49.

Chaiklin, A and Lave, J. (eds.) (1993). *Understanding Practice: perspective on activity and context*. Cambridge: Cambridge University Press.

Charny, I. W. (1986). What Do Therapists Worry About: a tool for experiential supervision. In: Kaslow, F. W. (ed.) *Supervision and Training: models, dilemmas and challenges*. New York: Haworth Press.

Collingwood, R. G. (2002 [1940]). *An Essay in Metaphysics*. Oxford: Oxford University Press.

Comaroff, J. (1985). *Body of Power, Spirit of Resistance: the culture and history of a South African people*. Chicago: University of Chicago Press.

Crapanzano, V. 2000. *Serving the World: Literalism in America From the Pulpit to the Bench*. New York: New Press.

Cremerius, J. (1990). Training Analysis and Power. *Free Associations*, 20:114-38.

Crichton-Brown, Sir J. (1920). Notes of Psychoanalysis and Psychotherapy. *Lancet*, 1: 1248-9.

Cross-National Collaborative Group (1992). The Changing Rate of Major Depression: cross-cultural comparisons. *JAMA*, 268: 3098-3104.

Csordas, T. J. (1993). Somatic Modes of Attention. *Cultural Anthropology*, 8(2): 135-156.

Csordas, T. J. (2002). *Body/Healing/Meaning*. Boston: Palgrave Press.

Deleuze, G. and Guattari, F. (1987). *A Thousand Plateaux*. Minneapolis: University of Minnesota Press.

Desjarlais, R. R. (1996). Presence. In: Laderman, L. and Roseman, M. (eds.) *The Performance of Healing*. London: Routledge.

Diller, J. V. (1991). *Freud's Jewish Identity: a case study in the impact of ethnicity*. London: Fairleigh University Press.

Dougherty, J. W. D. (1985) (ed.) *Directions in Cognitive Anthropology*. Urbana: University of Illinois Press.

Dow, J. (1986). Universal aspects of symbolic healing: a theoretical synthesis. *American Anthropologist*, 88 56-69.

Durkheim, E. (1957 [1915]). *The Elementary Forms of Religious Life*. (J. W. Swain Trans). London: George Allen and Unwin Ltd.

Durkheim, E. (1982 [1895]). *The Rules of Sociological Method*. (D. W. Halls Trans). New York: Free Press.

Ehernwald, J. (1966). *Psychotherapy: myth and method; an integrative approach*. New York: Grune and Stratton.

Eisenstadt, S. N. (1968). *On Charisma and Institution Building: selected papers/ Max Weber*. Chicago: University of Chicago Press.

Ellenberger, H. (1970). *The Discovery of the Unconscious: the history and evolution of dynamic psychiatry.* London: Penguin Press

Evans-Pritchard, E. P. (1977 [1937]). *Witchcraft, Oracles, and Magic Among the Azande.* Oxford: Oxford University Press.

Evans-Pritchard, E. P. (1951). *Social Anthropology.* London: Cohen and West.

Evans-Pritchard, E. P. (1956). *Nuer Religion.* Oxford: Oxford University Press.

Evans-Pritchard, E. P. (1961). *Anthropology and History.* Manchester: Manchester University Press.

Ewart, E. (2000). *Living With Each Other: Selves and Others Amongst the Panari of Central Brazil.* Ph.D. thesis, London School of Economics.

Eysenck, H. J. (1952). The Effects of Psychotherapy Evaluation. *Journal of Consulting Psychology,* 16: 319-24.

Falzeder, E. (2000). Profession—Psychoanalyst: A Historical View. *Psychoanalysis and History,* 2 (1): 37-60.

Fernandez, J. and Huber, M. T. (eds.) (2001). *Irony in Action: anthropology, practice, and the moral imagination.* Chicago: University of Chicago Press.

Ferris, P. (1997). *Dr Freud: A Life.* London: Sinclair-Stevenson.

Fiedler, F. (1950). A Comparison of Therapeutic Relationships in Psychoanalytic, Nondirective and Adlerian Therapy. *Journal of Consulting Psychology,* 14:436-445.

Figlio, K. (1993). The Field of Psychotherapy: conceptual and ethical definitions. *British Journal of Psychotherapy,* 9 (3): 324-334.

Forrester, J. (1994). A whole Climate of Opinion: rewriting the history of psychoanalysis. In: Micale, M. S. and Porter, R. (eds.) *Discovering the History of Psychiatry.* Oxford: Oxford University Press.

Foster, G. M. and Anderson, B. G. (1978). *Medical Anthropology.* New York: Wiley.

Fortes, M. (1945). *The Dynamics of Clanship Among the Tallensi: being the first part of an analysis of the social structure of a trans-Volta tribe.* Oxford: Oxford University Press.

Foucault, M. (1977). *Language, Counter-Memory, and Practice: selected essays and interviews.* Oxford: Blackwell.

Foucault, M. (1977b). *Discipline and Punishment.* London: Allen Lane.

Fox, R. (1957). Training for Uncertainty. In: Merton, R. Reader, G. Kendall, P. (eds.) *The Student Physician*. Cambridge: Harvard University Press.

Fox, R. (1980). The Evolution of Medical Certainty. In *Milbank Memorial Fund Quarterly*, 1: 1-49.

Frattoroli, J. (1992). Orthodoxy and Heresy in the History of Psychoanalysis. In: N. M. Szajnberg (ed.). *Educating the Emotions*. New York: Plenum Press.

Freidson, E. (1970). *Profession of Medicine: a study of the sociology of applied knowledge*. New York: Dodd and Mead

Freidson, F. (1994). *Professionalism Reborn: theory prophecy and policy*. London: Polity Press.

Frank, D. and Frank, J.B. (1993 [1961]). *Persuasion and Healing*. Baltimore: John Hopkins Press.

Freud, S. and Breuer, J. (1955 [1893-5]). *Studies of Hysteria* Vol. 2. London: Hogarth Press.

Freud, S. (1955 [1918]). *Lines of Advance in Psycho-Analytic Techinque*. Standard Edition. Vol 17. London: Hogarth Press.

Freud, S. (1955 [1920]). *Beyond the Pleasure Principle, Group Psychology, and Other Works*. London: Hogarth Press.

Freud, S. (1958 [1915a]). *Observations of Transference Love*. Standard Edition. Vol. 12. London: Hogarth Press.

Freud, S. (1975 [1917]). *Introductory Lectures*. Vol. 1. London: Penguin.

Freud, S. (1977). *Standard Edition of the Complete Works of Sigmund Freud* Vol. XX. London: Penguin.

Freud, S. (1977 [1932]). *New Introductory Lectures on Psychoanalysis*. London: Penguin.

Freud, S. (1979 [1909]). *Case Histories I: 'Dora' and 'Little Hans'*. London: Penguin.

Freud S. (1985). *The Complete Letters of Sigmund Freud to Wilhelm Fliess 1887-1904* (ed. Masson, J.). Cambridge: Belknap Press, Harvard University.

Freud, S. (1991 [1915]). *The Interpretation of Dreams*. London: Penguin. Fromm, E. (1959). *Sigmund Freud's Mission*. New York: Grove Press.

Fromm, E., De Martino, R., and Suzuki, D. T. (1960). *Zen Buddhism and Psychoanalysis*. New York: Harper and Row.

Fromm, E. (1972). *Fear of Freedom*, London: Routledge.

Frosh, S. (1999 [1987]). *The Politics of Psychoanalysis*. London: Macmillan Press.

Furedi, F. (2004). *Therapy Culture: cultivating uncertainty in an uncertain age* London: Routledge.

Furedi, F. (2005). *Where Have all the Intellectuals Gone?* London: Continuum.

Gabbard, K. and Gabbard, G. O. (1987). *Psychiatry and the Cinema*. Chicago: University of Chicago Press.

Gallop, J. (1985). *The Daughter's Seduction: feminism and psychoanalysis*. Ithica: Cornell University Press.

Gardner, F. (1995). Being in the Know: thoughts on training, prestige and knowledge. *British Journal of Psychotherapy*, 11(3): 427-435.

Garza-Guerrero, C. (2002a) 'The Crisis in Psychoanalysis': what crisis are we talking about? *International Journal of Psychoanalysis*. 83: 57-83.

Garza-Guerrero, C. (2002b) Organisational and Educational Internal Impediments of Psychoanalysis: contemporary challenges. *International Journal of Psychoanalysis*. 83: 1407-33

Gellner, E. (1985). *The Psychoanalytic Movement*. London: Blackwell.

Giddens, A. (1991). *Modernity and Self-Identity: self and society in the late modern age*. Cambridge: Polity Press.

Gluckman, M. (1963). *Order and Rebellion in Tribal Africa: collected essays with an autobiographical introduction*. London: Cohen and West.

Goffman, E. (1959). *The Presentation of Self in Everyday Life*. New York: Doubleday.

Goffman, E. (1961). *Asylums: essays on the social situation of mental patients and other inmates*. New York: Doubleday.

Goffman, E. (1968). *The Moral Career of the Mental Patient*. Harmondsworth: Penguin.

Goody, J. R. (1977). Against Ritual. In: Moore, S. F. and Myerhoff, B. G. (eds.) *Secular Ritual*. Assen and Amsterdam: Van Gorcum.

Gorer, G. (1962). The Psychoanalytic Study of Society. *International Journal of Psycho-Analysis*, XLIII, Vol. 1, Parts 2-3: 188-91.

Gouldner, A. W. (1979). *The Future of Intellectuals and the Rise of the New Class*. London: Macmillan Press.

Gray, A. (1994). *An Introduction to the Therapeutic Frame*. London: Routledge.

Grunbaum, A. (1984). Epistemology Liabilities of the Universal Appraisal of Psychoanalytic Theory. *Nous*, Vol. XIV, 3.

Grunbaum, A. (1984). *The Foundations of Psychoanalysis*, New York: Harbour.

Gusterson, H. (1996). *Nuclear Rites: a weapons laboratory at the end of the Cold War*. Berkeley: University of California Press.

Halmos, P. (1973). *The Faith of Counsellors*. London: Constable.

Haynal, A. (1993). *Psychoanalysis and the Sciences: epistemology—history*. Berkeley: University of California Press.

Heald, S. and Deluz, A. (1994). *Anthropology and Psychoanalysis*. London:Routledge

Heelas, P. (1996). *The New Age Movement: the celebration of the self and the sacralisation of modernity*. Oxford: Blackwell.

Heimann, P. (1954). Problems of the Training Analysis. *Int. J. Psycho-Anal*, 35:163-8.

Heimann, P. (1949-50). On Counter-transference. *Int. J. Psycho-Anal*, 31: 81-4.

Helman, C. (1984 [1994]). *Culture, Health, and Illness*. London: Reed Educational.

Herdt, G. (1987). *The Sambia: ritual and gender in New Guinea*. New York: Holt Rinehart and Winston.

Hillman, J. (1983). *Healing Fiction*. Woodstock: Spring Publications.

Hinshelwood, R. D. (1985). Questions of Training. *Free Associations*, 2: 7-18.

Hinton, L. and Kleinman, A. (1994) Cultural Issues and International Psychiatric Diagnosis. In: Costas Silva, J. A. and Naddson, C. (eds.) *International Review of Psychiatry*. Vol. 1. Washington DC: American Psychiatric Press.

Hobart, M. (2000). *After Culture: anthropology as radical metaphysical critique*. Yogyakarta: Wacana University Press.

Holmes, J., and Roberts, G. (1999). *Healing Stories: narrative in psychiatry and psychotherapy*. Oxford: Oxford University Press.

Holmes, J. (2000). NHS Psychotherapy—Past, Future, Present. *British Journal of Psychotherapy*, 16(4): 447-57.

Horney, K. (1942). *Self Analysis*. New York: Norton.

Horton, R. (1970). African Traditional Thought and Western Science. In: Marwick, M. (ed.). *Witchcraft and Sorcery*. Harmondsworth, Middlesex: Penguin Books

Hoshmand, L. T. (2001). Psychotherapy as an Instrument of Culture. In: Slife, B. D. *et al* (eds.). *Critical issues in Psychotherapy: translating new ideas into practice*. London: Thousand Oaks.

Houseman, M. and Severi, C. (1998). *Naven or the Other Self: a relational approach to ritual*. Koln: Brill Press.

Hsu, E. (1996b). The Polyglot Practitioner: towards acceptance of different approaches in treatment evaluation. In: Olsen S. G. and Hoeg E. (eds.) *Studies in Alternative Therapy III. Communication in and about Alternative Therapies*. Odense: Odense University Press.

Hsu, E. (1999). *The Transmission of Chinese Medicine*. Cambridge: Cambridge University Press.

Hsu, E. (2004). Other Medicines—Which Wisdom do they Challenge? (Unpublished Paper).

Hubert, H. and Mauss, M. (1981 [1964]). *Sacrifice: its nature and function*. Chicago: University of Chicago Press.

Hutton, R. (1999). *The Triumph of the Moon*. Oxford: Oxford University Press.

Jackson, M. (1989). *Paths Towards a Clearing: radical empiricism and ethnographic enquiry*. Bloomington: Indiana University Press.

Jacoby, R. (1975). *Social Amnesia*. Sussex: Harvester.

Jacobs, M. (2000). Psychotherapy in the United Kingdom: past, present, and future. *British Journal of Guidance and Counselling*, 28 (4): 451-66.

Jacobs, M. (2001). Reflections (Psychodynamic Psychotherapy). In: Spinelli, E and Marshall, S. (eds.). *Embodied Theories*. London: Continuum.

Jahoda, G. (1982). *Psychology and Anthropology: a psychological perspective*. London: Academic Press.

Jenkins, R. (1992). *Pierre Bourdieu*. London: Routledge.

Johnson, S. M. (1994). *Character Styles*. London: Norton

Johnson, T. (1972). *Professions and Power*. London: Macillan.

Jones, E. (1955). *Sigmund Freud: life and work*. Vol. 1. London: Hogarth Press.

Jones, E. (1957). *Sigmund Freud: life and work*. Vol. 3. London: Hogarth Press.

Kapferer, B. (1983). *A Celebration of Demons: exorcism and the aesthetics of healing in Sri Lanka*. Bloomingdon: Indiana University Press.

Kardiner, A. (1939). *The Individual and His Society: the psychodynamics of primitive social organization / by Abram Kardiner; with a foreword and two ethnological reports by Ralph Linton.* New York: Columbia University Press.

Katz, J. (1984). *The Silent World of Doctor and Patient.* New York: Free Press.

Katz, R. (1982). *Boiling Energy: community healing among the Kalahari Kung.* Cambridge, Mass.: Harvard University Press.

Keller, C. and Keller, J. D. (1993). Thinking and Acting with Iron. In: Chaiklin, S. and Lave, J. (eds.) *Understanding Practice: perspectives on activity and context.* Cambridge: Cambridge University Press.

Kernberg, O. (1986). Institutional Problems of Psychoanalytic Education. *Journal of the American Psychoanalytic Association,* vol. 34 (4): 799-834.

Kernberg, O. (1996). Thirty Methods to Destroy the Creativity of Psychoanalytic Candidates. *Int. J. Psycho-Anal,* 77: 1031-1040.

Kernberg, O. (2006) The Coming Changes in Psychoanalytic Education: Part 1. *International Journal of Psychoanalysis.* 87: 1649-73.

Kirsner, D. (2000). *Unfree Associations: inside psychoanalytic institutes.* London: Process Press.

Klein, M. (1975 [1952]). *Envy, Gratitude and Other Works.* London: Routledge.

Klienman, A. (1980). *Patients and Healers in the Context of Culture.* Berkeley: University of California Press.

Kleinman, A. (1991 [1988]). *Rethinking Psychiatry.* New York: Free Press.

Klienman, A., Das, V., and Lock, M. (eds.) (1998). *Social Suffering.* Oxford: Oxford University Press.

Laderman, C. (1986). The Ambiguity of Symbols in the Structure of Healing. *Social Science and Medicine,* 24 (4): 293-301.

La Fontaine, J. S. (1985). *Initiation.* London: Penguin Books.

Lambek, M. and Antze, P. (2004). *Illness and Irony: on the ambiguity of suffering in culture.* Oxford: Berghahn.

Larson, M. S. (1977). *The Rise of Professionalism: a sociological analysis.* Berkeley: University of California Press.

Larson, M. S. (1990). In the Matter of Experts and Professionals, or how Impossible it is to Leave Nothing Said. In: Torstendahl, R.

and Burrage, M. (eds.) *The Formation of Professions: knowledge, state, and strategy*. London: Sage.

Lasch, C. (1979). *The Culture of Narcissim American: life in an age of diminishing expectations*. New York: Warner Books.

Lave, J. and Wenger, E. (1991). *Situated Learning: legitimate peripheral learning*. Cambridge: Cambridge University Press.

Lave, J. and Chaiklin, S. (1993). *Understanding Practice*. Cambridge: Cambridge University Press.

Leach, E. R. (1954). *Political Systems of Highland Burma*. London: Routledge.

Levine, F. J. (2003) The Forbidden Quest and the Slippery Slope: roots of authoritarianism in Psychoanalysis. *International Journal of Psychoanalysis*. 85: 13-8.

Levi-Struass, C. (1967). *Structural Anthropology*. London: Basic Books.

Lewis, G. (1980). *Day of Shining Red: an essay on understanding ritual*. Cambridge: Cambridge University Press.

Lewis, I. M. (1977). *Symbols and Sentiments*. London: Academic Press.

Liberman, B. L. (1978b). The Role of Mastery in Psychotherapy: maintenance of improvement and prescriptive change. In: Frank, J. D. *et al. Effective Ingredients of Successful Psychotherapy*. New York: Brunner/Mazel.

Little, M. (1950). Countertransference and the Patient's Response to it. *Int. J. Psych-Anal*, 32: 32-40.

Littlewood, R. (1980). Anthropology and Psychiatry: an alternative approach. *Br. J. Med. Psychology*, 53: 213-225.

Littlewood, R. and Lipsedge, M. (1987 [1982]). *Aliens and Alienists: economic minorities and psychiatry.*. London: Routledge.

Littlewood, R. and Kareem, J. (eds.) (1992). *Intercultural Therapy: themes, Interpretations and practice*. Oxford: Blackwell Scientific Publications.

Littlewood, R., Jadhav, S., and Raguram, R. (1999) Circles of Desire: a therapeutic narrative from South Asia—translation to creolization. In: Holmes, J. and Roberts, G. (eds.) *Healing Stories: narrative in psychiatry and psychotherapy*. Oxford: Oxford University Press.

Littlewood, R. and Dien, S. (2000). *Cultural Psychiatry and Medical Anthropology: An introduction and reader*. London: Athlone Press.

Lock, M. and Scheper-Hughes, N. (1996). A Critical-Interpretive Approach in Medical Anthropology. In: Sargent, C. F. and Johnson, T. M. (eds.). *Handbook of Medical Anthropology: contemporary theory and method*. London: Greenwood Press.

Losche, D. (2001). What Makes an Anthropologist Laugh? The Abelam, Irony, and Me'. In: Fernandez, J. and Huber, M. T. (eds.) *Irony in Action*. Chicago: University of Chicago Press.

Lousada, J. (2000). The State of Mind We Are In. *British Journal Psychotherapy*, 16 (4): 467-76.

Luborsky, L. B. and Luborsky, S. (1975). Comparative Studies of Psychotherapy. *Archives of General Psychiatry*, 32: 995-1008.

Lurhmann, T. (1989). *Persuasions of the Witch's Craft*. London: Blackwell.

Luhrmann, T. (2001). *Of 2 Minds: the growing disorder in American Psychiatry*. New York: Borzoi Books.

MacClancy, J. (2002). *Exotic No More: anthropology on the front lines*. Chicago University of Chicago Press.

Macdonald, K. M. (1995). *The Sociology of the Professions*. London: Sage

Mechanic, D. (1972). *Public Expectations and Health Care: essays on the changing organisation of health services*. New York: Wiley-interscience.

MacIntyre, A. (2001 [1981]). *After Virtue*. London: Duckworth.

Malcolm, J. (2004 [1983]). *Psychoanalysis: the impossible profession*. London: Picador.

Malinowski, B. (1971 [1926]). *Myth in Primitive Psychology*. Westport: Negro Universities Press.

Malinowski, B. (1927). *Sex and Repression in Savage Society*. London: Kegan Paul.

Marcuse, H. (1966 [1955]). *Eros and Civilisation*. Boston: Beacon Press.

Marmor, J. (1962). Psychoanalytic Therapy as an Educational Process: common Denominations in therapeutic approaches of different therapeutic "schools". In: Masserman, J. H. (ed.) *Psychoanalytic Education*. London: Grune and Stratton.

Masson J. (1984). *Against Therapy*. London: Fontana Press.

Mayer, L. (2003) Subservient Analysis. *International Journal of Psychoanalysis*. 84: 1241-62.

McDougall, W. (1908). *Introduction to Social Psychology* London: Methuen.

Mechanic, D (1972) Social Psychological Factors Affecting the Presentation of Bodily Complaints. *New England Journal of Medicine*, 286, 1132-1139.

Meed, M. (1943). *Coming of Age in Samoa: a study of adolescence and sex in primitive societies*. Harmonsworth: Penguin.

Miller, A. (1994). *The Drama of the Gifted Child*. New York: Basic-Books.

Mills, C. W. (2000 [1959]). *The Sociological Imagination*. Oxford: Oxford University Press.

Morris, B. (1996 [1987]). *Anthropological Studies of Religion*. Cambridge: Cambridge University Press.

Moskowitz, E. (1990). *In Therapy we Trust: America's obsession with self-fulfilment*. Baltimore: John Hopkins University Press.

Needham, R. (1983 [1962]). *Structure and Sentiment: a test case in social anthropology*. Chicago: Chicago University Press.

Nurge, E. (1958). Etiology of Illness in Guinhangdan. *American Anthropologist*, 60: 1158-72.

Parson, T. (1964). *Essays in Sociological Theory*. New York: Free Press.

Parkin, D. (1995) Latticed Knowledge: eradication and dispersal of the unpalatable in Islam, medicine and anthropological theory. In: Fardon, R. (ed.) *Counterworks: managing the diversity of knowledge*. London: Routledge.

Parkin, F. (1979). *Marxism and Class Theory: A Bourgeois Critique*. New York: Colombia University Press.

Peck, S. (1978). *The Road Less Travelled*. New York: Norton.

Pedder, J. R. (1986). Courses in Psychotherapy: evolution and current trends. *British Journal of Psychotherapy*, 6 (2): 203-221.

Philips, A. (1995). *Terrors and Experts*. Cambridge: Harvard University Press.

Porter, R. and Hinnels, J. R. (eds.) (1999). *Religion, Health, and Suffering*. London: Kegan Paul International.

Porter, R. (1996) Two Cheers for Psychiatry! The Social History of Mental Disorder in Twentieth Century Britain. In: Freeman, H and Berrios, G. E. (eds.) *150 Years of British Psychiatry Volume II: the aftermath*. London: Gaskel.

Prince, R. (1980). Variations in Psychotherapeutic Procedures. In: Draguns, H. C. (ed.) *Handbook of Cross-Cultural Psychology: Psychopathology*. Boston: allyn and Bacon.

Pulver, S. E. (1995). The Technique of Psychoanalysis Proper. In: Moore, B and Fine, B. D. (eds). *Psychoanalysis: the major concepts*. New Haven: Yale Uni. Press.

Rapp, D. (1988) The Reception of Freud by the British Press: general interest in literary magazines, 1920-1925. *Journal of the History of the Behavioural Sciences*, xxix: 191-201.

Richards, A. (1956). *Chisungu: a girl's initiation ceremony in Northern Rhodesia*. London: Faber.

Rieff, P. (1966). *The Triumph of the Therapeutic: uses of faith after Freud*. London: Chatto and Windus Ltd.

Rivers, W. H. R. (1924). *Medicine, Magic and Religion*. London: Kegan Paul.

Rivière, P. (1984). *Individual and Society in Guiana: a comparative study of Amerindian social organisation*. Cambridge: Cambridge University Press.

Roberts, J. (2003 [1988]). Setting the Frame: definition, functions, and typology of rituals. In: Imber-Black, E. and Roberts, J. (eds.) *Rituals and Families in Family Therapy*. New York: W. W. Norton and Company.

Roith, E. (1987), *The Riddles of Freud: Jewish influences on his theory of female sexuality*. London: Tavistock Press.

Rose, N. (1990). *Governing the Soul: The Shaping of the Private Self*. London: Routledge.

Roseman, M. (1991). *Healing Sounds From the Malaysian Rainforest: Temiar music and medicine*. Berkeley: University of California Press.

Roth, A. and Fornagy, P. (1996). *What Works for Whom: a critical review of psychotherapy research*. London: Gilford Press.

Rudnytsky, P. L. (1987). *Freud and Oedipus*. New York: Columbia University Press.

Ruskin, M. (1985). The Social Organisation of Secrets: towards a sociology of psychoanalysis. *International Review of Psychoanalysis*,12: 143-159.

Russell, B. (1996 [1946]). *History of Western Philosophy*. London: Routledge.

Russell, D. (1986). *The Secret Trauma: incest in the lives of girls and women*. New York: Basic Books.

Russell, D. E. H. (1983). The Incidence and Prevalence of Intrafamilial and Extrafamilial Sexual Abuse of Female Children, *Child Abuse* 7: 133–46.

Rycroft, C. (1995 [1968]). *A Critical Dictionary of Psychoanalysis*. London: Penguin.

Samuels, A. (1989) *The Plural Psyche: personality, morality and the father*. London: Routledge.

Samuels, A. (1993). *The Political Psyche*. London: Routledge.

Samuels, A. (1993) 'What is Good Training'. *British Journal of Psychotherapy* 9: 3.

Schafer, R. (1978). *Language and Insight*. New Haven: Yale University Press.

Schultz, D. P. and Schultz, S. E. (2000). *A Modern History of Psychology*. University of South Florida: Harcourt College Publishers.

Scheff, T. (1979). *Catharsis in Healing, Ritual, and Drama*. Berkeley: University of California Press.

Seijas, H. (1973), 'El Susto Como Categoría Etiológica'. *Acta Científica Venezolana*, 23: 176-78.

Seligman, C. G. (1924). Anthropology and Psychology: a study of some points of comparison, *Journal of the Royal Anthropological Institute*, 94: 30-43.

Selvini Palazzoli, M., Boscolo, L., Cecchin, G., and Prata, G. (1977). The Treatment of Children Through Brief Therapy of Their Parents. *Family Process*, 13 (4): 429-442.

Sennett, R. (1976). *The Fall of Public Man*. New York: Knopf.

Seymour-Smith, C. (1986). *Macmillan Dictionary of Anthropology*. London: Macmillan Press.

Sharma, U. (1996). Bringing the Body Back into the (Social) Action: techniques of the body and the (cultural) imagination. *Social Anthropology*, 4 (3): 251-263.

Sharp, L. (1993). *The Possessed and Dispossessed: spirits, identity, and power in a Madagascar migrant town*. Berkeley: University of California Press.

Shorter, E. (1994) (ed.). The Face of Melancholy. In: *From the Mind into the Body: the cultural origins of psychosomatic symptoms*. New York: Free Press.

Shorter, E. (1997). *A History of Psychiatry*. New York: John Wiley and Sons.

Sinclair, S. (1997). *Making Doctors: an institutional apprenticeship*. Oxford: Oxford University Press.

Skorupski, J. (1976). *Symbol and Theory*. Cambridge: Cambridge University Press.

Smail, M. (2001). *The Origins of Unhappiness*: a new understanding of personal distress. London: Robinson.

Sperber, D. (1975). *Rethinking Symbolism*. Cambridge: Cambridge University Press.

Sperber, D. (2005). *An Epidemiology of Representations*. An Interview with John Brockman. Available at: www.edge.org/3rd_culture/sperber05/sperber05_ index.html. [Accessed Nov 2005].

Spitzer, R. L. *et al* (eds.) (1984). *International Perspectives on DSM III*. Washington: American Psychiatric Press.

Straker, G., Watson, D. and Robinson, T. (2003). Trauma and Disconnection: a trans-theoretical approach. *International Journal of Psychotherapy*, 7: 145-58.

Storr, A. (1979). *The Art of Psychotherapy*. London: Heinemann Publishing.

Storr, A. (1989). *Freud*. Oxford: Oxford University Press.

Szasz, T. S. (1979). *The Myth of Psychotherapy: mental healing as religion, rhetoric and repression*. Oxford: Oxford University Press.

Torrey, E. F. (1986). *Witchdoctors and Psychiatrists: the common roots of psychotherapy and its future*. New York: Harper and Row.

Turner, V. (1967). *The Forest of Symbols*. London: Cornell University Press.

Tyler, S. A. (1969). *Cognitive Anthropology*. London: Holt, Rinehart and Winston.

Valentine, M. (1996). The Abuse of Power in the Analytical Setting. *British Journal of Psychotherapy*, 19 (2): 174-181.

Van de Hart, O. (1993). *Rituals in Psychotherapy*. New York: Harper Collins.

Wallace, A. (1961). *Culture and Personality*. New York: Random House.

Webb, J., Schirato, T. and Danaher, G. (2002). *Understanding Bourdieu*. London: Sage.

Weber, M. (1947 [1922]). *The Theory of Social and Economic Organisation*. New York: Oxford University Press.

Webster, R. (1995). *Why Freud Was Wrong*. London: Harper Collins.

Wienmann, J. (1981). *An Outline of Psychology as Applied to Medicine*. Bristol: Wright.

Whan, M. (1999) Registering Psychotherapy as an Institutional Neurosis: or, Compounding the Estrangement Between Soul and World. *The European Journal of Psychotherapy and Counselling*. Vol. 2 (3).

Whiting, B. (1950). *Paiute Sorcery*. New York: Viking Bond.

Whiting, R. A. (2003 [1988]). Guidelines to Designing Therapeutic Rituals. In: Black, I. and Roberts, J. (eds.). *Rituals in Families and Family Therapy*. New York: W. W. Norton and Company.

Whitehouse, H. (1995). *Inside the Cult: religious innovation and transmission in Papa New Guinea*. Oxford: Clarendon Press.

Winnicott, D. W. (1947). Hate in the Countertransference. *Int. J. Psycho-Anal*, 30: 69-74.

Wittgenstein, L. (1946-7). *Lectures of the Philosophy of Psychology*. (Notes taken by Geach, P. T.). Oxford: Oxford University Press.

Yalom, I. D. (2001). *The Gift of Therapy*. London: Piatkus Books.

Young, A. (1983). The Relevance of Traditional Medical Cultures to Modern Primary Health Care. *Social Science and Medicine*, 17: 1205-11.

Young, R. (1996a). *The Culture of British Psychoanalysis*. Available from: http://human-nature.com/culture/paper5h.html [accessed Dec 2004].

Young, R. (1996b). *The Psychodynamics of Psychoanalytic Organisations*. Presented at the conference for the International Society for the Psychoanalytic Study of Organisations in New York City, 15 June 1996. Available at: http://www.sba.oakland.edu/ispso/html/young.html [accessed Dec 2004].

Zatzick, D. F. and Johnson, F. A. (1997). Alternative Psychotherapeutic Practice Among Middle Class Americans: some conceptual comparisons. *Culture, Medicine, and Society*, 21: 213-246.

INDEX